Mind and Spirit

T0385756

Journal of the Royal Anthropological Institute Special Issue Series

The *Journal of the Royal Anthropological Institute* is the principal journal of the oldest anthropological organization in the world. It has attracted and inspired some of the world's greatest thinkers. International in scope, it presents accessible papers aimed at a broad anthropological readership. All of the annual special issues are also available from the Wiley-Blackwell books catalogue.

Previous special issues of the *JRAI*:

Energy and Ethics, edited by Mette M. High and Jessica M. Smith
Dislocating Labour: Anthropological Reconfigurations, edited by Penny Harvey and Christian Krohn-Hansen
Meetings: Ethnographies of Organizational Process, Bureaucracy, and Assembly, edited by Hannah Brown, Adam Reed, and Thomas Yarrow
Environmental Futures, edited by Jessica Barnes
The Power of Example: Anthropological Explorations in Persuasion, Evocation, and Imitation, edited by Andreas Bandak and Lars Højer
Doubt, Conflict, Mediation: The Anthropology of Modern Time, edited by Laura Bear
Blood Will Out: Essays on Liquid Transfers and Flows, edited by Janet Carsten
The Return to Hospitality: Strangers, Guests, and Ambiguous Encounters, edited by Matei Candea and Giovanni da Col
The Aesthetics of Nations: Anthropological and Historical Approaches, edited by Nayanika Mookherjee and Christopher Pinney
Making Knowledge: Explorations of the Indissoluble Relation between Mind, Body and Environment, edited by Trevor H.J. Marchand
Islam, Politics, Anthropology, edited by Filippo Osella and Benjamin Soares
The Objects of Evidence: Anthropological Approaches to the Production of Knowledge, edited by Matthew Engelke
Wind, Life, Health: Anthropological and Historical Perspectives, edited by Elisabeth Hsu and Chris Low
Ethnobiology and the Science of Humankind, edited by Roy Ellen

MIND AND SPIRIT

A COMPARATIVE THEORY

EDITED BY T.M. LUHRMANN

This edition first published 2020
© 2020 Royal Anthropological Institute

Registered Office
John Wiley & Sons Ltd, The Atrium, Southern Gate, Chichester, West Sussex PO19 8SQ, UK

Editorial Offices
350 Main Street, Malden, MA 02148-5020, USA
9600 Garsington Road, Oxford OX4 2DQ, UK
The Atrium, Southern Gate, Chichester, West Sussex PO19 8SQ, UK

For details of our global editorial offices, for customer services, and for information about how to apply for permission to reuse the copyright material in this book, please see our website at www.wiley.com/wiley-blackwell.

The right of T.M. Luhrmann to be identified as the author of the editorial material in this work has been asserted in accordance with the UK Copyright, Designs and Patents Act 1988.

Library of Congress Cataloging-in-Publication Data

CIP data requested

9781119712886

A catalogue record for this book is available from the British Library.

Journal of the Royal Anthropological Institute.
Incorporating MAN
Print ISSN 1359-0987
All articles published within this special issue are included within the ISI Journal Citation Reports® Social Science Citation Index. Please cite the articles as volume 26(Supp) of the Journal of the Royal Anthropological Institute.

Cover image: Michelangelo, *Il Sogno*, copyright: Courtauld Institute, London

Cover design by Ben Higgins

Set in 10 on 12pt Minion by Aptara Inc.

Printed in Singapore by C.O.S. Printers Pte Ltd

1 2020

Contents

Notes on contributors

Felicity Aulino is a Five-College Assistant Professor based in the Department of Anthropology at the University of Massachusetts Amherst. She is the author of *Rituals of care: karmic politics in an aging Thailand* (Cornell University Press, 2019). *Department of Anthropology, University of Massachusetts Amherst, 212 Machmer Hall, 240 Hicks Way, Amherst, MA 01002, USA. felicity@anthro.umass.edu*

Josh Brahinsky is a biocultural anthropologist exploring relationships between minds, bodies, practices, and organization strategies of evangelicals and other contemplatives. He is currently a Research Associate in Anthropology at Stanford University. *Department of Anthropology, Building 50, Stanford University, 450 Jane Stanford Way, Stanford, CA 94305, USA. jbrahins@stanford.edu*

John Dulin is an Assistant Professor of Anthropology at Utah Valley University. He completed his Ph.D. in Anthropology at the University of California, San Diego, in 2016 and finished a two-year postdoctoral fellowship at Stanford University in 2018. He is an anthropologist of religion who has conducted research with multiple religious communities in the United States, Ethiopia, and Ghana. *Department of Behavioral Science, Utah Valley University, 800 W. University Pkwy, Orem, UT 84058, USA. John.Dulin@uvu.edu*

Vivian Afi Dzokoto is a cultural clinical psychologist and Associate Professor in the Department of African American Studies at Virginia Commonwealth University. Her research explores intersections between culture and financial behaviours in African settings. In other work, she studies the interplay between culture, emotion, and mental health. *Department of African American Studies, Virginia Commonwealth University, 816 W. Franklin Street, PO Box 842509, Richmond, VA 23284-2509, USA. vdzokoto@vcu.edu*

T.M. Luhrmann is the Watkins University Professor at Stanford University, in the Stanford Anthropology Department (and Psychology, by courtesy). Her work focuses on local theory of mind and the edge of experience: on voices, visions, the world of the supernatural, and the world of psychosis. She was elected to the American Academy of Arts and Sciences in 2003. *Department of Anthropology, Building 50, Stanford University, 450 Jane Stanford Way, Stanford, CA 94305, USA. luhrmann@stanford.edu*

Emily Ng is Postdoctoral Researcher at the University of Amsterdam. She is the author of *A time of lost gods: mediumship, madness, and the ghost after Mao* (University of California Press, 2020). *Amsterdam School for Cultural Analysis, University of Amsterdam, Spuistraat 134, Rm. 4.62, Amsterdam, North Holland, 1012 VB, The Netherlands. emily.ng@uva.nl*

Rachel E. Smith is a Research Associate at the Max Planck-Cambridge Centre for Ethics, Economy and Social Change ('Max-Cam'), based at the University of Cambridge. From September 2016 to August 2018, she was a Postdoctoral Fellow on the Templeton-funded Mind and Spirit project at Stanford University. *Max Planck-Cambridge Centre for Ethics, Economy and Social Change, Department of Social Anthropology, University of Cambridge, Free School Lane, Cambridge CB2 3RF, UK. res84@cam.ac.uk*

Kara Weisman completed her Ph.D. in Psychology at Stanford University, where she is currently a postdoctoral researcher in the Department of Anthropology. Her work focuses on intuitive theories, conceptual change, and 'folk philosophy of mind' – how children and adults come to understand things like mental life, sentience, and personhood. *Department of Anthropology, Building 50, Stanford University, 450 Jane Stanford Way, Mall, Stanford, CA 94305, USA. kweisman@stanford.edu*

Mind and Spirit: a comparative theory about representation of mind and the experience of spirit

T.M. LUHRMANN *Stanford University*

This special issue reports the findings of the Mind and Spirit project. We ask whether different understandings of 'mind', broadly construed, might shape the ways that people attend to and interpret thoughts and other mental events – and whether their judgements affect their experience of (what they take to be) gods and spirits. We argue in this collection that there are indeed cultural differences in local theories of minds, in the way social worlds draws the line between interior and exterior, and that these differences do affect the way people sense invisible others. This introduction lays out the ideas that inspired the project and the methods that we used. This is the first report on our work.

The Mind and Spirit project is a Templeton-funded, Stanford-based large comparative and interdisciplinary project under my direction, drawing on the expertise of anthropologists, psychologists, historians, and philosophers. The project asks whether different understandings of 'mind', broadly construed, might be related to the ways that people experience what they take to be real. We looked specifically at gods and spirits because the evidence for invisible others often comes from anomalous thoughts and awarenesses, so that someone feels spoken to or senses a presence. If what counts as thought is different in different social worlds, so might the sense of what comes from outside.

We took a mixed-method, multi-phase approach, combining participant observation; long-form semi-structured interviews; more structured epidemiological interviews in the general population about spiritual experience; large-scale surveys among local undergraduates; and psychological experiments with children and adults. Our fieldworkers were skilled ethnographers and researchers, competent in the local language, and experienced in local research. We worked in five different countries, which we chose because we took them to have different traditions in thinking about thinking: China, Ghana, Thailand, Vanuatu/Oceania, and the United States, with some work in the Ecuadorian Amazon. In each country, we included a focus on an urban charismatic evangelical church with additional work in a rural charismatic evangelical church, as well as another urban and rural religious setting of local importance. The team shared a conceptual framework, a common design, and a thematic focus. We held

Journal of the Royal Anthropological Institute (N.S.), 9-27
© Royal Anthropological Institute 2020

weekly discussions during fieldwork and interpreted our observations together. This approach – not only using mixed methods, but also integrative, multidisciplinary, and explicitly comparative – is unusual in anthropology, but we believe that it enables us to make a more powerful case for our anthropological observations.

At its core, this is a study of a basic tenet of our discipline: that the ways humans interpret their world change their experience of the world. Anthropologists have a deep intuition that ideas matter. That is indeed one definition of culture: 'Culture consists of patterns, explicit and implicit, of and for behavior acquired and transmitted by symbols' (Kroeber & Kluckhohn 1952: 181). For Kroeber and Kluckhohn, these were shared ideas, inferences from what people saw, and expectations on which they acted. Anthropologists also see that humans live in worlds structured by power relationships, by the violence done by people to each other, by the health of their bodies, and by the way they manage to rear new generations. They assume that what Durkheim called their collective representations arise out of their experience of social worlds, and that bodies are the products of history.

Not everyone agrees. Particularly in the domain of the mind, it is easy for sceptics to say that these collective representations may feel important, but that they do not change anything fundamental about human experience. Many psychologists and many psychiatrists treat culture as superficial – as facepaint, not as in the bones of what it is to be human. We argue in this special collection that there are indeed differences in local understandings of minds, and that these differences are associated with significant differences in the way people experience thought and make judgements about what feels real to them – particularly in the domain of what we call spiritual experience. In this introduction, I describe what motivated the project, what we as a team sought to do, and how we did it. Our primary project goal was to establish that differences in the way a social world thinks about thinking seem to matter. The conclusion summarizes our findings, and then raises questions about where these cultural differences come from and how they might arise. Here, I describe what we did.

Towards an anthropology of mind

It can be hard to study thought. The Enlightenment model of mind presents thinking as so fundamental that it can be seen as a-cultural – as part of the apparatus of being human, rather like the structure of the inner ear. In the Enlightenment tradition, thinking is being. To be human is to think. *Cogito ergo sum*.[1] Thinking is not imagined as something culture can alter, or as a preference you choose, like deciding that you will learn to paint or ride a bike. Thinking is just something you do, as naturally and automatically as breathing.

That presumption of acultural inevitability is what gives rise to the sceptical challenge. Anthropologists have observed for many years that the way people think about and experience emotions, intentions, desires, and so forth, differs in different social worlds. The field takes for granted that local meaning changes experience. Our intellectual forebears – Émile Durkheim, A.R. Radcliffe-Brown, Ruth Benedict, Margaret Mead – all grounded their theories on the presumption that an outer social world shapes inner awareness in ways that are consequential for human life.

But it has sometimes proved difficult to persuade other people that these differences do more than change the surface of what it is to think. There was a striking exchange when the psychologist Angeline Lillard (1998) wrote an article that reviewed a rich array of anthropological observations and suggested that the way psychologists had represented the mind was distinctly provincial. Two well-respected psychologists responded:

> The cross-cultural differences catalogued by Lillard explicitly include differences in religious beliefs, and beliefs in phenomena such as witchcraft, magic and karma. As such, her view of cross-cultural ToM [theory of mind] differences pertains only to the inessential fluorescence of mature ToM competence, rather than to its essential character in early acquisition ... in general, Lillard seems to be looking at differences in *specific beliefs*, rather than at the *concept* of belief (Scholl & Leslie 1999: 137; emphasis in original).

As Rita Astuti (2012) pointed out in an essay discussing this exchange, these scholars treated anthropological observations as if anthropologists were looking at cultural ideas about vision, while psychologists were studying the biological mechanisms of the retina. They did science, we did fluff.

They were arguing over what is called 'theory of mind'. The phrase is associated with a research paradigm which, until recently, has been focused on tasks assumed to demonstrate that by the age of 5, more or less, toddlers understand that people can have different beliefs from one another (Gopnik & Meltzoff 1997; Wellman, Cross & Watson 2001). The classic experiment is the 'false belief' task, which younger children 'fail' and older children 'pass'. A child looks at a dollhouse. The researcher makes one doll (often called Sally) place a toy in a drawer and then leave the room, after which another doll (often called Ann) moves that toy to another hiding place. Then the researcher asks the child this question: when Sally returns to the room, where will she think the toy is hidden? Younger children point to the second hiding place, because that is where the toy actually is. The standard interpretation of this behaviour is that the younger child presumes that all people know what the child takes to be true about the world. Older children understand that the doll Sally does not know that the toy has been moved, and so they point to the first hiding place.

Brian Scholl and Alan Leslie are able to claim that theory of mind, in this specific sense, is acultural, because all children, everywhere we have looked, pass the false belief test at some point in their development. To be sure, it is true both that children pass the false belief task everywhere, and that developmental psychologists – now influenced by anthropologists – have begun to see culture at work within it. Henry Wellman (2013) and others have demonstrated that there are culturally different kinds of understandings of mental states, and children master these understandings in different sequences depending on their social worlds. In the Pacific, children master the false belief task at an older age than their Western counterparts (Wassman, Träuble & Funke 2013). Those same Pacific children, however, find it easier than Western children to understand hidden emotions (the man doesn't like the gift, but does not want to show his disappointment) (Dixson, Komugabe-Dixson, Dixson & Low 2018; see also Harris & Tang 2018).

Yet in none of these cases is the child in the false belief experiment in fact thinking about the mind. The child is drawing inferences about knowing, believing, wanting, intending. 'Mind' is the word English-speaking adults use as the collective noun for mental processes. In the United Kingdom and the United States, the word also connotes a place-like domain associated with the brain, private but knowable, and extremely important. In these social worlds, in many ways the mind gives individuals their identities. Your feelings, your beliefs, your ideas – in those social worlds, they make you *you*.

This is not so in many other worlds. Godfrey Lienhardt famously characterized the Dinka this way:

> The Dinka have no conception which at all closely corresponds to our popular modern conception of the 'mind' as mediating and, as it were, storing up the experiences of the self. There is for them no such interior entity to appear on reflection, to stand between the experiencing self at any given moment and what is or has been an exterior influence upon the self (1961: 149).

Lienhardt wrote that because the Dinka did not imagine a 'mind' as separate from a 'world', one could not suggest to a Dinka person that a powerful dream is 'only' a dream. The Dinka, he wrote, 'do not make the kind of distinction between the psyche and the world which would make such interpretations significant for them' (1961: 149).

Are those sorts of differences meaningful in human experience? Scholl and Leslie would likely be right to argue that Dinka children would pass false belief tests. (Dinka children do not appear to have been tested.) There is much about minds and brains that remains more or less the same for all humans, regardless of their social location. However, Scholl and Leslie are wrong to imply that different representations of mind have little significance for mental experience. And yet anthropologists have not yet developed this domain as a site for the development of theory, for comparison, and for the exploration of human diversity.

To be sure, anthropological work does offer evidence that local thinking about thinking has an impact on human experience that seems more fundamental than superficial, closer to the structure of the retina than to fireside musings about the nature of vision. I will mention only two.

First, medical anthropologists have shown that different models of mental action alter the symptoms of disease. Those who struggle with despair but do not imagine sadness as a legitimate cause of illness (as, for example, in China) are more likely to focus on joint pains and to experience them more intensely than those who take the mind's action to be central (Kirmayer 2001; Kitanaka 2011; Kleinman 1986). Those with psychosis may not experience thought insertion if, like the Iban of Borneo, they do not imagine the mind as a container (R. Barrett 2004). If the mind is a place where feelings can be held down like a monster under a trap door, then you should be able to help someone by talking with them: you need to help them see that they are the keeper of the keys. If the mind is the emergent epiphenomenon of a pulsating brain, unhappiness is best treated by chemicals that alter those neural connections (Lakoff 2005; Luhrmann 2000; Makari 2015). With the advent of biomedical psychiatry, those with schizophrenia became imagined as people with 'broken brains'. The social meaning of their diagnoses may even play a role in the poor outcome of the disorder in the West because the symptoms of schizophrenia, interpreted as the signs of a broken brain, become harsher and more caustic (Hopper 2004; Luhrmann & Marrow 2016; Luhrmann, Padmavati, Tharoor & Osei 2015; Sousa 2011). This work finds that cultural representations shape bodily experience in specific, identifiable ways.

Second, anthropologists and historians have shown that Christianity's doctrine of inner assent contributed to a new individualism, although these scholars debate when the effect became evident. 'Inner assent' refers to the Christian insistence that inner thought is in some ways more important than outward behaviour.[2] Weber (1930 [1905]), of course, located one shift at the birth of Protestantism, with what he called its unprecedented inner loneliness. Webb Keane (2007) follows his lead in focusing on Reformation efforts to purify the relationship between human and God so that it was not tainted by people, practices, and even words. Louis Dumont (1986) saw the individualism in early Christianity but then emphasized the Enlightenment and its aftermath.[3] Medieval historians Colin Morris (1972) and Caroline Walker Bynum (1982) identify the shift in the tenth and twelfth centuries, with the new emphasis on the inner propelled both by theology and by the emergence of guilds and other groups. But – as Mauss (1985 [1938]) pointed out – the idea of moral person as an individual is explicit in the New Testament. Romans 10:10: 'For it is with your heart that you believe and are justified'. The classical historian Robin Lane Fox, in his magisterial *Pagans and Christians* (1986), makes much of the fact that pagans were offended less by Christian non-belief in Romans gods than by their willingness to let an inner conviction affect their outer compliance.[4] The main point is that the idea that inner thought is more important than outward behaviour – in conjunction with some other changes – changed the way people thought about who they were.[5]

Yet anthropologists have not yet systematically organized these and other efforts around the question of how models of the mind might be related to human experience. For example, one might ask what kind of observation Lienhardt was making. He was not claiming that the Dinka did not think or feel. Lienhardt's book is, as William James said in another context, bathed in sentiment, and his interlocutors were quite thoughtful. Lienhardt could have meant that the Dinka had few words to describe their mental life, as Bruno Snell (1960) observed about the language of the *Iliad* and as Signe Howell (1981) found among the Chewong of Malaysia. Howell set out to identify all mental process terms among the Chewong, a tribe on the Malaysian peninsula. She found five (want, want very much, know, forget, and miss or remember). There was, she reported, no word for 'think'. Lienhardt could also be claiming that among the Dinka it was socially inappropriate to interpret what is in other people's minds, an orientation anthropologists have come to describe as 'opacity of mind': 'the assertion, widespread in the societies of the Pacific, that it is impossible or at least extremely difficult to know what other people think or feel' (Robbins & Rumsey 2008: 407). Lienhardt could have meant that imagination was not a salient concept for the Dinka – as Suzanne Gaskins (2013) and Eve Danziger (2006) have shown, in different ways, for different groups of Maya. These different claims generate different hypotheses, and different questions to explore.

The anthropological opportunity here is to ask how local theories of the mind differ, and to explore whether those differences can be related to differences in human experience.[6] This is what Rita Astuti (2012) challenges us to do in her reflections on the Scholl/Leslie/Lillard exchange, and what Webb Keane (2015) invites us to do through his explorations of the ways in which ethical reasoning utilizes the capacities that cognition affords. It is also what Joel Robbins urges us to do in his initial discussion of the opacity of mind when he observes how difficult it is for many anthropologists to take seriously ethnographers who work in Melanesia when they say that the people they study (e.g. the Urapmin) do not make assumptions about what other people intend.

> Anthropologists who raise such doubts draw on the deeply held Western assumption that those mental states we call intentions are crucial to the meaning of speech ... [W]hat kind of data could we provide that would convince our colleagues (and perhaps ourselves) that such language ideologies do profoundly shape the way the people we study handle language both mentally and socially, and as both producers and interpreters of speech? (2008: 422-3).

What kind of data indeed?

Journal of the Royal Anthropological Institute (N.S.), 9-27
© Royal Anthropological Institute 2020

The challenge is to make a plausible claim for a relationship between what people say about what we could call 'mind' and what we take to be their mental experience. We cannot simply assert that local models of mind change human experience; we need careful, systematic evidence of the sort that the medical anthropologists used to make the argument that different ways of thinking about emotion (different local theories of mind) are associated with different symptom expression. Arthur Kleinman (1986) interviewed around 100 Chinese patients diagnosed with neurasthenia who complained primarily of headaches and joint pains, and found that the great majority of them (87) also met criteria for depression according to the *Diagnostic and statistical manual of mental disorders* (*DSM-III*). He knew also that sadness was not seen, in this social world, as a legitimate cause of illness. That evidence, embedded in a rich ethnographic and historical context, was sufficient to persuade not only anthropologists but also psychiatrists that it was plausible that, in general, Chinese patients experienced depression more through bodily symptoms than through the emotional sadness that American patients emphasize. This kind of evidence did not make medical anthropology into a handmaiden of medicine – it persuaded medical scientists to take anthropological evidence seriously, and it became a remarkably influential study within anthropology. Anthropological evidence powerful enough to speak to other fields can re-energize our own.

Representations of mind and the experience of spirits

Why should the way someone thinks about thinking affect their experience of spirit? Some years ago I wrote a book, *When God talks back*, about the charismatic evangelical Christianity practised by maybe a quarter of Americans (Luhrmann 2012).[7] In these faiths, people seek out a personal relationship with an interactive God. They imagine God not only as supernaturally powerful but also as intimate. In this kind of Christianity, God talks back. People talk about hearing God 'speak'. Yet God is immaterial, not available to the senses. I wanted to know what Christians meant in saying that they heard God speak and how they came to be able to do so.

What I discovered was that knowing God in this way was not so much a matter of belief as a matter of skill – something that someone learns to do – and that the main vehicle for the learning was prayer. People usually prayed informally, and in that prayer they conducted daydream-like conversations with God in their minds. The church invited people to develop these daydream-like dialogues in particular ways. First, it invited them to think about their minds not as private, but as containing thoughts and images and sensations they might once have understood to be internally generated but were in fact communications from God. Second, it invited them to practise their dialogue with God in their mind by in effect pretending that God was present: by going for a walk with God, or by asking God what shirt he wanted them to wear. Third, it invited them to practise being loved unconditionally by God by learning to experience God in their minds in particular ways. In short, I saw that the social world of the church led congregants to focus on their own mental experience in highly structured, socially choreographed ways.

This practice of attending to inner experience seemed to change congregants' inner experience. Newcomers to this kind of church would begin by saying that God didn't talk to them. Yet after some months they would sometimes report that they could recognize God's voice the way they recognized their mother's voice on the phone. They said that their prayer experiences were more vivid and that God felt more real to them in their minds. Sometimes they reported that they heard God speak in a way they could hear with their ears, and I observed that those who prayed more actively were more likely to report that God's voice sometimes had an audible quality.

I could see, then, that learning was involved, and that it was not just about learning to say certain things – to adopt a certain discourse – but also changed something substantive about the experience of mind. Some of my work became an effort to demonstrate that paying attention to what one imagines ('training') makes some inner experiences more vivid, so that inner representations of God feel more powerful, more sensory, and more real. I also found that people who have a propensity for being absorbed in inner experience are more likely to have vivid inner experiences and more unusual experiences; they are also more likely to enjoy the inner attention that this kind of prayer demands (Luhrmann, Nusbaum & Thisted 2010). Yet it also seemed that there was something about the experience of hearing God that was hard for Christians in the secular American context. They would talk about struggling to experience God as real in their thoughts. They would say things like, 'You'll think I am crazy' or 'You don't need to send the white coats for me'. The fear of being crazy was even more pronounced when they reported hearing God speak with their ears. These hesitations seemed to be related to the ways they thought about their minds: as bounded, private, and secular – the mind-as-mechanism model of modern psychology.

That suggested to me that there was a scholarly and scientific story not only about the consequence of giving inner experience increased significance through prayer, but also about the consequences of the way that inner experience was understood in a specific social world. In other words, it seemed that there was an important and untold anthropological story about the specific way people learned to pay attention in particular social worlds. It seemed likely that different social groups encourage people to attend to their mental activities in different ways – that in different social settings, people imagine what we call mind differently, that they imagine thought differently, and that they have different assumptions about what happens when you think and about what thought can do. And so it seemed quite possible that different patterns of attention would lead to different patterns of experience.

In the Mind and Spirit project, we set out to explore whether we might see a relationship between local thinking about thinking and the experience of gods and spirits. We use the term 'local theory of mind' to refer to cultural differences about how mind – loosely, inner events – is imagined, what can be shared about inner thoughts and feelings, and what those inner thoughts and feelings are thought to do (see also Luhrmann *et al.* 2011). In doing this, the work starts from the same place as the developmental psychologist: with how humans learn about thought. But where the developmental psychologist focuses on when the developing child learns about the limitations of the mind, the anthropologist focuses on the way local social worlds invite people to make sense of their contradictory ideas about thoughts and feelings.

What anthropologists see is that adult humans continue to have conflicting intuitions about thought events, and that cultural practices encourage them to understand these intuitions in different ways. By 'intuition' here I mean the ideas people generate when they think, as we say, with their guts: quickly, automatically, without rechecking and analysing and laying the logic out on the page (Kahneman 2003). Snap judgements are intuitions. The self-critical thoughts that come to mind, even though we know we are too self-critical – those are intuitions. So are thoughts that we should jump out of the way of a moving car and pull someone out of danger. And all humans continue to have the conflicting ideas about thought that they struggle with during development, even if some of those ideas are ones they don't 'really' believe in. All of us, I suspect, have had moments – standing by a hospital bed, staring at an unopened email, listening to an election result – when we've wished hard to change an outcome even though we know, on some level, that wishing cannot change it. We've had anger wash over us so powerfully it felt as if the anger was not ours. We've had the thought that we knew something that we could not know, as if the knowing came to us from outside, and we've felt our minds being read even though we don't believe that can happen. Most people who lose loved ones have had the sense, at one time or another, that their loved one still is there. Even in the secular United States, many people never quite lose the sense that their thoughts affect the world, that others can read their minds, that they can read other minds, and that some thoughts (like inspiration) can come to them from outside.

People may have these ideas only on occasion and likely with only certain kinds of thoughts. But they do have them – and different social settings invite them to take some intuitions more seriously than others. For example, the cultural practice of prayer encourages the idea that wishing affects the world – when it is the right kind of wishing, and when there is thought to be a god who has the actual power to bring about the results. The cultural practice of burying the dead or even banishing them (A.-M. Taylor 1993) encourages the idea that the dead are truly gone.

I use the phrase 'cultural invitations' to describe these features of the social world, what one might call the 'affordances' that the social world offers (Gibson 1986). The reason to use the word 'invitation' is that any social world offers many ways to understand one's own experience. In the secular English-speaking West, for example, people have a saying: 'Sticks and stones may break my bones but words will never hurt me'. It's a taunt a child yells to the playmate who has just insulted them to tell that playmate that the insult has no force. The cliché invites the hearer to assume that what a person thinks and says can have no physical impact on a material world. Yet sports commentators also regularly say that they jinx athletes when they comment too positively on them and then the athlete flubs a move – as if saying the praise aloud caused the athlete to fall. And some invitations are more present in some worlds than in others.

At the heart of this project is the person making judgements about thoughts and perceptions: about which thoughts and perceptions they generated, and which thoughts and perceptions may have come from others; about which thought-like events are truly interior, and which more exterior; about what effects a thought may have had. I see humans as always making subtle judgements about what is real, as learning to interact with others in the environment and learning from the interaction how to interpret the experience of their own inner awareness, their own consciousness of thought events. I envision a person developing skills in interpreting their own thoughts and skills in drawing inferences about the thoughts of others, and doing so in different social worlds. The project hypothesis is that different cultural invitations lead people to develop different theories of mind; these affect the way that people experience their own thoughts and understand the thoughts of others; and these differences are significant enough to have consequences that matter.

Now I will explain what the project did.

Journal of the Royal Anthropological Institute (N.S.), 9-27
© Royal Anthropological Institute 2020

Comparison

When we think about difference, we compare. The Mind and Spirit project chose to make that comparison explicit. We chose five countries that we took to have different traditions in thinking about mind: China, Ghana, Thailand, the United States, and Vanuatu, with some work in Amazonian Ecuador not reported in this volume. We appointed ethnographers competent in the local language and experienced in local research to spend nine months in the field and two years (and more) on the project. We found a church in each setting like the one in which I did the work that inspired this project: an urban charismatic church with specific features – congregants were middle class/aspirational middle class; they were relatively well educated; the church was relatively high tech (e.g. using PowerPoint), with contemporary amplified Christian music; charismatic experiences were encouraged, and tongues were spoken, at least in private; and God would speak back to congregants and have a personal relationship with each one. All churches are different, but Pentecostal and neo-Pentecostal congregations have been described by some anthropologists as having a more similar – more portable – culture than many. Neo-Pentecostal churches are 'third-wave' charismatic churches: churches that adapted Pentecostal practices for middle-class congregants during the last third of the twentieth century and are now highly visible around the world (Bialecki 2017; Miller 1997; Miller & Yamamori 2007). (In this context, the early twentieth-century Protestant revival that led to Pentecostalism is referred to as the first wave; the 1960s Catholic charismatic revival is the second wave.) These churches are sometimes described as 'hard' cultural forms: a culture within a culture that spreads vigorously around the world in a surprisingly stable manner (Felton 2013; Robbins 2004).

The grant which gave rise to the project conceptualized the work as an attempt to answer three questions:

1. *Are there cultural differences in local understandings of mind?*
2. *Are there cultural differences in the way people experience the supernatural/spiritual?*
3. *Does the relationship between local understandings of mind and the experience of the supernatural vary by culture in systematic ways?*

The advantage of this three-part conceptualization was that even if the work found no relationship between experience of the supernatural and local understanding of mind, we would still learn something.

We were acutely aware of one of the main challenges of anthropological work, and indeed of much research in this domain. To understand an individual's spiritual/supernatural experience, you must talk to them. One can learn about what a church teaches by attending the church, and by watching the way experts behave. But you cannot know whether a particular individual has had those experiences without talking to them. This is particularly true for more subtle events, like talking to God in the mind, which simply are not accessible to behavioural observation, and in any event often take place in private. Yet interviews can be unreliable, and intensive interviews can be done only with a small number of people.

We used multiple methods to bolster our confidence that what we saw in the interviews was representative. I will list them here, even though we report in this volume only on our fieldwork and our intensive interviews.

(a) Ethnographic research done by the fieldworker and also by previous anthropologists and scholars. As above, this work – both observations and interpretations – was done collaboratively, with a shared focus and continual dialogue across sites.

(b) Intensive semi-structured interviews. There were twenty in each urban charismatic evangelical 'apple' and forty or more in three other settings: a rural charismatic evangelical church and an urban and rural religious setting of local importance (Methodism in the United States; Buddhism in Thailand; Buddhism and rural spirit possession in China; Presbyterianism and 'kastom' [revived traditional religion] in Vanuatu; 'traditionalist' religion in Ghana).

(c) A 'spiritual epidemiology': 200 similar but shorter interviews in each country in an urban location like the local Department of Motor Vehicles, where many people from the general population pass through.

(d) Surveys on mind and spirit: packets of pen-and-paper surveys (over thirty in total) on mind and spirit with 100 local undergraduates in each setting.

(e) Developmental tasks: three tasks with children and adults.

(f) A structured 'ontology' task in which we systematically asked adults a series of questions about what they take to be real and how confident they are about its realness.

Why bother with these other methods? We do not assume that the more quantitative findings are required to validate our intensive interviews, or that they replace them. But if we found (for instance) that the Ghanaian participants in our long-form semi-structured interviews consistently affirmed sensory experiences of the supernatural more readily than participants in the United States – and if they also did so in the short face-to-face interviews and in the surveys – we would feel more confident that our interviews represented a common local response. Each method was conducted with a different population in each country: the intensive semi-structured interviews with committed adult practitioners; the spiritual epidemiology and ontology tasks with the general population; the surveys with undergraduates; the developmental work with children. In each case, the team came up with shared expectations for the kinds of participants we sought. Our goal was not to see whether 'Ghana' was different from 'the United States', as if we were comparing two objects, an orange and a pear. Our goal, rather, was to feel more certain that the differences between what participants said in Ghana and in the United States was not arbitrary, but a reflection of common local understandings.

Now I will turn to the way we decided to structure our intensive semi-structured interviews, which are the basis of the work presented in this volume. Each participant was interviewed twice: first about spiritual/supernatural experience, and then about the mind.

Asking about spiritual/supernatural experience

What is spiritual experience? Our approach followed religious studies scholar Ann Taves's emphasis on attribution: that spiritual experience is experience deemed spiritual (Taves 2009). We built our intensive semi-structured interview protocol on the foundations of my own experience in talking with charismatic evangelical Christians in Chicago, on the San Francisco South Bay peninsula and in Chennai and Accra. The Mind and Spirit team spent four months together prior to the field research discussing the way those questions might be received by Christians and people who were not

Christians in our different settings and revising the interview protocol accordingly. We piloted in the United States, and when the fieldworkers arrived in their sites, we piloted and revised again.

In our intensive interviews, each fieldworker asked about roughly thirty spiritual events, with many follow-up questions. Our questions included both general probes about commonplace experiences (e.g. 'Do you ever pray/communicate to [the most salient invisible other]? Can you say something about why you do this?'; 'How do you usually feel the presence of [that invisible other]?'; 'Does the [invisible other] ever communicate to you through other people? Through the sacred text? In your mind?') and more specific probes about experiences often described as 'anomalous': voices, visions, and other sensory experiences; the sense of an invisible presence; sleep paralysis; out-of-body events; and others. These events seem to occur in many cultures; they seem to occur in some people independently of prior expectation; and they seem to form distinct patterns with stable traits. They are often 'deemed religious' – so commonly that the folklorist David Hufford (1982) calls them 'core' religious experiences and Ann Taves (2009) describes them as among the 'building blocks' of religion. There are ardent debates about whether these episodes do create stable categories, just as there are ardent debates about psychiatric categories (Borsboom & Cramer 2013; Kirmayer & Crafa 2014). Nevertheless, because these events appear to be recognizable across cultural and historical boundaries, we chose to include questions about them. We also included more open-ended questions such as: 'What has been your most memorable [spiritual] experience?', to evoke memories other questions did not.

These interviews were phenomenologically quite detailed. We asked people whether the invisible other spoke in their minds – and then how they knew that the voice came from the invisible other. This question, 'How did you know it was God?', was central to our work. We asked people to imagine a conversation they had had earlier in the day with a human person, and then asked them to think about the experience of hearing an invisible other speak in their mind – and to describe the difference. We asked people to distinguish a voice from God in their mind from a thought in their mind that God might have given them. We asked people if the invisible other had ever spoken in a way they could hear with their ears, and if so, where the voice came from; whether they had turned their head to see who had spoken; whether they had been fully awake or were falling asleep at the time; and how often events like that had happened to them. We asked people whether they had ever experienced a vision, and if so, whether it was directly in front of their eyes or more distant.

We describe our method here as *comparative phenomenology*.

Comparative phenomenology

By 'comparative phenomenology', we mean an approach to interviewing that zeroes in on felt experience with the aim of understanding that experience more deeply by exploring the event through comparison to other experiences in order to elicit more phenomenological detail. The method takes a phenomenon-focused, experience-near approach. That is, the goal is to understand the specific details of the event as individuals feel it in the moment – from their perspective, as the event unfolded. At the same time, the interviewer asks for more detail, based on his or her knowledge of other possibly related events. Comparative phenomenology interviewing is akin to clinical interviewing, although it does not presume pathology. Someone comes in to a clinician's office to complain about back pain. It is the clinician's task to consider a host of possible causes – along with the possibility that this back pain is explained by none of them. And so the clinician asks follow-up questions about the pain that draw from his or her knowledge of these causes but are open to other interpretations. The clinician asks where it hurts, how it hurts, whether it hurts when the person turns this way or that. This knowledgeable but open-ended approach is particularly important when studying religious experience because reports of such experiences are often laden with theology. Just as someone at a lecture might tell a friend more about the content of the lecture than about the timbre of the speaker's voice, people who experience the presence of God often want to say more about their views of who God is than about what they actually experienced that led them to think that God was speaking.

Comparative phenomenology assumes that there may be dimensions of an experience that people don't always bother to describe, and that we can learn from careful interviewing more about what people experience. For example, people of faith sometimes say that God 'spoke' to them. But what does that mean? Did the person hear with their ears? Turn his or her head to see who was speaking? The more a participant says yes to these questions, the more confident the interviewer feels that there may have been an auditory dimension to the experience. When people said that a spirit appeared to them, we were less interested in their theology than we were in the way the spirit manifested: where it was in the room; whether they could feel it and smell it as well as see it.

We set out to design interviews that were as phenomenologically precise and as descriptively grounded as possible, in ways that enabled us to compare. It is a phenomenological approach more bluntly empirical than continentally philosophical, more William James than Merleau-Ponty.[8] The challenge was to allow initial questions to be as open as possible, so that we did not foreclose what people had to say, while using follow-up questions that might capture phenomenological dimensions of events people do not always describe, and doing so systematically enough so that we could feel reasonably confident that we were asking similar questions to people in different settings. Here is an example of the way I have used this method:

Pastor J.:	The second step was – I was clearly hearing the voice of God saying that – this question was put into my ears very clearly. God –
Tanya:	Did you hear it with your ears? Or – ?
Pastor J.:	Yes. Yes. With my ears.
Tanya:	Oh. Audibly.
Pastor J.:	Audibly, I heard [God speak]. I heard this question: 'Do you want to be in a job, working for a company? Or do you want to be my servant feeding my sheep? Or do you want to be a pastor working with the church?'
Tanya:	That's amazing! So did you like turn your head to look to see who was speaking? Or did you know it was God?
Pastor J.:	No. No. No. What I mean by audible is not a sound that is coming from outside. I could clearly *know in my spirit sense* this question coming through my mind – that I'm hearing a clear stated question that's coming to my mind.

This exchange teaches us two things. Pastor J. does not appear to be reporting an auditory experience – even though he has been insisting that it was. It also teaches us that in his social setting, there seems to be this category of a domain that is not in the world (the voice is not sensory) but also not in the mind, which he calls the 'spirit sense'.

Searching for models of good questions, over the years I have read hundreds of standard interviews whose questions explore voices, visions, awe, pain, imagination, despair. I have read widely in the phenomenological literature of anthropology (e.g.

Journal of the Royal Anthropological Institute (N.S.), 9-27
© Royal Anthropological Institute 2020

Csordas 1993; Desjarlais & Throop 2011) but also in the phenomenological tradition in psychiatry, psychology, and philosophy (e.g. Berrios 1982; Parnass 2004; Petitimengin 2006; Sass 2014). These traditions are important resources for this kind of work.

Asking about mind/mental experience

In exploring the mind, we began with a heuristic: an analytic distinction between the human experience of thinking, intending, believing, wanting, feeling, and so forth, and the culturally specific representations of those acts. We came to distinguish them conceptually as terrain and map: the terrain as what humans experience and the map as the way those phenomena are represented in a local social world – understanding that such a distinction is always limited and always fallible, but that it enables us to formulate a comparison. We presumed that not all the terrain is locally mapped as 'mind' – that specific kinds of mental events, like anger, might be mapped more as part of body or of spirit, as indeed we found. As Serge Moscovici remarked in his foreword to a remarkable early collection about cultural variety in minds and selves, *Indigenous psychologies* (Heelas & Lock 1981), 'The domain of the psychological is bounded by culture and evolves with history' (1981: ix).

Our questions focused on what we took to be three dimensions of mind that we believed, based on the ethnographic and historical literature, to vary in different social worlds: porosity versus boundedness; interiority; and the epistemic status of the imagination (see also Luhrmann 2011).

The degree to which the mind is 'bounded' or 'porous'. Are other minds (gods, spirits) understood to be able to be present inside the mind? Charles Taylor (2007: 37-41) distinguished 'porous' from 'buffered' to capture the way selves were experienced in different social worlds. The 'porous' self is vulnerable to spirits, demons, and cosmic forces; the source of its most powerful emotions comes from outside the mind. The 'buffered' self, by contrast, feels a clear boundary between mind and world, and mind and body. While Taylor's distinction provoked controversy (e.g. Meyer 2012), it captures real differences in understanding what thoughts in the mind can do. We take the dimension of porosity to describe the degree to which an imagined wall between mind and world is permeable and whether thoughts and spirits can pass from mind to world, or world to mind, and whether such thoughts have causal power.

The degree to which inner experience is presumed to be important. Should thoughts and feeling be shared with others? Are they salient to explaining behaviour? Might they in fact even be unknowable to observers? Some social worlds – most famously in the Pacific, but one can find doctrines of opacity in Amazonia and elsewhere – have so strong a prohibition on inferring inner experience that people say that someone else's intentions cannot be known (Robbins & Rumsey 2008). All social worlds have expectations about what and when to share. We take the dimension of interiority to describe the degree to which inner experience should be shared and whether an observer should (and even can) know what others think.

The epistemic stance. To what degree are thoughts which do not represent the world as it is – we often describe this as imagination or fantasy – represented as 'real'. The imagination has had different statuses with respect to the real across Western history. In the medieval European era, the imagination was presumed to be the route to true reality. The ephemeral, non-factual nature of what the mind imagines was emphasized in the post-Enlightenment period (Abrams 1953). More recently, scholars have argued that adults in agricultural settings are less likely to encourage fantasy play than adults in modern industrial societies (Gaskins 2013). These different implicit theories of play, fantasy, and make-believe might well be related to the way people learn to ascribe truth status to assertions. We take this dimension of epistemic stance to be the degree to which the imagination is treated as real, and the degree to which it is treated as important.

In our intensive semi-structured interviews, we explored these dimensions with short vignettes which we used to probe our participants' understandings, and through direct questions. The advantage of these vignettes is that in discussing stories, people may reason differently than they imply when spelling out what they think they ought to think. (Good examples of this technique include Astuti & Harris 2008 and J. Barrett & Keil 1996.) We gave people stories about neighbours, such as the following.

> Suppose that in a distant community that is very much like this one, there is a woman named Jane. One day, Jane realizes that her neighbour Mary is really, really angry at her, and she has been angry for a long time.

There were three similar stories: one in which the neighbour was angry; another in which she was caring; and another in which she felt envious. (We varied the gender between male and female, and the order of the presentation of the stories.) Then we asked, in an open-ended way, whether Mary could affect Jane with her feelings, just by thinking those thoughts; whether she could if she were a special sort of person, or whether spirits might use those feelings to affect Jane; and whether Mary's feelings could make Jane sick or well. The goal was to understand when and how these thoughts (anger, envy, caring) could be causally powerful.

Then we asked people a series of direct questions about, for example, whether feelings should be shared, and with whom and when; and whether it was more important to express feelings directly or to maintain social harmony. (For these, we did not use vignettes, which now I regret.)

Finally, we gave our participants a series of vignettes about play (modelled on the work of Gaskins n.d.) and asked them whether that kind of play happened where they were and whether they would encourage it. For example:

> Albert has a small stuffed teddy bear, named Furry, that he takes everywhere with him. One day, Albert sets an extra place at the dinner table. His mother asks him who the place is for. Albert says, 'Furry wants to join us for dinner'.

> Thomas is alone, watching cartoons on TV. He turns to one side and says, 'Do you like the cartoon?' His mother comes into the room and sits down next to Thomas. Thomas says, 'Please be careful not to sit on my friend Tippy'.

The goal of all these stories was to create an opportunity to explore the way people understood those different events. Interviews asked in detail about the circumstances in which one person's thought could affect another, or whether imaginary friends aided or thwarted a child's development. In his foreword to *Indigenous psychologies*, Moscovici wrote that the solution to what he called the universalistic malady of psychology was to see how people in different worlds lived. 'Give [psychology] a phenomenology rather than an epistemology, and so allow in a breath of fresh air' (1981: x). This is what we set out to do.[9]

The essays that follow present our initial observations. Most are single-authored, but the authorship belies the degree to which we worked together. We presented as a team many times. We are, also, an interdisciplinary team. Two scholars here are psychologists, and their influence in thinking about what counts as evidence runs throughout the work of the anthropologists, as the anthropological orientation runs through theirs. The Weisman and Luhrmann essay describes how powerful these cross-currents were for the team, and how we think our respective fields would benefit from each other. The other essays – by Aulino, Brahinsky, Dulin, Dzokoto, Ng, and Smith – each spell out their author's central observations about the ways their participants seemed to map the terrain of the mind and how that related to their experience of spirit.

We appear to have a finding: that the more a person imagines the mind-world boundary as porous (as permeable), the more they report vivid, near-sensory experiences of invisible others. We see this in the interviews, and while we are not reporting our quantitative data here, it holds up as well in data generated by these other methods. We seem to see, in short, that ways of representing the mind (which we take to be cultural ideas) appear to be related to ways of experiencing spirits (which appear to reflect experience, and not just a culturally shaped way of talking). There is more work to do. The next challenge is to understand the social and historical conditions of these cultural differences in thinking about thinking, a task I take up in the conclusion. It seems clear to us, however, that this relationship between porosity and a more sensory spiritual experience is real. We feel that we show, in this volume, that cultural differences in the way people think about thinking really matter to the way they experience what they deem real, even in so basic a realm as sensory experience.

NOTES

It is an enormous pleasure to thank the John Templeton Foundation for its generous support of this project (#55427).

Without the hard work of the research teams in each of our fieldsites, and the generous co-operation of participating institutions, this work would have been impossible.

The US team was led by Nikki Ross-Zehnder and Josh Brahinsky, and included Lucy Monctezuma Chen Tan, Dominic Locantore, and Maria Russo, who were responsible for most of the data entry and some of the data collection. Other data collectors included Sean Wallace, Shantell Missouri, Norman Mortello, Noah Anderson, Mark Swerdlow, and Elizabeth Michael. Nana Ansuah Peterson, Viet-Co Audrey Tran, and Amy Wissenbach played especially critical roles in data collection and our work would not have been possible without them. The team would also like to thank the churches involved in this work, the Los Gatos Department of Motor Vehicles, and San José State University.

The Ghana team was led by John Dulin and Vivian Dzokoto. The team would especially like to thank Joseph Ansah, Ebo, Eunice Otoo, Mohammed Bosu, and Mankradohene of Mankessim.

The Thailand team was led by Felicity Aulino, and included Cheewintha Boon-Long, Pattaraporn Tripiyaratana, and Sangwan Palee. The team would also like to thank Adisorn Juntrasook.

The China team was led by Emily Ng, and included Tiange Zhang, Yifan Yang, and Xinyue Hu.

The Vanuatu team was led by Rachel Smith, and included Lavinia Mahit, Jerry Mala, Lana Takau, Jill Hinge, and Polinda Lango.

The Mind and Spirit project also benefited from the administrative support of Emily Bishop and Jen Kidwell as well as the wisdom of a group of advisers who convened annually for three years to provide feedback on the project, including (in alphabetical order) Rita Astuti, Jon Bialecki, Julia Cassaniti, Joanna Cook, Martin Fortier, Suzanne Gaskins, Nicholas Gibson, Alison Gopnik, Courtney Handman, Paul Harris, Adisorn Juntrasook, Lianne Kurina, Hazel Markus, Francesca Mezzenzana, Padmavati Ramachandran, Joel Robbins, Andrew Shtulman, Ann Taves, Hema Tharoor, Michiel Van Elk, Neil Van Leeuwen, Tom Weisner, Henry Wellman, and Ciara Wirth.

Finally, I would like to thank Nick Long for his excellent editorial advice, along with Justin Dyer and the rest of the *JRAI* team, including the helpful anonymous reviewers.

[1] The Enlightenment tradition is, of course, more complex than these sentences might suggest. Descartes was by no means the sole voice. The Stanford Encyclopedia is a useful starting point (*https://plato.stanford.edu/entries/enlightenment/*), as is Macdonald (2003). Nonetheless, it does seem as if the legacy of the Enlightenment has been the centrality of mind.

[2] The phrase 'inner assent' itself appears to come from Rousseau, from his *Reveries of a solitary walker* (I 1018, viii 23) and was developed by Paul de Man (1979).

[3] 'To state this thesis in approximate terms, I submit that something of modern individualism is present with the first Christians and their surround world, but that is not exactly individualism as we know it. Actually, the old form and the new form are separated by a transformation so radical and so complex that it took at least seventeen centuries of Christian history to be completed' (1986: 24).

[4] Some anthropologists have argued more broadly that inner assent altered the way Christians imagined the very composition of the mind, so that as philosophy and eventually psychology emerged from within Christian societies, philosophers and psychologists could simply take for granted that knowledge was propositional – that it was based on sentence-like structures such as 'I believe that it will rain tomorrow', or 'I know that cows eat grass and give milk', and that propositions were the basis of action (Asad 1993; cf. Smith 1998). Others have shown that the attempt to reach God directly – to really reach God through the deceiving entanglements of mind, language, and society – leads Christians to constantly reinvent faith and practices (Barker 2012; Engelke 2007; Handman 2015).

[5] In his wide-ranging study of liberal individualism, the sociologist Larry Siedentop remarks: 'The interiority of Christian belief – its insistence that the quality of personal intentions is more important than any fixed social laws … made the west what it is' (2014: 353).

[6] In using the term 'local theory of mind' here, I am rendered more confident by the developmental psychologist Henry Wellman's (2013) insistence that these ideas about mind really are theories, and that the term 'theory of mind' should not be limited to these very specific false belief tasks.

[7] A 2006 Pew Research Center survey found that they could identify 23 per cent of Americans as 'renewalist' Christians who sought an experientially vivid relationship with a personal God.

[8] Maurice Merleau-Ponty draws directly on the European phenomenological tradition, which almost invents a new language to help the researcher see (e.g. *noema*, *epoché*, bracketing), while William James sought to describe precisely with plain-language prose. He later described this approach as radical empiricism.

[9] He actually spoke of social psychology rather than psychology; but the phrase 'social psychology' meant something different in 1981. He clearly intended to refer to the field as a whole.

REFERENCES

ABRAMS, M.H. 1953. *The mirror and the lamp: romantic theory and the critical tradition.* Oxford: University Press.

ASAD, T. 1993. *Genealogies of religion: discipline and reasons of power in Christianity and Islam.* Baltimore, Md: Johns Hopkins University Press.

ASTUTI, R. 2012. Some after dinner thoughts on theory of mind. *Anthropology of This Century* 3 (available online: *http://aotcpress.com/articles/dinner-thoughts-theory-mind/*, accessed 7 January 2020).

——— & P. HARRIS 2008. Understanding mortality and the life and the ancestors in rural Madagascar. *Cognitive Science* 32, 713-40.

BARKER, J. 2012. The politics of Christianity in Papua New Guinea. In *Christian politics in Oceania* (eds) M. Tomlinson & D. McDougall, 146-70. Oxford: Berghahn Books.

BARRETT, J. & F. KEIL 1996. Conceptualizing a nonnatural entity: anthropomorphism in God concepts. *Cognitive Psychology* 31, 219-47.

BARRETT, R. 2004. Kurt Schneider in Borneo. In *Schizophrenia, culture and subjectivity: the edge of experience* (eds) J. Jenkins & R. Barrett, 87-110. Cambridge: University Press.

BERRIOS, G.E. 1982. Tactile hallucinations: tactile and cognitive aspects. *Journal of Neurology, Neurosurgery and Psychiatry* 45, 285-93.

BIALECKI, J. 2017. *A diagram for fire: miracles and variation in an American Charismatic movement.* Berkeley: University of California Press.

BORSBOOM, D. & A.O.J. CRAMER 2013. Network analysis: an integrative approach to the structure of psychopathology. *Annual Review of Clinical Psychology* 9, 91-121.

BYNUM, C.W. 1982. Did the twelfth century discover the individual? In *Jesus as mother: studies in the spirituality of the High Middle Ages*, 82-106. Berkeley: University of California Press.

CSORDAS, T. 1993. The somatic mode of attention. *Cultural Anthropology* 8, 135-56.

DANZIGER, E. 2006. The thought that counts: understanding variation in cultural theories of interaction. In *The roots of human sociality: culture, cognition and interaction* (eds) S. Levinson & N. Enfield, 259-78. Oxford: Berg/Wenner-Gren Foundation for Anthropological Research.

DE MAN, P. 1979. *Allegories of reading: figural language in Rousseau, Nietzsche, Rilke, and Proust.* New Haven: Yale University Press.

DESJARLAIS, R. & C.J. THROOP 2011. Phenomenological approaches in anthropology. *Annual Reviews in Anthropology* **40**, 87-102.

DIXSON, H.G.W., A.F. KOMUGABE-DIXSON, B.J. DIXSON & J. Low 2018. Scaling theory of mind in a small-scale society: a case study from Vanuatu. *Child Development* **89**, 2157-75.

DUMONT, L. 1986. *Essays on individualism: modern ideology in anthropological perspective.* Chicago: University Press.

ENGELKE, M. 2007. *A problem of presence: beyond scripture in an African church.* Berkeley: University of California Press.

FELTON, P. 2013. The future of Pentecostalism in Brazil: the limits to growth. In *Global Pentecostalism in the 21st century* (ed.) R.W. Hefner, 63-90. Bloomington: Indiana University Press.

FOX, R.L. 1986. *Pagans and Christians.* New York: Knopf.

GASKINS, S. n.d. Cultural differences in parental beliefs about play and imagination. Unpublished typescript.

——— 2013. Pretend play as culturally constructed activity. In *Oxford handbook on the development of imagination* (ed.) M. Taylor, 224-47. Oxford: University Press.

GIBSON, J. 1986. *The ecological approach to visual perception.* New York: Psychology Press.

GOPNIK, A. & A. MELTZOFF 1997. *Words, thoughts and theories.* Cambridge, Mass.: MIT Press.

HANDMAN, C. 2015. *Critical Christianity: denominational conflict in Papua New Guinea.* Berkeley: University of California Press.

HARRIS, P. & Y. TANG 2018. Peering into the opaque mind. *European Journal of Developmental Psychology* **15**, 631-42.

HEELAS, P. & A. LOCK (eds) 1981. *Indigenous psychologies: the anthropology of the self.* New York: Academic Press.

HOPPER, K. 2004. Interrogating the meaning of 'culture' in the WHO International Studies of Schizophrenia. In *Schizophrenia, culture and subjectivity: the edge of experience* (eds) J. Jenkins & R. Barrett, 62-87. Cambridge: University Press.

HOWELL, S. 1981. Rules not words. In *Indigenous psychologies: the anthropology of the self* (eds) P. Heelas & A. Lock, 133-44. New York: Academic Press.

HUFFORD, D. 1982. *The terror that comes in the night: an experience-centered study of supernatural assault traditions.* Philadelphia: University of Pennsylvania Press.

KAHNEMAN, D. 2003. Maps of bounded rationality: psychology for behavioural economics. *American Economic Review* **95**, 1449-75.

KEANE, W. 2007. *Christian moderns: freedom and fetish in the mission encounter.* Berkeley: University of California Press.

——— 2015. *Ethical life: its natural and social histories.* Princeton: University Press.

KIRMAYER, L.J. 2001. Cultural variation in the clinical presentation of depression and anxiety: implications for diagnosis and treatment. *Journal of Clinical Psychiatry* **62**: suppl. 13, 22-30.

——— & D. CRAFA 2014. What kind of science for psychiatry? *Frontiers in Human Neuroscience* **8**, 435 (available online: *https://www.frontiersin.org/articles/10.3389/fnhum.2014.00435/full*, accessed 7 January 2010).

KITANAKA, J. 2011. *Depression in Japan: psychiatric cures for a society in distress.* Princeton: University Press.

KLEINMAN, A. 1986. *Social origins of disease and distress: depression, neurasthenia and pain in modern China.* New Haven: Yale University Press.

KROEBER, A.L. & C. KLUCKHOHN 1952. *Culture: a critical review of concepts and definitions.* Cambridge, Mass.: Harvard University Peabody Museum of American Archeology and Ethnology Papers **47**.

LAKOFF, A. 2005. *Pharmaceutical reason: knowledge and value in global psychiatry.* Cambridge: University Press.

LIENHARDT, G. 1961. *Divinity and experience.* Oxford: University Press.

LILLARD, A. 1998. Ethnopsychologies: cultural variations in theory of mind. *Psychological Bulletin* **123**: 1, 3-32.

LUHRMANN, T.M. 2000. *Of two minds: the growing disorder in American psychiatry.* New York: Knopf.

——— 2011. Towards an anthropological theory of mind: overview. *Journal of the Finnish Anthropological Association* **36**: 4, 5-13.

——— 2012. *When God talks back: understanding the American evangelical relationship with God.* New York: Knopf.

———, R. ASTUTI, J. ROBBINS, *et al.* 2011. Towards an anthropological theory of mind. Position papers from the Lemelson Conference [includes introduction, individual essay and edited collection]. *Journal of the Finnish Anthropological Association* **36**: 4, 5-69.

——— & J. Marrow (eds) 2016. *Our most troubling madness: case studies in schizophrenia and culture.* Berkeley: University of California Press.

———, H. Nusbaum & R. Thisted 2010. The absorption hypothesis: hearing God in evangelical Christianity. *American Anthropologist* 112: 1, 6-78.

———, R. Padmavati, H. Tharoor & A. Osei 2015. Differences in voice-hearing associated with psychosis in Accra, Chennai and San Mateo. *British Journal of Psychiatry* 206, 41-4.

Macdonald, P. 2003. *History of the concept of mind: speculations about soul, mind and spirit from Homer to Hume.* Burlington, Vt: Ashgate Publishing.

Makari, G. 2015. *Soul machine: the invention of the modern mind.* New York: Norton.

Mauss, M. 1985 [1938]. A category of the human mind; the notion of the person; the notion of self. In *The category of the person: anthropology, philosophy, history* (eds) M. Carrithers, S. Collins & S. Lukes, 1-25. Cambridge: University Press.

Meyer, B. 2012. Secularization and disenchantment. *The Immanent Frame,* 25 October (available online: https://tif.ssrc.org/2012/10/25/secularization-and-disenchantment/, accessed 25 February 2020).

Miller, D.E. 1997. *Reinventing American Protestantism: Christianity in the new millennium.* Berkeley: University of California Press.

——— & T. Yamamori 2007. *Global Pentecostalism: the new face of Christian social engagement.* Berkeley: University of California Press.

Morris, C. 1972. *The discovery of the individual 1050-1200.* Toronto: University Press.

Moscovici, S. 1981. Foreword. In *Indigenous psychologies: the anthropology of the self* (eds) P. Heelas & A. Lock, vii-xi. New York: Academic Press.

Parnass, J. 2004. Belief and pathology of self-awareness: a phenomenological contribution to the classification of delusions. *Journal of Consciousness Studies* 11: 10-11, 148-61.

Petitmengin, C. 2006. Describing one's subjective experience in the second person: an interview method for the science of consciousness. *Phenomenology and the Cognitive Sciences* 5, 229-69.

Robbins, J. 2004. *Becoming sinners: Christianity and moral torment in a Papua New Guinea society.* Berkeley: University of California Press.

——— 2008. On not knowing other minds: confession, intention, and linguistic exchange in a Papua New Guinea community. *Anthropological Quarterly* 81, 421-9.

——— & A. Rumsey 2008. Introduction: Cultural and linguistic anthropology and the opacity of other minds. *Anthropological Quarterly* 81, 407-20.

Sass, L. 2014. Delusion and double book-keeping. In *Karl Jaspers' philosophy and psychopathology* (eds) T. Fuchs, T. Breyer & C. Mundt, 125-47. New York: Springer.

Scholl, B.J. & A.M. Leslie 1999. Modularity, development and 'theory of mind'. *Mind and Language* 14, 131-53.

Siedentop, L. 2014. *Inventing the individual: the origins of Western liberalism.* Cambridge, Mass.: Harvard University Press.

Smith, W.C. 1998. *Believing: an historical perspective.* Oxford: One World.

Snell, B. 1960. *The discovery of mind: the Greek origins of European thought.* New York: Dover.

Sousa, A.J. 2011. Pragmatic ethics, sensible care: psychiatry and schizophrenia in North India. Ph.D. dissertation, University of Chicago.

Taves, A. 2009. *Religious experience reconsidered: a building-block approach to the study of religion and other special things.* Princeton: University Press.

Taylor, A.-M. 1993. Remembering to forget: identity, mourning and memory among the Jivaro. *Journal of the Royal Anthropological Institute* (N.S.) 28, 653-78.

Taylor, C. 2007. *A secular age.* Cambridge, Mass.: Harvard University Press.

Wassman, J., B. Träuble & J. Funke 2013. *Theory of mind in the Pacific: reasoning across cultures.* Heidelberg: University Press.

Weber, M. 1930 [1905]. *The Protestant ethic and the spirit of capitalism* (trans. T. Parsons). London: George Allen & Unwin.

Wellman, H.M. 2013. Universal social cognition. In *Navigating the social world: a developmental perspective* (eds) M. Banaji & S. Gelman, 69-74. Oxford: University Press.

———, D. Cross & J. Watson 2001. A meta-analysis of theory of mind development: the truth about false belief. *Child Development* 72, 655-84.

Esprit et esprit(s) : une théorie comparative de la représentation de l'esprit et de l'expérience des êtres spirituels

Résumé

Ce dossier rassemble des contributions au projet « Esprit et Esprit(s) » dont l'objet porte sur la question de savoir si différentes acceptions du mot « esprit » (*mind*), au sens large, peuvent modeler la manière dont les pensées et autres données mentales sont vécues et interprétées, et si ces jugements affectent la perception des entités considérées comme des divinités et des esprits. Il existe bel et bien des différences culturelles dans les théories locales de l'esprit, selon la manière dont les mondes sociaux délimitent l'intérieur et l'extérieur, et ces différences affectent la manière dont les « autres » invisibles sont perçus. Cette introduction expose les idées qui ont inspiré le projet et les méthodes utilisées. Il s'agit d'un premier compte-rendu des travaux menés dans ce cadre.

1

From karma to sin: a kaleidoscopic theory of mind and Christian experience in northern Thailand

FELICITY AULINO *University of Massachusetts Amherst*

In this essay, I argue for a 'kaleidoscopic' theory of mind implicit in people's common-sense awareness of themselves, others, and reality in northern Thailand. Phenomenal experience is here generally understood as contingent on a host of factors, from personal habits to the influence of others, such that sensory perceptions themselves are in part a consequence of prior action (karma) with moral import. When Thai people convert to Christianity, they reject karma in favour of a God who will absolve a believer of all offence. Drawing on both neo-Pentecostal and Buddhist Thais' rich descriptions of their encounters with the divine and a host of other 'supernatural' experiences, I show how many Thai Christians maintain an abridged sense of karmic contingency. With attention to local theory of mind, non-monotheistic knowledge formations come into focus, highlighting the unique nature of the individualism emerging among Thai congregants and the stakes such individuation has for them.

Johnny Srisak[1] explained his conversion from Buddhism to Christianity as the result of a single Bible verse: Romans 8: 5. He was a young man at the time – before his marriage, before the launch of his successful architecture career, before the birth of his now teenaged sons. First his older sister had converted, which was an anomaly then in a northern Thai family. He and his father eventually followed her lead. As we talked in the open-air portico of his now long-established Pentecostal church in the urban centre of Chiang Mai, he recalled a question that had haunted him in his youth. Was there no power in the universe that could change our fate and clear us of our wrongdoings? The question was a rail against karma, the force taken for granted in his social world, that which can limit one's life chances regardless of even the most active striving. Then one day his sister presented him Romans 8: 5: 'But God demonstrates his own love for us in this: While we were still sinners, Christ died for us'. It was the answer to his rail. Christ could alleviate all the moral wrongdoing that could not be undone directly and immediately by any other means. Johnny traded karma for sin and felt himself absolved. He has remained a Christian ever since.

In 2017, I spent nine months in northern Thailand as a field researcher for the Mind and Spirit project, investigating, in part, experiences like Johnny's. The Mind and

Spirit project is a Templeton-funded, Stanford-based comparative and interdisciplinary project under the direction of T.M. Luhrmann (PI), drawing on the expertise of anthropologists, psychologists, historians, and philosophers. The project asks whether different understandings of 'mind', broadly construed, might shape or be related to the ways that people attend to and interpret experiences they deem spiritual or supernatural. We took a mixed-method, multi-phase approach, combining participant observation, long form semi-structured interviews, quantitative surveys among the general population and local undergraduates, and psychological experiments with children and adults. We worked in five different countries: China, Ghana, Thailand, Vanuatu, and the United States, with some work in the Ecuadorian Amazon. In each country, we included a focus on an urban charismatic evangelical church, with additional work in a rural charismatic evangelical church, and in another urban and rural religious setting of local importance.[2] For Thailand, the local majority in both the city and the countryside were Theravada Buddhists.[3]

In this essay, I aim to show how a local theory of mind provides distinct insight into Thai neo-Pentecostal experience, its cultural kindling (Cassaniti & Luhrmann 2014) and its consequences. While Christianity is rare in Thailand (0.63 per cent of the population as a whole), Chiang Mai, the northern region in which the research for this essay took place, is now around 6 per cent Protestant (both in the city and in the province as a whole, accounting together for approximately one quarter of the Christians in the country).[4] The urban neo-Pentecostal church with which I primarily worked was in its seventh year, newly splintered from the more famous (and contentious) Hope Church network. Upwards of 200 people appeared regularly for its Sunday services, which migrated weekly to various city venues. And there were other large congregations of upwardly mobile evangelical charismatic Thai Christians in town. Some have standing structures of their own (like Johnny's, which celebrated its twenty-fifth anniversary with a renovation and expansion of its home church), and others fill hotel banquet rooms and convention centres every weekend. Nevertheless, it bears repeating that the prevalence of Christianity among Thai and Sino-Thai populations has historically been low. In this essay I focus on first-generation converts.

Like neo-Pentecostal services elsewhere around the world, these Chiang Mai venues exude a modern feel through a mass of audiovisual equipment, from mics and amps for the band (complete with guitars, drums, keyboards, bass, violins, and multiple vocalists) to overhead projectors for song lyrics and sermon slides. Big services use earpieces and Lavalier microphones to co-ordinate through the resounding production. But even with a wall of speakers, the volume of these events remains relatively muted. No ringing in the ears follows any service here; one Chiang Mai church even seats its drummers behind Plexiglas walls to dampen the sound. Rapturous elements of a service, such as fast tempos or periods in which congregants speak in tongues as a group, are kept to a minimum. At a recent Pentecostal revival in Chiang Mai – held yearly with thousands in attendance, from the very affluent to the very poor – such moments never lasted longer than two minutes. Thai preachers also modulate their voices, so that even when they utter their most passionate cries from the pulpit, their voices are held back, as if released first in their throats, with the emphasis pronounced in pitch but the volume kept in check. The God these Thai congregants come to know is gentle and loving, literally soft spoken. And unlike the obsession with damnation and sin that Joel Robbins (2015) speaks of among the Urapmin of Papua New Guinea, the Thai Christians with whom I worked were focused to a much greater degree on God's love and forgiveness.

Journal of the Royal Anthropological Institute (N.S.), 28-44
© Royal Anthropological Institute 2020

What makes the insistence on calm, modulated experience so persistent in a Christian practice better known globally for its noise and rapture? I argue that a local theory of mind helps answer such a question by providing an experience-near sense of the karmic logic at the root of widespread common-sense, psychosocial norms, and perceptual experience alike.

A kaleidoscopic theory of mind as entrée to experience

To start, I develop the claim that karma is part and parcel of a working model of mind prevalent in Thai contexts. In broad strokes, karma refers to a theory of cause and effect across lifetimes. While it is usually thought of in behavioural terms of moral or immoral actions and their consequences, there are ramifications of karma in terms of the very make-up of the mind itself. In this section, I briefly give a sense of the ubiquity of karmic logic in Thai social worlds. I then present the implications of this logic in technical detail following Maria Heim's masterful elaboration of Buddhaghosa's fifth-century commentaries on the Pali Canon and its Abhiddhammic theory of mind. I go on to show how these erudite philosophical foundations manifest in modern lay people's overarching sensibilities and mundane interactions, with or without direct reference to this tradition. There are wide-ranging ramifications of this understanding of the mind, not only for Buddhist soteriological goals, but also for everyday social affect management and everyday notions of cause and effect. The karmic logic found in Theravada thought, I argue, has profound resonance with common-sense reasoning in contemporary Thailand across religious registers and provides a useful analytic framework for understanding Thai Christian experience. One would miss some important dimensions of neo-Pentecostalism in Thailand without it.

'The Buddha said that actually … if you try to find the real cause and effect of karma, there's no end'. Dtutong sat opposite me on a mat in his living room as he spoke these words, his long thin legs easily folded across one another, each foot resting on the opposite thigh. An urban Buddhist, he sprinkled reference to dharmic teachings throughout his explanations of his personal experiences:

> The Buddha told that it's, what do they call it?, *patjadtdtang* (ปัจจัตตัง), it's really *individuality*. If you want to track the reason of karma, you'll go crazy because it's very complex. It doesn't only have an X and Y axis; it has dimensions x, y, z, a, b, c, d … there's so many.

Dtutong reported that the wise may gain insight into such origins, while an ordinary person can only catch glimpses. Once, for instance, he had been hospitalized for severe gastrointestinal pain; as a tube was sent down his throat for a diagnostic test, he had a flashback of a fishing incident from his youth. He saw clearly in his mind's eye a picture of his violent treatment of a fish, hooked and thrown unnecessarily, and he thereby understood there to be a relationship between his harsh treatment of the fish and his pain. Similarly, when his house flooded, he saw a vivid image of a time he poured water down the hole of a cricket in his childhood.

A continuous stream of popular programming dramatizes and affirms the sense that the present has roots in the past. *Dharma life stories* (*lakorn thamnamcheewit*, ละครธรรมนำชีวิต) is a prime-time example, appearing on public channel 3 (with a string of its four-minute segments available on YouTube). With a refrain of 'karma is real' (*waen gaam keu jing*, เวรกรรมคือจริง), episodes of trauma and suffering are linked (explicitly, by the concluding narration of a monk) to the immoral actions of the protagonists, committed in this lifetime or in a distant past. A daughter-in-law, for instance, mistreats her comatose mother-in-law, only to fall into the same state herself and have her caretaker commit similar abuse. *Burning merit* (*plaengbun*, เพลิงบุญ), a twenty-five-part miniseries first aired in 2018, exemplifies karmic logic in racy soap opera storylines. An ancient-sounding proverb explains the drama playing out between the leading females: 'Too much *metta* [misplaced loving kindness], you'll keep meeting bad people'.[5] And with over 16 million views on YouTube, Atom's hit song 'Chuang nii' (ช่วงนี้) – translated as 'Karma' in English – croons that, 'at this time (*chuang nii*) you better watch out, go to the temple a lot to make merit, at this time your merit has nearly run out', as the lead actress in the video finds herself face-to-face with ghosts and apparitions at every turn.

These are but a few examples of the widespread promulgation of karmic logic in Thai media, beyond explicitly 'religious' contexts. Dtutong takes his visual memories as insight into his karmic burdens along such lines. But more than simply a tit-for-tat gloss on negative life circumstances, what's important to note is how people feel their sensory perceptions spring forth from karmic connections. To understand such sensibilities, I turn now to particular philosophical terms with which they resonate.

The Pali Canon is the tripartite set of texts composing the textual core of Theravada Buddhism, the overarching religion claimed by roughly 93 per cent of Thais.[6] The Canon includes sermons of the Buddha (*Suttas*), a code of conduct for monks (*Vinaya*), and an in-depth treatise on the mind (*Abhidhamma*). Buddhaghosa remains one of the most notable commentators on this core set of texts. Heim (2014) renders Buddhaghosa's work accessible as a philosophical system itself, without much of the modernist projection that many twentieth-century scholars brought to the task of translation. To be clear, I am not claiming textual doctrine as ethnographic fact; rather, I seek to bring Buddhaghosa's theory to bear on contemporary experience, allowing it to do analytic work bringing to light a local theory of mind along with fundamental ways of understanding the world and engaging with it.

The basic components of 'mind' are identified in the *Abhidhamma* as individuated entities, which are bundled together in any given instance to comprise experience. That is to say, mind is an umbrella term for the many parts that come together in various combinations.[7] The *Abhidhamma* consists of list upon list of these mental factors and functions – from sensory contact and conscious awareness to myriad forms of pleasure and energy – a daunting challenge for anyone wishing to map and master its content. Instead of scoffing at the lists as some remnant of failed taxonomical rationality, Heim shows that the form as well as the content of the manual are vital to its comprehensibility. That these various factors appear across lists and in reference to different phenomena reflects the many ways in which these factors can come together, depending on the particular circumstance. This is not a Linnaean-style classification system, not a hierarchical logic scheme in which lower-order components nest under higher-order categories. The possible combinations of component parts (i.e. of possible mind states) are functionally infinite – contingent on particular circumstances.

Like a turning kaleidoscope, the 'mind' here is understood to draw together component elements in an endless array of richly textured combinations. Of course, certain patterns arise with greater frequency, and the ever-changing unfolding of existence is in turn shrouded by a powerful illusion of continuity. The ultimate aim of the Theravada tradition stems ambitiously from here: to escape from the cycle of

Journal of the Royal Anthropological Institute (N.S.), 28-44
© Royal Anthropological Institute 2020

suffering that results from attachments in a world of constant change indexed by the
kaleidoscopic mind.

The point I want to make here is that these are not merely old philosophical tenets.
I heard echoes of these ideas from research participants again and again. Noi, an urban
Buddhist practitioner, explained:

> If our mind is sensitive enough, I mean if we have enough *samadhi* [สมาธิ, meditative concentration],
> we'll see how *jit* [จิต, mind] comes into existence, prevails, and perishes. And we will see that there's
> actually nothing in this world. Therefore, at this moment, what is important is how we can be most
> useful for ourselves and other people, those who are related to us (29 August 2017).

The composition of one's mind in this framework is both active and passive, with
past actions determining which combinations are possible in any given instance. Even
perceptions themselves – what people can and do perceive through their senses – are in
part a function of the conditioning of karma, as previous actions and their consequences
set certain parameters for mental combinations. This includes perceptions of the so-
called 'natural' and 'supernatural' realms alike. As one monk described for me, one
person may see a ghost in front of them while another may not; sensing an otherwise
unseen entity is a matter of a person's mind. 'We have to examine the factors for each
person'.[8]

Heim (2014) describes Buddhaghosa's philosophy as a 'moral phenomenology',
which proves instructive when considering the ways the Theravada tradition is variably
promoted and policed in Thai contexts. By moral phenomenology, she means a training
of awareness towards ethical goals: that is, Buddhaghosa's commentaries are meant not
as a description of how the world is, but as how it should be perceived as being.
As evidenced through popular programming, public education, and myriad other
mundane influences (see Aulino 2019), contemporary Thai social worlds train people's
awareness in ways that allow them to feel themselves as part of a natural order of co-
constitution and to take their spiritual encounters as part of the continual unfolding of
karmically contingent ordinary experience.

Karma, intention, and moral agency

In Western folk psychology models, people are understood to be more or less
autonomous 'belief-desire agents'. Intentions, beliefs, and desires are key to the root
'theory of mind' in the developmental psychology literature (e.g. Wellman 2013), taken
as self-evident mental faculties, properties, or states. What serves to constitute said
intentions, beliefs, and desires, or from where they stem, is not the focus of Western
folk models. By contrast, the Abhidhammic theory of mind focuses precisely on the
causal chains that create these prefigured mental properties, via the combination of
component parts (Heim 2014: 129). An individual's 'choices' retain an element of
'patiency', Heim's term for the non-agentive or passive aspect of lived experience.
Thus it is important to note that intention – that which classically anchors conscious
choice and arguably enables motivating desires, as well as that which forms the basis of
sincerity in post-Reformation Protestantism – is never considered in isolation in these
Pali sources or in most Thai people's casual consideration. In this Abhidhammic theory
of mind, intention and experience alike are necessarily and fundamentally affected by
karmic results, habit, and the influence of others.

Consider again Dtutong's contentions. He *saw* a link between his mistreatment of
animals and an acute *experience* of illness. His visual images flag a particular type of

attention to the present and the past, with emphasis on all that may predicate current circumstances. Dtutong had, in another instance, understood his desire for certain friendships in karmic terms as well. Once he had a vision of himself walking in India with two new acquaintances. Appearing somewhat foggier than flashes or memories from this lifetime, this visual perception confirmed his attraction to the relationships, and he explained this with a direct reference to reincarnation: 'We met again. We had known each other before'. Again, this reflects a social training of awareness towards recognition – often in the form of perceptual cues – of karmic antecedents to current circumstances.

The kaleidoscopic theory of mind also helps decipher norms of psychosocial support in northern Thailand (Aulino 2019). As others have noted, most forcefully Julia Cassaniti (2015), Thai social worlds generally favour a type of placidity or even-temperedness, with low arousal states preferable to excited emotions of any variety and frequent encouragement/admonishments to keep a 'cool heart' (ใจเย็น, *jai yen*). In contrast to hydraulic notions of 'letting off steam', psychotherapeutic ideals of sharing emotional tumult, or even Christian hermeneutics of confession and the ferreting out of impurity, Thai forms of reticence map closely onto ideals set out in the Pali Canon.[9] Ill temper or other excessively emotive states are thought to affect negatively the experience or composition of oneself and those in close proximity, thereby producing more karmic burdens as well as proving the poor state of one's own current karmic conditioning. Therefore, pleasing environs and light-hearted moods are privileged. Following social dictates for harmonious relations, distracting others from troubles, removing oneself from tumultuous situations, and other strategies for letting painful or disturbing emotional states pass can all be understood in relation to the kaleidoscopic logic of continual recombination and co-dependent origination.

On one hand, mind in this framework is not bounded or separate from the world. One is subject to a constant flux of influences, internal and external, along a karmic time continuum. On the other hand, individuals and individual minds are bounded. People talk and behave as if these influences should not upset one's mental state. Here lies the heart of ethical obligation. One should strive for – and the social world should support – actions and affects that minimize increases in karmic burdens. The power of underlying social values of equanimity and aesthetic appeal stems from this: at root, such states are conducive for the alleviation of karma on the road to liberation from suffering.[10]

Constitutive porosity

Mind in this tradition is thus defined by what we could call a constitutive porosity: it is porous to factors that serve to make it up. Usually the term 'porosity' refers to a stable thing that is permeable: a porous mind would be a thing permeable to other things. But in this case, the thingness of the mind (and, by extension, the self) is not constant or stable. Rather than a mind that is porous, with elements passing in and out, this constitutive porosity is part and parcel of the continual making of the kaleidoscopic mind itself. Porosity in this sense is not driven by or expressed in, for instance, a fear of sorcery or a vulnerability to spirit possession, though such manifestations are possible. The permeability of the mind is fundamental to its combinatory constitution.

In Thai social worlds, such constitutive porosity is understood as best regulated with equanimity. Equanimity is highly esteemed, both as a virtuous practice to curb the continued creation of negative karma and as a marker of religious attainment. Letting certain stimuli pass by or through you is a valued achievement given one's self is not bounded to a single lifetime or to the confines of one's own mind space, which again is inherently constituted with and through contingent influences.

One might liken one's constitution to a telephone network, as several of my interlocutors did; the service depends on the network. You can try to do good, stay calm, and 'make merit'[11] to gain access to a better provider, but you cannot simply decide and switch plans by your desire and volition alone. This brings us back to the overlapping lists of the *Abhidhamma*. Intention (เจตนา, *cetanā*) may be ever-present in all mind states, along with sensory contact, feeling, perception, and conscious awareness, but these elements are altered and take shape with other factors, such as initial thinking, sustained thinking, joy, pleasure, faith, energy, mindfulness, and so forth – with good, bad, and neutral elements affecting the tenor, the trajectory, and the very substance of all experience.

'Spiritual' experience and the kaleidoscopic mind

In my interviews, Buddhist participants often denied the extraordinariness of what might be deemed spiritual experiences, insisting instead that they felt indifferent (เฉย ๆ, *cheeuy cheeuy*) to close encounters with spirits or to meditative attainments. Such indifference reflects an understanding of both the constitutive porosity of the mind and corresponding ideals of composure. Encounters with spirits can reflect back to the observer something about their karmic condition. These encounters often mark an obligation to make merit on an unseen entity's behalf, and attaching to such things – or even attaching to positive achievements for that matter – is karmically burdensome. In terms of this local theory of mind framework, one could say that being overly concerned with or attached to any given encounter adds components to future iterations of the mind, which could serve to worsen circumstances (though a protective talisman or two or three never hurts).

Some people broke the kaleidoscopic elements of the mind down to some extent in interviews; others simply acknowledged the process. Noi, the cosmopolitan urban Buddhist quoted above, provides a good example of the former. She dedicates a lot of time to meditation, merit making, and formal Buddhist studies, in addition to her successful business ventures and volunteer activities. She described mind (จิต, *jit*) as sense and sensor, and then explained it has various 'subsets'. She went on, 'The *jit* works very fast. For example, I see a picture of you once, there are 17 *jits*. We perceive all the time. It changes all the time. We hear something, this is another *jit*. It keeps changing'. Indeed, she later evoked *jit* in another sense, as distinct from *cetasika* (เจตสิก) or mental states, for which she named another four conditions. Each set of components she named was distinct, yet inseparable, like body and sense overall. If and when one can become aware of the process, she said, one can gain some power over the lure of the senses, conditioned as they are at times by unwholesome factors. And as a trained person, Noi even felt able to 'tune in' to waves sent from other realms, like those from *praeta* (เปรต) or ghosts of relatives in need and 'in her network', precisely because she had some awareness, some power of discernment, of these distinct components.[12]

The kaleidoscopic theory of mind thus contours the spiritual events that the Thai people with whom I worked recognize, report, and experience. In a general sense, people refer to the characteristic of a 'weak' or 'pliable' mind (จิตอ่อน, *jit awn*) as leading to encounters with spirits; or, the inverse: one has a 'hard' mind (จิตแข็ง, *jit kaeng*) that is not susceptible to run-ins with ghosts – or, by the same token, has difficulty believing in God.

Thai Christian experience

A kaleidoscopic theory of mind helps bring into view the distinctly 'Thai' qualities of charismatic Christianity in northern Thailand. People aim for calm, for equilibrium. The God who offers an escape from karma is not a harsh judge; He takes on existing social values of equanimity and placidity and imparts such to followers. Still, Christian theology shapes Thai congregants' experience in distinctive ways. Some, like Tanwa, who converted to join his urban congregation over ten years ago, endorsed karma as a gloss for scientific cause and effect in line with church doctrine, with Christian sin a particular kind of karma. Others refused karma to a greater or lesser extent. Gail, a rural congregant also over ten years a Christian, fully denied karma in favour of 'sins of humans caused by Adam and Eva [Eve]'. The idiom of original sin captures for her the ultimate cause of all suffering, and Christianity, in turn, the sole means of redemption. But karma here is not merely illustrative of what Edwin Zehner (2005) calls 'transitional hybridities' – components of other traditions allowable despite evangelical anti-syncretism. Rather, karmic-style logics and related modes of moral behaviour are an indication of the persistence of the kaleidoscopic theory of mind even amid the 'hard' forms of evangelical Christianity (Robbins 2001). In turn, this local theory of mind helps highlight intimate elements of Christian experience in northern Thailand; what's more, this framework can help to identify and eschew common analytic presumptions, themselves rooted in monotheistic paradigms, as explored below.

Contracted contingency and God's guidance

In the context of Christian conversion, a kaleidoscopic theory of mind remains salient, but the factors felt to be conditioning experience are simplified or contracted by the presence of God. That is, God is understood by converts to be the most important and powerful 'condition' affecting you.[13] Being cool, collected, and even-tempered remains a signal of religious achievement: for a Christian, it is taken as a sign of God's work in you. One might say, because God works in you, understanding these constitutional processes and witnessing them is less important than having God do so for you. In fact, people said exactly that. One interviewee, Gong, went so far as to say 100 per cent of people can be helped by God, whereas only about 1 per cent can actually follow the Buddha's teachings. God is like a raft that must not be discarded, providing a permanent touchstone in inherent flux.

This 'contraction' of contingency – whereby God becomes the primary influence in life – also allows for a genre of spiritual experience to arise with great frequency for Christians without a Buddhist counterpart: namely, a sense of guidance. The Mind and Spirit project asked people whether they had ever felt guided by God through thoughts arising in their minds, through reading the Bible, or through other people. Around the world, Christians understood these questions and often endorsed a set of experiences in which they felt guided by a higher power. What was striking in the Thai context was Christians' ready attribution of guidance by one specific powerful cause to circumstances ordinarily understood to be contingent on a host of many varying factors. Nat, an active member of a Chiang Mai congregation for four years, provided a classic illustration of such guidance at work. Like so many other Thai participants, there was a distinct visual aspect to his cognition. A designer by trade, he could narrate, for instance, the subtle differences in imagery between memory and speculation – the former playing in his mind like a smooth and vivid video, the latter like a series of still images. So when it came to guidance from God, internal images were also key. As an example, he told me about a period when he was not attending to his clients with much care. He said he had lost contact with one client in particular, but God kept prodding Nat to think of him. One particular day, 'I saw him in my head; even though I had other work to do, all I saw was his face, so I decided to go to him'. Nat happened to catch the man leaving his house after lunch. It turns out he was headed out that very moment to another design shop. He told Nat so directly, remarking, 'If you hadn't come right now, you would have lost me [as a customer]'. Nat was astonished, and his first reaction was to thank God, this good fortune being confirmation that the thought had been sent as guidance by the almighty.

Such an elaborated Christian answer stands in stark contrast to the blank stares this type of question elicited from Buddhists. Queries about 'guidance' were largely unintelligible to them, even when framed in terms of spirits, ancestors, or other familiar non-Christian entities. Some quipped back, guided where? In Buddhist contexts in which the kaleidoscopic mind finds full expression, there is no one dominating guiding force in these situations, but rather a co-constituting porosity at play.

Pivotal orientations: Christian relations with spirits
Accepting God as an all-powerful personal saviour, Christians disavow forms of co-constitution with other spirits. That is, they must take a particular orientation to the unseen, as a 38-year-old rural Christian named Mimi helped me understand. We were sitting across from one another at a wooden café table, flanked on three sides by thick green rice fields. It was a hot and hazy day, and the ceiling fans beat steadily from high overhead, offering a soft breeze to the art space in which we had gathered to discuss spiritual experience. We were about an hour in to our long-form interview when she cast her doe-like eyes downward, her jovial disposition shifting ever so slightly, as the topic of dreams came up.

Many of the Thai Christians with whom I spoke claimed they had stopped dreaming. Some explained they felt no longer subject to spiritual interlopers in their sleep. Most claimed they had not been subject to night terrors or sleep paralysis since their conversion either. In the churches in which I worked, as with the other aspiring middle- and upper-class congregations in the city and rural congregations with which I was familiar, no one was 'slain in the spirit', an otherwise common Pentecostal experience of being knocked over by the power of the Holy Spirit. While church leaders explicitly endorsed the *possibility* of connecting with God in this way, being slain in the spirit was not encouraged (or witnessed) during services. Not only does falling over and/or quaking read as antithetical to Thai higher-class notions of decorum and control, such behaviour also mirrors familiar forms of spirit possession. Church leaders expressed the fear that people would mimic and become attached to having those experiences. From the vantage point of a kaleidoscopic understanding of the mind, such permeability and attachment are better tempered or overcome by faith.[14]

Mimi echoed much of this. As for dreams in particular, she professed that she did not dream regularly and generally did not put much stock in them. She speculated that dreaming most likely reflected what a person was focused on in their life. But she began to voice some uncertainty, the possibility of something special, in regard to dreams about her mother. In the two years since her mother passed away, Mimi had dreamt of her twice. The first time had been when she returned home after the funeral; she dreamt of her mother calling to her, something like, 'Oh! You are back home, darling'. In that dream, she had heard her mother's voice, sensed her there. The second time was after her own son was admitted to the hospital for a frightening childhood illness, when her mother 'came to her' again, asking after the baby's well-being.

Christianity presents a problem here. Many Thai Buddhists had talked to me with reverence about communicating with their mothers after death.[15] Often through vivid dreams, these connections were taken as an indication of motherly love and a signal to make merit at the temple for a departed parent. 'But as a Christian', Mimi said, 'I don't believe in spirits'. Here she lowered her eyes. Raised Buddhist along with everyone else in her community, she had converted to Christianity in college nearly two decades earlier. 'So', Mimi went on, 'I wondered if my mother really came to me'. As a tear glinted in her eye, she went on to concede it was not that spirits do not exist; rather, she had committed to the Christian idea that virtuous spirits/souls went to another realm. So she asserted that it must have been an evil spirit that she saw in her dream, an illusion made by some ghost pretending to be her mother, trying to elicit her trust and intimacy.

Mimi's dream helps bring out the stakes of this new religion in the northern Thai context. Had Mimi's mother come into her experience prior to conversion, whether or not she was real would not be of primary concern. While proof might be considered and evidence sought to confirm, taking steps to make merit or otherwise appropriately respond would be prioritized. Indeed, I found little of the 'ontological anxiety' Joshua Brahinsky (this volume) finds so rampant in US evangelical contexts. My Thai interviewees did not strive to ensure their answers to me were consistent, nor were they fixated on proving or convincing anyone of the reality of unseen forces. Yet Mimi was certainly ambivalent about whether these visitations were from her mother or not. As a Christian, she did not question the existence of spirits per se, but her conversion prompted her disavowal of any potentially positive, constitutive relationships with them. Mimi was no longer the sum of the same component parts as she was when she was a Buddhist.

Aspiring individuals, constitutive relations

I often heard Thai Christians and Buddhists alike characterize Buddhism as self-orientated and Christianity as centred on doing for others. In some ways, this was perplexing. Many observers have suggested that Christianity is a religion that encourages individualism. What's more, the focus of many Thai Buddhist experiences is on providing for others, seen and unseen. 'Supernatural' encounters derive much of their meaning from what they oblige the experiencer to do. The bulk of spiritual practices relayed to me by Buddhists involved tending to multitudes of beings through transfers of merit. Even in more cosmopolitan meditation practices, placidity was an ideal in part because it was thought to foster a proper attunement to the world and to the spirits and ancestors to whom one was legitimately obliged.

When observers assert the self-orientation of Thai Buddhism, they pivot on a particular sense of an individual self. I see this as linked to Sanit Samarkangaan's claim that *individuals* in Thai society are largely responsible for meeting their own needs by forging *relationships* (Sanit 1975). 'Individualism' here does not refer to independence, self-reliance, or the 'moral worth of the individual'.[16] Instead, it refers to a social system that relies on relationships for social functioning, and individual responsibility to seek out and depend upon proper relations with others therein. Noi's claims for being useful to others can be understood in this way; as she said, 'what is important is how we can be most useful *for ourselves* and other people, *those who are related to us*'. Yes, a type of self-interest drives the need to care for and assess others carefully: one must, for instance, associate with 'good' people in order to avoid the pitfalls of others' ill will. Yes, placidity can lead to an increase in one's personal power of attracting positivity. But even more so, given the constitutive porosity of mind presented above, such associations can be understood as karmically constituted and fundamentally constituting of one's self. Individualism in this sense rests not on autonomous individuality, but rather on an individuality composed of relations – with others as among its component parts.

Thai Christians do appear more 'individualistic' in the sense often described in the anthropological literature (Bialecki & Daswani 2015). Even so, the way they become more individualistic reveals the karmic bones of the Buddhism from which they converted. Obligation and relationality are evident at the core of a great deal of Buddhists' extraordinary experience and ritual work. For Buddhists, one's continual fashioning is subject to effort (a function of what one does and seeks to do, as well as what one has done and obligations incurred in past lifetimes). Many visit fortune-tellers or play the lottery as a diagnostic of sorts, a means of assessing the status of their fate or the type of ecological niche they currently occupy. They might then follow prescribed dictates in an attempt to alter their fate, whether for this lifetime or for the next. And still there remains an understood 'patiency' to ethical life, a type of fatefulness to existence and experience unalterable by intention and action alone.

For new Thai Christians, spirits are no longer assisted in mutually beneficial ritual practices; they are instead categorized en masse as demons to be cast out in the name of Jesus Christ. Christians must rely on themselves to make relationships with other people, many of them Christian. For the congregants I knew, this primarily involved providing support for newer converts to Christianity within their church's structured shepherding system. What's more, they promoted being a good person as a form of aid, their individual behaviour – particularly actions of grace, honesty, calmness, and generosity – a powerful example to others capable of attracting and converting the unsaved. When someone socialized with what I am calling a kaleidoscopic model of mind becomes a Christian, it is as if they can 'do for others' by way of becoming impermeable, God-cloaked, individuated entities in their own right, then making a great effort to be in relationship with others, whom they help.

Inner assent is generally understood as key, for historical reasons, to the importance of belief in Christianity and the impetus for increased individuation (Asad 1993; Keane 2002). I am suggesting that in a context with an operating kaleidoscopic theory of mind, indications of individuation appear at an intimate level that has to do with how relationships are experienced, and the ways the world itself is understood and engaged. Further, as Saba Mahmood points out, owing to the 'Christian structure' of dominant analytic frames, often 'certain differences are more legible than others' in the examination of religiously based difference (2010: 298). I am arguing that the kaleidoscopic theory of mind and its historical lineages is a powerful way to attune to other horizons.

Monotheism, ontological pluralism, and the kaleidoscopic mind
When Thai Buddhists convert to Christianity, something fundamental changes in the way they are invited to understand reality itself. In Buddhist thought, the constant flux

and contingency intrinsic to the model of mind described above mirrors the dhammic workings of existence overall. Indeed, when I asked people for metaphors for the mind, or similes to help relate the way the mind works, Thai Christians and Buddhists alike most often offered natural exemplars: water, waves, the four elements (water, fire, earth, air – depending on circumstances), or all of the natural world itself. They spoke about cause-and-effect logics, though for Buddhists such logics were not compelled by a sense of a bounded, linear creation. Experience was felt to unfold in karmic time, with multiple truths and multiple realities not only possible but potentially co-present.[17] After conversion to Christianity, while the 'natural world' mind metaphors remained, both the time-frame and the field of cause and effect were bounded.

When God becomes the primary influence of note, the effort of deciphering signs from the social and natural environment is narrowed. And as God takes the place of karmic retribution, a person's trained attentiveness to actions and their consequences readily transfers to the neo-Pentecostal sense of constant intimacy with God. This intimacy reflects a type of individualism previously uninhabited. God renders other antecedents largely irrelevant.

This shift contracts felt multiplicity in a broader sense. This was true for Mimi, when she felt she had to deny the possibility of her mother's return in a dream. A challenge we encountered in our research helps bring this fundamental issue further to the surface. In surveying people for our 'spiritual epidemiology' – an attempt to gauge the rates of various types of phenomenal events experienced in the population – people would deny categorically types of events with which they nonetheless had personal experience. For instance, a respondent might claim that spirits cannot communicate through dreams, but then report that the dream of a friend's dead father had been a direct threat in their own life; another might say that spirits categorically cannot affect people, but then later explain that the spirit of a friend's friend had previously sabotaged their business. The specific relationship was key, with the proximal cause of utmost importance, not the generic type of event it 'represents'. Any particular relation creates a cascading set of possibilities that may not be captured by an umbrella category. If the kaleidoscope clicks into view in this way, this set of elements is possible; if another way, another set. Both are real. They can contradict. And they can both be true at the same time.

In research conducted within church congregations, we did not encounter this issue to the same degree. As one Christian research assistant suggested, with conversion, by default you are put into relationship with all demons, by virtue of your allegiance with God (whereas in the past you might not have had any karmic connections to such entities). Some Christians even related a marked increase in encounters with spirits immediately after their conversion (especially when they had never had such experiences before). They sometimes attributed this to their new visibility to evil spirits, as if they had been put into relationship by fiat as a target in spiritual warfare. So while a type of contingency remains in Christian spiritual life, co-constitutionality is simplified and constricted in a way that alleviates certain relational burdens and karmic obligations. This also serves to create categories of beings that can uniformly be understood as operating in the same way. Christian cosmology bounds reality into a singular creation, supporting Linnaean-type typologies in the process.

The first night I brought my Thai research assistants to church – our first outing together, their first exposure to Christian worship – their main shock came from the repeated notion that God created everything. It had been a rousing service, an event quite different from anything they had experienced theretofore. A famous preacher was in from Bangkok and congregations from all over the region had gathered for the occasion. Hands were raised. Eyes were shut. Tears flowed. Donations were welcomed. Afterwards, as we collected ourselves in the car, my assistants' reactions poured out with little prodding. That God created and was evident in everything was the most outrageous element to them – even more than the weeping and the money, which elicited cynicism but less outright contempt.

To a convert, the notion that God created the world bounds reality into a singular creation; to a non-convert, experience is not felt to unfold as such. When non-Christian Thai respondents spoke of feeling obligation to a spirit, they felt it as a requirement for well-being, even if it did not matter (or even exist) on another plane of existence. Mimi does not simply put faith in God as opposed to previous belief in the spirit of her mother; the two must now become mutually exclusive.

What my work suggests is that non-monotheistic traditions like those found in Thailand at times recognize multiple natures – overlapping, contradictory, but not mutually exclusive planes of existence – rather than merely elaborating different epistemologies within a singular nature. What's more, Thai Buddhists' spiritual and extraordinary experiences do not lend themselves to a standard taxonomy, characterized by ideal types and sub-categories. I would go so far as to argue that such taxonomical thinking generally relies on a singular sense of reality that can be known and mapped. This sense of knowledge is fostered by a bounded cosmos like that espoused by monotheism, which does not have an easy parallel in the multiplicity of possibilities composing the Buddhist cosmos to which my interviewees pointed.[18] Paul Unschuld suggested something similar when comparing Western and Chinese medicine and philosophy across two millennia: 'Western civilization has been and remains a culture searching for, and believing in, the existence of one single truth. This attitude is reflected in Western monotheistic religious culture, and it is reflected in a continuous attempt to build one coherent scientific paradigm' (1992: 57). Despite the limitations of such broad strokes, Unschuld productively suggests from Chinese knowledge systems an instrumental approach in which knowledge depends on desired ends. Similar to how relations structure what is and is not possible and perceptible in my Thai colleagues' renderings, Unschuld finds in Chinese medical renderings that 'different truths may coexist if their application results in a successful manipulation of a perceived reality' (1992: 58).[19]

A kaleidoscopic theory of mind implies this orientation of multiplicity, so marked among Thai Buddhist participants. The *Abhidhamma* can here, then, be an important guide. But rather than reading the *Abhidhamma* as a taxonomy of the fixed parts of the mind, we would do well to read Buddhaghosa's philosophy as a manual for how to train one's awareness in order to achieve liberation from suffering. Whether listening to temple dharma talks or to talk radio, watching popular evening television programming or flipping through dime-store paperbacks, Thai social worlds propagate such training. They teach people to understand and experience mental states as transient. People are trained to seek equanimity by not attaching to tumult, itself the result of or causing future karma. Similarly, people are encouraged not to dwell upon supernatural encounters (television dramas and ghost stories notwithstanding). Understanding that one's perceptions are conditioned, in part, by obligatory relationships, one is taught to feel such encounters are 'no big deal'. What is instructed is basic ritual acknowledgement, so that further seeds of karma need not be unduly sowed. This is a moral training of awareness, not a set of axioms of what is unequivocally true.

The *Abhidhamma* is geared towards a subtle analysis of the minutiae that come to comprise any given moment of experience in the human mind. But at another level of analysis, the mind itself is an epiphenomenon, an illusory result of spirit and body conjoining.[20] Inherent in this kaleidoscopic theory of mind is mind's existence and lack of existence, simultaneously. And, indeed, whether in clerical or layman's terms, people spoke as if the nature of reality necessarily depended on the level of analysis deployed. Hence we see an ontological plurality at play – akin more to quantum than classical mechanics; more about the simultaneous existence of wave and particle than a fixed and ordered world. Indeed, Heim encourages resistance to the 'ontological reflex' – the habit of reckoning back to a presumed singular reality, or the urge to provide an overarching meta-narrative or logic – when working through this Pali tradition.[21] Ontological plurality instead can provide fertile ground for understanding how people attest to one set of understandings fully, and at the same time conceive of another level of analysis (perhaps pertaining to a different set of circumstances or a level of analysis they themselves are unable to achieve) that renders their current understanding obsolete. And yet it also stands, compelling and necessary. Ontological pluralism in Thai contexts embraces such multiplicity, supporting and promoting an appreciation of plurality and an acceptance of any contradiction stemming therefrom.

Monotheism supports what amounts to locking in to one orientation: God renders other antecedents largely irrelevant and drives all influences into a singular plane of God-created existence. The conditioned nature of the mind described above, by contrast, reflects the multiplicitous nature of reality in Buddhist cosmology: kaleidoscopic minds engage multiplicities for insight, mutual aid, and ecologically attuned experience.

Onward

The kaleidoscopic theory of mind presented here brings out key elements of people's common-sense awareness of themselves, others, and the nature of reality in northern Thailand. Resonating with philosophical tenets found in the *Abhidhamma*, my interviewees narrated their phenomenal experience as contingent on a host of factors: past and present, material and immaterial. For Buddhists, karma provides a moral 'patiency' to experience, with perception itself understood at least in part as a function of prior actions and one's fated position. For Christians, this moral understanding is explicitly displaced when converts take God as the primary influence on experience. Sin can be atoned for and forgiven. And yet northern Thai churches can also be understood to maintain an implicit link to the logic of karmic conditioning. Their aesthetic sensibilities appeal to overarching social ideals of equanimity. While the obligation to maintain decorum for one's own well-being and for others can be explained in many ways, the convergence of influences on inner states marked by the *Abhidhamma* is a philosophically rich and locally relevant theoretical orientation that helps unearth abiding moral touchstones. Discomfort with high arousal here has deep roots.

Christian faith has worked miracles in the lives of many of the individuals with whom I worked. Depressions lifted, terminal illnesses abated, addictions overcome, jobs secured: people's lives can be remarkably altered with Christianity. And yet much can be flattened or eradicated in the Christian world-view as well, including a broad-ranging ecological sensitivity and a deep (and at times consoling) appreciation of multiplicity. What's more, secular analytic frames, derived from monotheistic philosophical lineages, can limit appreciation of the stakes of such transformations. The current encounter between Thai Buddhism and Christianity is unprecedented in its conversion rates and social proliferation. What this encounter will engender, near and far, and what will become of a kaleidoscopic theory of mind in sustained intimate contact with Christianity in Thai contexts remains to be seen – and remains worthy of sustained attention.

NOTES

My deepest gratitude to Cheewintha Boon-Long, Pattaraporn Tripiyaratana, and Sangwan Palee, who were invaluable to this article and the overarching project alike.

[1] All names are pseudonyms.

[2] This paragraph is based on a description drafted collectively by the Mind and Spirit team and used to illustrate the joint nature of the research.

[3] We matched Buddhists to their Christian counterparts in age and neighbourhood and general class standing. This did not equate to a particular temple community, akin to a church congregation, though a network of local temples and teachers emerged as touchstones among the Buddhist sample. Also noteworthy, 'spirit cults' are subsumed by Theravada Buddhism in the Thai national imagination (see Endres & Lauser 2012), and questions about God were paralleled with Buddhists largely through questions about spirits and other 'supernatural' entities along with other Buddhist religious attainments.

[4] The majority of Christians reside in the country's three northernmost provinces. See *http://estar.ws/ harvest/christian-presence-map.html* (last accessed 8 January 2020) for details, though those numbers include Hill Tribe populations. For historical context, see the OMF (Overseas Missionary Fellowship) (*https://omf.org/thailand/north-thailand*), the Digital Library of Christian Resources (*http://www.thaicrc. com/*), and Thaichurchhistory.com.

[5] เมตตาจนเกินการณ์ < . . . > จะพบคนพาลอยู่ร่ำไป.

[6] The very categories of the Pali Canon and Theravada Buddhism are not without their pitfalls (see Collins 2013); Heim (2014) goes a long way in moving through these tensions.

[7] It is worth noting that 'mind' can be used in numerous ways, with varying degrees of specificity and/or concreteness, depending on the level of analysis deployed. Certain adepts are thought able to discern the operations of karma across lifetimes; for others, acknowledgement of the general process suffices.

[8] The monk went on, probing: 'But *do they [spirits] exist?* That is also linked to our minds. If we believe they exist, then they do; if we say they don't exist, then they don't. But they do'.

[9] For another contrast, see Tooker (2018) for Akha notions of balancing or levelling, as opposed to depth-based metaphors of self, in northern Thailand.

[10] In the cycle of conditioning, every action – of body, speech, and mind – is said to beget more karma; all, that is, except for those that do not bear karmic fruit, the *kiriya*. While such states are considered beyond the reach of most humans, the possibility of *kiriya* further reinforces the ideal of equanimity and social markers of prestige. But supposed attributes of adepts can be manipulated in the social world and contribute to repressive social conditions, as I discuss at length elsewhere (Aulino 2019).

[11] Merit making generally involves composing an offering of flowers, food, basic necessities for monks, and/or money to offer at a temple.

[12] Noi also evoked the *Triphum Phra Ruang* (*Three worlds according to King Ruang*), a cosmological text read as part of Thailand's national education, in a similar fashion: listing not only various mental factors but also multiple realms of existence.

[13] There is an elite stratum of Thai Christians whose families have been Christian for multiple generations; more work is needed to understand the influence of Protestantism and Catholicism in the upper echelons of Thai society.

[14] I encountered only one urban church that endorsed being slain in the spirit: the self-proclaimed 'poor people's church' across town. I found no significant differences in this regard across rural and urban settings – though one of the more established and upper-class churches had increasing ties to Bethel Redding, an American, non-denominational charismatic megachurch, inviting more unusual experiences (after much internal debate). A preacher's wife explained to me that cultural associations were the impediment to accepting God's presence in being slain in the spirit.

[15] Major bookstores provide clues to the rank and religious profile of mothers, with a section alongside the Buddhism books dedicated to the spiritual importance of mothers. People told me that mothers are your closest Buddha, the Buddha inside you (*Pra nai keu mae*, พระในคือแม่).

[16] See *http://www.britannica.com/EBchecked/topic/286303/individualism*. Note Sanit was writing prior to the introduction of Thailand's sweeping social welfare reforms; nevertheless, his insights regarding hierarchy and relationality remain salient.

Journal of the Royal Anthropological Institute (N.S.), 28-44
© Royal Anthropological Institute 2020

[17] Recall here the monk noting that a spirit could be not real and real at the same time.

[18] Monotheism may seem too blunt a category, as opposed to the inner assent of the post-Reformation. But it is precisely such a blunt concept that can reflect different starting presumptions and their variant ontological openings. Don Handelman makes parallel points in regard to both 'monotheism' (2008) and the 'lineal hierarchy' taken for granted in monotheistic logic (2012).

[19] This resonates with Yongsak Thantiphidok's depiction of Thai medicine (Yongsak 2007), and, intriguingly, with Marisol de la Cadena's description of Andean sensibilities as well. De la Cadena also invokes the 'kaleidoscopic' to portray the 'simultaneity of similarity and difference' (2015: 32).

[20] This understanding – that mind is the result of spirit (วิญญาณ, winyaan) and body (กาย, gai) conjoining – came through in my interviews, and was also evident in dharma talks and radio broadcasts and in the general Thai Buddhist ethos.

[21] The 'ontological turn' in anthropology is susceptible to this reflex, if and when the ontological reality of the 'other' is presumed singular by default. See also Premawardhana's discussion of 'polyontological mobility' (2018).

REFERENCES

ASAD, T. 1993. *Genealogies of religion: discipline and reasons of power in Christianity and Islam*. Baltimore, Md: Johns Hopkins University Press.

AULINO, F. 2019. *Rituals of care: karmic politics in an aging Thailand*. Ithaca, N.Y.: Cornell University Press.

BIALECKI, J. & G. DASWANI 2015 What is an individual? The view from Christianity. HAU: *Journal of Ethnographic Theory* **5**: 1, 271-94.

CASSANITI, J. 2015. *Living Buddhism: mind, self, and emotion in a Thai community*. Ithaca, N.Y.: Cornell University Press.

——— & T.M. LUHRMANN 2014. The cultural kindling of spiritual experiences. *Current Anthropology* **55**: S10, S333-S43.

COLLINS, S. 2013. *Self & society: essays on Pali literature and social theory 1988-2010*. Chiang Mai: Silkworm Books.

DE LA CADENA, M. 2015. *Earth beings: ecologies of practice across Andean worlds*. Durham, N.C.: Duke University Press.

ENDRES, K.W. & A. LAUSER 2012. *Engaging the spirit world: popular beliefs and practices in modern Southeast Asia*. New York: Berghahn Books.

HANDELMAN, D. 2008. Afterword: Returning to cosmology – thoughts on the positioning of belief. *Social Analysis* **52**: 1, 181-95.

——— 2012. Postlude: Framing hierarchically, framing moebiusly. *Journal of Ritual Studies* **26**: 2, 65-77.

HEIM, M. 2014. *The forerunner of all things: Buddhaghosa on mind, intention, and agency*. Oxford: University Press.

KEANE, W. 2002. Sincerity, 'modernity', and the Protestants. *Cultural Anthropology* **17**, 65-92.

MAHMOOD, S. 2010. Can secularism be other-wise? In *Varieties of secularism in a secular age* (eds) M. Warner, J. VanAntwerpen & C. Calhoun, 282-99. Cambridge, Mass.: Harvard University Press.

PREMAWARDHANA, D. 2018. *Faith in flux: Pentecostalism and mobility in rural Mozambique*. Philadelphia: University of Pennsylvania Press.

ROBBINS, J. 2001. Introduction: Global religions, Pacific Island transformations. *Journal of Ritual Studies* **15**: 2, 7-12.

——— 2015. Dumont's hierarchical dynamism: Christianity and individualism revisited. HAU: *Journal of Ethnographic Theory* **5**: 1, 173-95.

SANIT SAMARKANGAAN (สนิท สมัครการ) 1975. Concerning the 'face' of Thai people: analysis according to the linguistic anthropology approach (เรื่อง 'หน้า' ของคนไทย วิเคราะห์ตามแนวคิดทางมานุษยวิทยาภาษาสาสตร์). *Thai Journal of Development Administration* **15**, 492-505 (in Thai).

TOOKER, D. 2018. Rethinking depth metaphors with a cosmocentric self: the 'steep' and the 'level' in Akha emotional practices. *Ethos* **47**, 346-66.

UNSCHULD, P. 1992. Epistemological issues and changing legitimation: traditional Chinese medicine in the twentieth century. In *Paths to Asian medical knowledge* (eds) C. Leslie & A. Young, 44-61. Berkeley: University of California Press.

WELLMAN, H.M. 2013. Universal social cognition: a childhood theory of mind. In *Navigating the social world: a developmental perspective* (eds) M. Banaji & S. Gelman, 69-74. Oxford: University Press.

YONGSAK THANTIPHIDOK (ยังศักดิ์ ตันติปิฎก) 2007. Epistemology and local medicine: disappearing elements in the study of Thai health (ญาณวิทยากับการแพทย์พื้นบ้าน: มิติที่ขาดหายไปของการศึกษาภูมิปัญญาสุขภาพไทย). In *Thai health, Thai culture* (สุขภาพไทย วัฒนธรรมไทย) (eds) Komatra Cheungsatiansap (โกมาตร จึงเสถียรทรัพย์) & Yongsak Thantiphidok (ยังศักดิ์ ตันติปิฎก), 145-78. Bangkok: Institute of Research on Society and Health (สวสส) (in Thai).

ZEHNER, E. 2005. Orthodox hybridities: anti-syncretism and localization in the evangelical Christianity of Thailand. *Anthropological Quarterly* **78**, 585-617.

Du karma au péché : une théorie kaléidoscopique de l'esprit et du vécu des chrétiens dans le nord de la Thaïlande

Résumé

Dans cet essai, l'autrice avance des arguments en faveur d'une théorie « kaléidoscopique » de l'esprit, implicite dans la conscience ordinaire de soi, des autres et de la réalité, dans le nord de la Thaïlande. Dans cette région, l'expérience phénoménologique est généralement comprise comme liée à de multiples facteurs, habitudes personnelles aussi bien qu'influences des autres, de sorte que les perceptions sensorielles à proprement parler sont en partie la conséquence d'actions antérieures (*karma*) ayant un retentissement moral. Lorsqu'ils se convertissent au christianisme, les Thaïs réfutent l'idée du karma pour se tourner vers un Dieu qui absoudra les croyants de tout péché. À partir des riches descriptions faites par des Thaïs, néopentecôtistes aussi bien que bouddhistes, de leur rencontre avec le divin et de nombreuses autres expériences « surnaturelles », l'article montre comment les thaïs chrétiens gardent souvent la notion, certes tronquée, de la contingence karmique. La théorie locale de l'esprit intègre des régimes de connaissance non monothéistes, mettant en lumière la nature unique de l'individualisme qui émerge parmi les fidèles thaïs et les enjeux qu'implique pour eux cette individuation.

2

Crossing the buffer: ontological anxiety among US evangelicals and an anthropological theory of mind

Joshua Brahinsky *Stanford University*

Scholars describe the dominant model of mind in the United States as secular: bounded, private, supernaturally inert, and the locus for self and identity. I argue that US charismatic evangelicals live with the secular sense of a seemingly immutable boundary between the immaterial mind-self and the material world – what Charles Taylor might call 'boundedness' – but at the same time, their commitment to supernatural connection means they imagine the mind-world boundary as porous under certain circumstances: a brittle, fragile buffer between the natural and the supernatural. To allow this porosity, charismatics develop strategies for crossing the buffer, which include spoken prayer, powerful emotions, playful modes of pretend, and bodily rupture or 'breaking in'. These strategies provide evidence that the supernatural is real. Yet practitioners remain anxious about the relationship between these supernatural experiences and the scepticism around them. This 'ontological anxiety' becomes visible in three ways. First, charismatics cultivate intense bodily sensations that demonstrate the reality of God. Second, they describe their experience with a 'common-sense realism'. Finally, charismatics are disturbed by the incoherence between their evangelical and secular impulses around the possibility of mental action.

James[1] hears a voice, 'Now go and be a man of God'. He turns his head to locate the source. The voice seems audible – it shakes him to the core. As he explained, 'Those were the exact words . . . I can hear them clearly in my head today . . . I just felt like it was a voice that pierced through all the doubt and stuff that I had in my mind about who I was, completely shattered the wall'. In his personal life, he had reached the bottom. He had been kicked out of his home because he stole from his parents. He was asked to leave the homeless shelter owing to his addiction. The voice that felt as if it were from outside his mind enabled him to believe both that he was renewed and that God was real. Now his doubts were gone. This moment that the wall was breached became a pivot in his testimony, which then moved from a story of misery and degradation to one in which he was renewed and flying upwards, freed from the chains of doubt and en route to an intimate relationship with God. He had broken the through the buffer.

The wall described in James's testimony sounds remarkably similar to Charles Taylor's (2007) depiction of a barrier – the 'buffer' – between the secular world and the sacred that Taylor sees as common to people in the West, and the United States in particular. Among charismatic evangelicals in the United States, spiritual experience is all about crossing this buffer. Charismatic evangelicals (most of whom probably have not read

Journal of the Royal Anthropological Institute (N.S.), 45-60
© Royal Anthropological Institute 2020

Taylor) explicitly describe a wall: as James said, God's voice 'pierced through all doubt [and] completely shattered the wall'. They come to imagine the wall as a brittle, fragile barrier between the natural and the supernatural which they can breach with specific activities, and which God, too, seeks to cleave in turn. They have developed detailed practices to enable themselves to break through the barrier. These include spoken prayer, powerful emotions, playful modes of pretend, and bodily rupture or 'breaking in'. These strategies generate evidence that the supernatural is real. In this process, the boundary between the inert Western psychological mind and self and the supernatural is seen as imposing but also fragile, and especially vulnerable to activities outside the mind in the material world that might shatter the buffer and break in. This essay sets out to understand the way this imagined buffer both reflects and shapes evangelical experience.

James described his experience of rebirth in Glad Tidings, a San Francisco church within the Assemblies of God (AG), the largest charismatic evangelical formation in the world, involving over 69 million people. He told me his story during my research with the Mind and Spirit project, a Templeton-funded, Stanford-based comparative and interdisciplinary project under the direction of T.M. Luhrmann (PI), drawing on the expertise of anthropologists, psychologists, historians, and philosophers. The project asks whether different understandings of 'mind', broadly construed, might shape or be related to the ways that people attend to and interpret experiences they deem spiritual or supernatural. We took a mixed-method, multi-phase approach, combining participant observation, long-form semi-structured interviews, quantitative surveys among the general population and local undergraduates, and psychological experiments with children and adults. The research took place in five different countries: China, Ghana, Thailand, Vanuatu, and the United States, with some work in the Ecuadorian Amazon. In each country, we included a focus on an urban charismatic evangelical church, with additional work in a rural charismatic evangelical church, and in another urban and rural religious setting of local importance.[2] In the United States, our comparative group were Methodists; the historian Ann Taves had persuaded us that they were an example of the centre of US spirituality – in terms of practice, politics, and sociology. This essay, however, focuses on the urban charismatics, although the Methodists do appear at times.[3]

Our research was implemented by non-evangelicals. Because evangelicals have embraced Israel and Judaism as an important part of the process described in the Book of Revelation, my Jewish background provided me with a modicum of acceptance that initially opened access in my previous seven years of ethnography with AG participants. Even so, it seems possible that evangelical efforts to demonstrate the realness of their spiritual experience were somewhat pronounced owing to my position as an outsider. Yet because so many of the tales were formed in public testimony designed for other church members, I am confident that this ontological anxiety was more than simply a side-effect of the interview process.

The church

An early version of charismatic evangelical practice appeared in the 1800s with Methodist revivals in the United States. Revivalists saw themselves as creating new forms of community that brought them closer to God and, in the process, resisted the daily grind and the increasing commodification of life within the newly formed capitalist workforce (Johnson 1978). At the same time, from secular capitalism Methodists borrowed a careful structuring of time, methodical attention to cultivating an inner self, and a utopian approach to community building through carefully planned small-group meetings and preacher visits (thus the name 'Methodists') (Taves 1999; Wigger 1998). One could argue that in these settings, ideas about 'selves' and 'minds' and the relationships between them were shaped through a close dialogue with modern secular thinking but also via a commitment to the importance of supernatural experience. By the mid-1800s, evangelicalism was among the most vibrant movements in the United States. Its leaders were like today's movie stars, and its churches were at the centre of every major social movement. By the early twentieth century, Methodists had moved on to less charismatic forms of worship, although several waves of charismatic practices then washed through the country, with a third wave starting in the 1970s that remade these practices into a form that was more acceptable to middle-class white Americans (Bialecki 2015; Luhrmann 2012b; Wagner 1989). In the relatively portable 'hard cultural form' (Appadurai 1996; Robbins 2003) that we now call charismatic evangelicalism, participants reach for an intimate, personal relationship with God; they take the Bible to be literally or near-literally true; and they embrace what are called the 'gifts' of the Holy Spirit: prophecy, faith healing, and being filled by the Holy Spirit as manifested by speaking in tongues, a form of non-linguistic speech which is thought to communicate directly to God. In the past 100 years, charismatic evangelicalism has expanded to include over half a billion people and in the process has brought its practice into a dialogue with the local models of mind and self among converts across the globe (Cox 1995).

Glad Tidings Church in downtown San Francisco was at the heart of this twentieth-century revival as the headquarters of the California Assemblies of God in the 1930s. It was an urban charismatic centre where people came to Jesus, went off on missionary tours, and felt moved by the spirit. After a period of near slumber in the 1970s when it shrank to fifty or so members, Glad Tidings was itself reborn in the 1990s with a youthful third wave 'neo-Pentecostal' style and, over the next decade, grew to its current size of close to one thousand. Today, the church is busy, filled with between two hundred and four hundred people on Wednesdays and Sundays, and with forty live-in pastors, a vibrant youth group, Friday-night rehabilitation services, and constant activity the rest of the week. When I showed up, I was greeted at the entrance and then again every 20 feet until I found my way into the pews. I visited Glad Tidings many Sunday mornings and many afternoons for about three years and regularly saw a multi-ethnic, multi-aged group of urban professionals singing their hearts out to a heavy backbeat with their hands held high to open themselves to God. The band played loudly and the church was often filled with people speaking in tongues, with occasional exorcisms and faith healings. And after the service, as was their practice, several people came by to say hello and ask me to lunch. It was a place where people believed that it was important to convey how very active the spirit can be.

Minds and selves and theory of mind

Across the globe, people imagine the 'mind' – the locus of thoughts, feelings, intentions, beliefs, desires, and other mental 'stuff' – in ways that are culturally particular (Lillard 1998). This means also that we differ in the ways we imagine relationships between minds and the rest of the world. After all, concepts of minds only exist in relationship with selves, bodies, and spirits. Our goal in this research is to develop an 'anthropological theory of mind' which will trace the various ways these elements function and how they are blended into and/or separated from each other (Luhrmann 2011). Especially important for this essay, anthropological theories of mind generally discuss variations in the kinds of boundaries, if any, between minds and the other elements of the person and community and the ways that these boundaries might be more or less porous. Charles Taylor (among others) has argued that in North America, or even in the West more broadly, the dominant representation of mind sees it as fully bounded, and fully congruent with the self. Taylor describes a sharp boundary between self and other, individual and society, subject and world. He argues that this self comes to seem as if held within the mind. 'It comes to seem axiomatic that all thought, feeling and purpose, *all the features we normally can ascribe to agents, must be in minds,* which are distinct from the "outer" world' (2007: 539, emphasis added). From this perspective, spirits are outside the mind, and quite confusing. 'The buffered self begins to find the idea of spirits, moral forces, causal powers with a purposive bent, close to incomprehensible' (2007: 539). T.M. Luhrmann offers a resonant characterization:

> The Euro-American modern secular theory of mind: In this theory of mind, people treat the mind as if there is in effect a clear boundary between what is in the mind, and what is in the world. Entities in the world, supernatural or otherwise, do not enter the mind, and thoughts do not leave the mind to act upon the world (2011: 6).

Luhrmann also touches on the Western investment in a strong boundary between real and unreal such that Westerners might imagine that 'what is in the mind is not real in the way that tables and chairs are real; one can speak of "mere" imagination' (2011: 6). In other words, in the United States, the self and the mind are imagined as an interior sharply separated from an exterior real world, and held apart from it by a buffer.

The charismatic evangelicals I came to know at Glad Tidings shared this model of mind – except that they also thought that the mind (and self) was porous in specific ways: permeable for God; for the Holy Spirit; and often, but in more limited ways, for demons. When asked directly about the possibility that our thoughts could travel out from our minds, they responded that this was absurd: everyone (within this secular model of the mind) knows it is impossible. Yet, at the same time, their daily prayer included a call for the Holy Spirit to come and inhabit their innermost self. Worship was in many ways a demonstration of their interest in openness. Pastor Beiser regularly called participants to expand their availability and make more space for God to enter. 'Go for it! Let God in!' he would call. And then there was the ever-present danger that one might become too available and a demon might influence one's mind, perhaps shaping lustful or angry thoughts that would not occur otherwise. Yet because of this dual commitment to a mind both secular and porous, for these Christians, porosity was limited to very specific moments. Even so, they worried about whether those experiences were real.

That is, in spite of very active supernatural connections, doubt here is quite common. In the United States, when adults are surveyed, 80 per cent claim to believe in God and 28 per cent say that they talk to God – and God talks back (Pew Research Center 2018). At Glad Tidings, where some of the church's' participants feel God communicating with them almost daily, this sense of God's importance is felt even more strongly. Yet doubt was common even among these US charismatic evangelicals. The stories I heard of encounters with God all included extensive caveats about how 'strange' and 'crazy' the encounter was, with constant self-reflexive anxiety about whether or not they could maintain a coherent world-view while holding onto both scepticism and faith. The details of their narratives were intended to show that there were no plausible explanations other than the reality of the supernatural. In addition, these stories were often presented as believable because of hard-to-deny physical experiences that forced practitioners to renounce their own past scepticism. I began to think of charismatic evangelicals as 'anxiously supernatural' – this might also describe the broader US mix of supernaturalism and secularism, which differs from Europe's more straightforward secularism. At Glad Tidings, congregants' practices appeared to be designed to reassure themselves about the realness of God.

Perhaps ironically, a strong commitment to the division between an ephemeral inside and a concrete outside may mean that for charismatic evangelicals the outside – the body and the senses in particular – plays an especially important role. While some evangelical theorists argue that evangelical bodily practices provide a holistic approach to mind-body and spirit (Lord 2005), I observed that mind-body divisions matter in evangelical practice. The Protestant tradition certainly has exhibited tendencies towards denigrating the body and bodily functions, although it has imagined them in different ways at different times (Schmidt 2000). I have come to believe that, aside from the simple fact that bodies provide intimate feedback which is often difficult to deny, in the case of charismatic evangelicals within the secular US world the body offers a place from which God can cross the buffer and affect the otherwise supernaturally inert mind and self. George Marsden (2006) calls this reliance on everyday experience the 'common sense realism' that underpins fundamentalism. Webb Keane observed that Protestantism makes the body especially visible as its dualist dividing lines 'restore all things to their proper sides' of the material-spiritual opposition (2007: 200). I saw that charismatic evangelicals invest bodies with the power to bring the spirit across the buffer to the person. My participants spoke repeatedly about the body: what they felt in the body, how the body reacted. If they felt something in their body, they thought it was important.

In the following pages, I describe four strategies of barrier crossing among US evangelicals: expressive emotion, audible speech, playing pretend, and, finally, somatic rupture which breaches the wall. Following this, I demonstrate that charismatic evangelicals worry about their imagined barrier between the real-unreal or nature-supernature – they are especially ontologically anxious. Together, these stories make the case that cross-cultural variations in the ways people imagine the mind and self relate to the ways in which they imagine that they access the supernatural.

Strategies for crossing the line
Emotions

Charismatic evangelical practice is intensely emotional. Through a secular lens, these emotions appear as if generated outside of the mind. For charismatics, they provide a path across the buffer to the inner self. To be 'drunk in the spirit', for instance, means to be awash with laughter and giggling incessantly. Many of the people I interviewed regularly spoke about bawling like a baby – evangelical churches are among the few places in the United States where crying men can keep their sense of masculine charm. At the close of Glad Tidings' services, Judy, a regular attendee on Wednesdays, came to hug me and check on my spiritual progress. Through her warm smile I saw her face streaked with tears. She walked with the relaxed gait of one who has just been crying. It had not been a particularly powerful service for me, but she was deeply experienced at worship and often seemed to come out of a session looking as if she had been run over and then lovingly picked up off the ground. She seemed both exhausted and eager, emotionally drained and inspired.

Nash, a Glad Tidings participant and part-time carpenter, recalled an evening when he lived in a Christian rehabilitation centre and experienced 'true' worship. 'There was this band – the prophetic worship band – and I was on my face, just praying at the altar and all of a sudden, people started speaking these words from Matthew, "I have prepared a place for you, that you know not of, at my father's house"'. The words struck him as appropriate to his immediate situation and he felt deeply touched. 'It was so piercing and so for me at that moment I was crying, but it was different, it was not like weeping, it was more like literally when I looked down, it was projectile tears. It was projecting off my face. I had never had that happen before'. Crying transformed his deepest sense of stability. 'I felt like my whole body was being turned inside out and I heard an other-worldly scream that I thought was coming from across the room. There was a second of realization that it was me. It was crazy'. The sense of complete emotional release, of being turned inside out and losing control of his actions, was, for Nash, in some sense terrifying. But also, as he later explained, it gave him a wild, yet concrete, sense that God was actually present in his life.

Emotions are so central to the process that charismatics have developed a protective discourse to shield themselves from the ever-present criticism that they are too emotional. Indeed, one of the famous descriptions of early evangelicalism was that they were overly 'enthusiastic'. Critics argued that evangelical prayer was not only dangerous to social peace, but also a form of mental disorder (Knox 2000 [1950]). And so evangelicals go out of their way to decry excessive emotionalism. Dr Stewart, a former AG missionary, explained: 'Some see [us] swinging from the chandeliers and all that good stuff . . . watching folks running in the aisles, the pastor's wife jumping across the pews'. As another former missionary related, 'Wacky things can happen, you've got to admit that it's not the Spirit, it's some emotion. It's something else'. At times, they draw sharp lines to differentiate between authentic practice and something to be rejected: 'I think I'm gonna say, "You know that person's a nut!"'

Speech

'The Bible says there's power in words', said David, a charismatic evangelical in the Central Valley. For many charismatic evangelicals in the United States, audible speech matters. In explaining this, David joined a secular psychological model to a charismatic evangelical one as he added that, 'In [scientific] studies, positive language changes how people behave or act'. In other words, he argued, the Bible and science both agree on the power of audible speech to affect the world. For evangelicals, speech out loud provides a crucial method of crossing the barrier between mind and God. The key, it seems, is that speech happens outside the mind-self. The simplest versions are the command to heal – in the name of the father, son, and holy ghost – and the audible curse.

We can see this clearly in faith healing. Donald, a member of Glad Tidings, described to me what happens in the faith healing session he attends every Saturday: 'When someone says they are sick, . . . and another person is like, "All right, I'm going to pray for you right here", and then they use, "In the name of Jesus, I command this person to be healed"'. The 'you are healed' is imagined as operating like one of Austin's (1962) speech acts: like the 'I do' that enacts a marriage. It is similarly dependent upon the context – a wedding or a church adds a layer of authenticity and power, and more authoritative speakers (pastors, deacons) are sometimes treated as more powerful. To be clear, I interviewed dozens of charismatics about their prayer practices who spoke as if prayer was often effective whether spoken in the mind or out loud. Yet they behaved as if the vocalization was more powerful when the barrier needed to be broken dramatically.

This was true also in demonic exorcism. Halley, who had significant experience in demonic exorcism, told me a story of one afternoon at Glad Tidings when a woman up front was so agitated that she disturbed an admittedly already high-energy practice. 'During the altar call they're screaming ... screeching, and all this stuff', she explained. Halley walked the woman, who was deeply upset, down the stairs behind the band to a long room where a team of pastors work to exorcize demons from souls that need deliverance. Exorcism occurs more often on missions trips, but San Francisco has its share of demonic powers and so there are often staff in this room during prayer sessions. The challenge is to differentiate the demonic from mental illness or everyday anger and distress. Halley said that most of the signs are physical: vomiting that seems not to be induced, intense agitation in response to an increase in God's presence, super-strength, posture and personality changes, and even changes in physiology– 'I've seen times where people's eyes turn gray, completely gray'.

In this story, the woman's great strength was taken to be a sign of possession. 'There were probably five of our strongest guys trying to hold her down. She would whip them off with one arm – like that kind of thing. I'm seeing it with my own eyes where I literally feel like am I in a movie?' They held her down for a while. Deliverance often relies on loud verbalized prayers that call Jesus' power to bear immediately on the situation. Halley hollered, 'In the name of Jesus I drive you out. Demons begone!!' The woman's body went slack. It seemed to have worked. But within seconds, the possessed woman sat up and a fresh angry character replaced the old one. A new demon had apparently taken over, as different taunts emerged in a wholly altered tone. As Halley told it, the voice shifted from deep and guttural to high and raspy, the personality from angry to taunting – and then later to sly and seductive. Over several hours of prayer, the team moved their patient through six demonic iterations until she was freed.

Glad Tidings participants call these events 'spiritual warfare'. This is a model of the world drawn from third-wave charismatic evangelical thinkers like C. Peter Wagner (1996) who describe a globe in which multiple demonic powers vie with God and Christians for control. Christians battle demons through individual exorcisms, and also through corporate prayer when evangelicals ask God to support cleansing themselves, the city, the country, and the world. Halley explained that in contrast to a God who knows all our thoughts, demons or the Devil can't just read our minds or plant thoughts in our heads. They first require someone to open a door to their spirit and provide access. Given the right opening, the mind-self becomes porous to their manipulations. The best remedy is forceful spoken prayer. In a similar vein, curses also need to be spoken out loud.

Webb Keane's *Christian moderns* (2007) opens the door to the importance of speech within charismatic authority. For Keane, most Protestants find interior sincerity as the central, and perhaps only, mode of power. Of course, charismatic evangelicals do assume that intentions matter – deception about one's orientation towards God or the Devil is *verboten*. Yet, as Keane recognizes, charismatic evangelicals differ from other Protestants in their emphasis on outside material as a crucial element of everyday spiritual potency. Intention, for charismatics, becomes a necessary but insufficient condition for access

Journal of the Royal Anthropological Institute (N.S.), 45-60
© Royal Anthropological Institute 2020

to power. Audible speech, then, might be important in helping a curse, healing prayer, or demonic exorcism to cross the buffer and connect to the spirits.

Pretend

Charismatic evangelicals understand themselves to access the supernatural through at least two distinct versions of pretend. For some, pretending works in a secular context to enable the person to feel more confident that God is present. Others work with a 'fake it till you make it' strategy that helps them learn to speak in tongues. Both techniques involve cultivating an attitude of openness. Yet they do so in distinct ways – one more cognitive and the other more somatic.

For some, pretend can be used deliberately as a practice of training the mind, a means of attuning and refining thoughts to focus them more firmly on God, despite the doubt they feel. Lisette is a small, young Latina woman, upwardly mobile, working her way through graduate school in psychology, very much in the world of everyday secular experiences. Yet she is in constant contact with what she takes to be divinity. Jesus is present to her while eating breakfast, on the bus, and in class. Her primary outreach tool is imagination. She describes this as pretending – but not pretending, because Jesus is real. 'I just imagine when I'm driving that Jesus is in the passenger seat', she explains. I ask her if it works. 'Sometimes', she replies, 'when I remember ... Yes, [call me] crazy lady, but I'll talk like he's there, and when he's not, I'm looking up because I'm constantly in conversation'. In other words, Lisette aims at uninterrupted pretending that Jesus is present. I ask her if Jesus is really there, or if this is pretend. 'Both', she replies. 'I pretend that Jesus is there, but I'm not pretending'. This is the 'double epistemological register' of US evangelical pretend described by Luhrmann (2012a). Lisette both asserts the pretending and denies it. She does this because she aspires to cross from the pretend to the real. At times the pretence does fully lift. 'Sometimes I feel like I'm pretending that he's there, but then I just throw that out ... I don't need to pretend [anymore] because he *is* there'. Here, one half of the double register drops out.

When people set out to learn to speak in tongues (if it doesn't come spontaneously), they do something related, although more somatic. Speaking in tongues describes an expression of syllables and phonemes that sound language-like, but are not language (Samarin 1972). The experience is often portrayed as feeling automatic, passive, unchosen. Congregants refer to the experience of speaking in tongues as a 'gift', to indicate that the events simply happened to them – it was given by God. And yet nearly every person I interviewed described a period in which they deliberately made nonsense sounds (Brahinsky 2012; 2013). They 'pretended'. Although it was physical, people could not see the pretend underlying speaking in tongues; it was hidden. While most people said they had faked it at some point, I have never heard an evangelical say in public that they had only been pretending. Picture a group of people in a circle surrounding a person learning to speak in tongues. They pray in tongues towards the person in the middle to encourage their participation. Some of the trainees fake it. Throughout, members of the outer circle might also be faking it, but they don't discuss it. Most of the people I interviewed described a moment when they moved from pretend to what seemed like genuine experience. The project here is similar to Lisette's pretending that Jesus is pretend. People 'fake' speaking in tongues and in the process enable their body to develop the skill to experience speaking in tongues as if automatically. Crossing the line from doubt to what can be felt as genuine experience involves cultivating an ability to let things flow, in the imagination, or in the body.

Journal of the Royal Anthropological Institute (N.S.), 45-60
© Royal Anthropological Institute 2020

Rupture

The practice of buffer crossing most visible in Glad Tidings involves the experience of what I call 'rupture'. By this, I mean a bodily experience of an intense shift involving otherness – a radical difference from the everyday that signals a complete change in a person's trajectory. In Glad Tidings, nearly every person I interviewed reported several, if not many, dramatic experiences in which they felt a tremendous wash of feeling in their body that they experienced as generating a sense of spontaneous and complete renewal of their relationships to themselves, God, and the world. As many scholars have noted (e.g. Robbins 2003), this sense of rupture and immediacy permeates charismatic evangelical practice. From baptism and conversion, to being born again, charismatic evangelicals worship through a never-ending series of small ruptures (little rebirths). Speaking in tongues, faith healing, and being 'slain in the spirit' (see below) are the exemplars. In each, the model is Paul on the road to Damascus, hit suddenly and transformed fully. These ruptures occur most visibly in the body and thus, for those steeped in the US theory of mind, they take place outside of the mind and self. They often engender intense and powerful sensation, followed by a rapid shift as participants hit 'the wall' and make it through. Sometimes God will speak. Sometimes his presence is powerfully felt. But it nearly always comes on with a bang. In these cases, the experience is of God as 'breaking in': piercing the barrier that is presumed to separate the human from the divine, and, in the process, confirming that the divine is real.

These ruptures can be seen to be part of an evangelical rhythm, a pattern of ups and downs that begins with the lows. Since Jonathan Edwards first perfected 'hellfire-and-brimstone' preaching in the mid-1700s, evangelicals have imagined everyday life as regularly involving deep agony and angst. These depths allow for the transition to godliness. A Christian farmer and missionary, Shane, explained, 'I was at a really broken spot in my life you know, super broken'. He then returned to church, which generated a release of tremendous pent-up suffering, which in turn invited a palpable sense of God's love. 'I literally started bawling and I could feel peace come on me'. He felt freed from the despair that had brought him back to church. 'I wanted to stay the night in the church, it felt so good, you know? ... I felt like I was being set free'. He had achieved a moment of rupture, at once both the nadir and the peak of the cycle.

Rupture is often felt acutely in the body. The paradigmatic experience here is being 'slain in the spirit', in which someone suddenly falls down because they experience the overwhelming force of the Holy Spirit. My first encounter with a person slain in the spirit was at a Vineyard church in Scotts Valley, California. There a woman started jumping up and down yelling her love for Jesus, before stopping abruptly to stare at the wall and then falling flat as a board, straight towards the ground. Her head would have smashed onto the concrete floor if a neighbouring worshipper had not caught her adroitly. Most interviewees at Glad Tidings had been slain at least once, many several times. They described concern about the impetus behind falling over because often the proximate cause was a touch from a pastor and they worried that therefore they were just being compliant. Yet the physical sensations of partial consciousness, intense heat, or washes of tingles across their skin gave a sense that something other than manipulation was occurring.

Many described being slain in the spirit as if it came on spontaneously. Shane talked about supporting a person being slain. 'As soon as I put my hand on him, he instantly falls down ... boom, boom. Boom!' The 'boom' is the key element here. These are not subtle transitions. In this high-arousal version of Christianity, change comes in bursts of intense feeling. Jimmy, a young lawyer, described a prayer session breakthrough: 'I was in my car driving home, and I just felt the presence of God, overwhelming ... he must have been resting right on top of me, in my car or whatever. It was so powerful, it was hard for me to drive the car'. Once home he could fully let go.

> I get on my knees and I just fall to the ground. I say, 'God, have your way' ... I have never felt this again, like something resting on my chest and then this stirring from my belly, it was so intense. I am crying, I am sobbing, it's all these sensations of joy. I am laughing uncontrollably. It was so powerful ... It was like my body couldn't handle what he was doing to me. When it was done, it was like, I just felt peaceful.

Each of these moments reaffirms the realness of God, expressed by rupture in the body and intense emotional release

The sense that these experiences come on spontaneously has enabled a mode of being in the world that permeates charismatic evangelical experience. The goal of the 'theology of immediacy' (McClung 1984: 53) is 'spontaneity in personal conduct as well as corporate worship' (Spittler 1988: 409). Even the most meticulous and systematic theorists of charismatic evangelical training insist upon the spontaneity of the practice. AG missionary theorist Grant McClung, for instance, titled his central essay the 'Spontaneous Strategy of the Spirit' (1984: 101). Likewise, Russell Spittler, a well-known Pentecostal theorist, wrote that a message in tongues 'comes unplanned, unprogrammed' (1988: 415). Even Donald MacGavran, a scholar best known for joining rationalized sociology and theology, called charismatic evangelical practices spontaneous: '[The] principle of spontaneous action under the control of the spirit of Jesus as revealed in the scriptures lies at the heart of the Pentecostal faith' (MacGavran, Huegel, Taylor & Yoder 1963: 114-15). Perhaps this is not surprising in a tradition where the founding missiological text is Roland Allen's *The spontaneous expansion of the church: and causes which hinder it* (1927). Similarly, when missionary theorists delineated four core elements of Pentecostal practice, the first was 'the priority of the event' (McClung 1984: 5). 'Event' here is the name for a single surprising moment of transformation. For Paul Pomerville, another AG missiologist, 'the immediacy of God' (1985: 9) was the key to 'the event'. Pomerville also described 'the event' as enabling change beyond the immediate moment: '[T]he great commission [to evangelize] derives its meaning from the internalizing event. The Pentecostal event, then, is decisive for an understanding of the spiritual role in initiating and universalizing mission' (1985: 73). Pomerville explained also that in non-Pentecostal theology, reason or rationality limits connection with God. Instead of this contained perspective, what he termed the 'noetic principle of theology (inflection, reason, epistemology, propositional statements on the confrontation of being)', he called for a Pentecostal return to immediacy, what he described as 'the ontic principle (immediacy, presence, "the earnest" of God, confrontation with reality)' (1985: 68). Put more simply, for Pomerville, modern approaches to spirituality that focus on reason to access God are not effective. By reversing this pattern and focusing on immediacy, he writes, charismatic evangelical practice enables modern rational people to know God.

The evangelical rhythm of ups and downs became especially visible when compared to the contemporary Methodists I interviewed. Unlike charismatic evangelicals, the Methodists did not imagine God as involved in everyday life. Yet, surprisingly, they described themselves as more certain that God was real. Doubt was not central to their narratives. This evoked a different approach to worship. Instead of high-arousal evangelical rupture to break the brittle wall of doubt, Methodists' practice involved lower levels of arousal, which were more stable and sustained across time. Here, the wall is imagined as always somewhat porous and prayer as simply another form of thinking. In other words, US supernaturalism can involve various rhythms depending upon the importance of doubt.

Ontological anxiety

I saw in US-based charismatic evangelical participants an intense concern with the question of whether God is real, and a determination to prove his realness to themselves and to others. This worry about the bounds of the real and unreal I call 'ontological anxiety'. It was a concern that was less evident in our other sites – even among charismatic evangelicals – and in fact in Thailand the Western need for ontological clarity rarely appeared. Instead, people often reflected an openness to multiple realities, what Felicity Aulino (this volume) calls 'ontological pluralism'. I take the US charismatic evangelical focus on rupture and bodily events to be the most dramatic expression of ontological anxiety since explosive experiences are especially adapted to calm the anxious question of God's reality and its emphasis on bodily confirmation bypasses the bounded mind. Now I will describe another strategy: rational argument, in which talk of God is presented as part of a scientific evaluation. The strategy does not always work. In fact, my subjects were often uncomfortable when they recognized that their supernatural commitments ran counter to their own intuitions about their minds.

When people say, 'I know it when I see it', they are participating in what scholars call 'common-sense realism'. Here, direct sensory experience becomes the basis for all claims. It is a philosophy for the common person, a democratic approach to knowledge, one in which anyone can participate equally. This was the drive behind the Common Sense Philosophy of late 1700s Scotland, and also for its populist iteration in the late nineteenth-century United States. For Marsden (2006), the common-sense realism of Charles Hodges and other mid-nineteenth-century theorists was central to the emergence of fundamentalism and posed a direct challenge to more theoretically based approaches to scientific rationality (see also Kazin 1995). Common-sense realism is an often cranky but down-to-earth approach to understanding the world from inside the bodies that we trust. When my subjects used this strategy, they often did so within a framework of scientific inquiry and causal logic which cast miracle and conversion stories as sounding a bit crazy and presented themselves as especially sceptical' not at all prone to emotionalism or fantasy. The most fantastic story needed to be told like a police report – 'just the facts, ma'am'. When the stories got a bit wild, narrators introduced multiple caveats, and they searched for confounds. This may seem obvious in the United States – if you tell a story about demons or spirits, you have to answer to the sceptical people who are listening and prove it to them. But people in our other fieldsites seemed more concerned about their obligations to spirits, or worried about what spirits might be thinking or doing, rather than anxious about whether they existed or not.

My favourite illustration of the US orientation comes from an interview in the Central Valley. Phil travelled west as a 20-year-old Christian rap musician, and then again a few years later as a youth pastor. He is now married with several kids. Like many of the charismatic evangelicals who used this common-sense, fact-based strategy, he prefaced his stories of the supernatural with the rational. He is all about the nitty-gritty of the real.

Journal of the Royal Anthropological Institute (N.S.), 45-60
© Royal Anthropological Institute 2020

Phil explained that he was highly educated, had been to college, had studied the science of history. He understood that Jesus doesn't fit the secular sensibility. 'I'm going to tell you my craziest Jesus story', he said. He had visited a revival led by an evangelist with the biggest drum kit in the world. People reported that these worship sessions would engender an inspiring smell that seemed to come from nowhere. He got there and his friend handed him a baby, who proceeded to throw up all over Phil's shirt. In the bathroom, Phil tried to wash the vomit off but he was smelling it all over. Returning to worship, he turned his attention to God, and, surprisingly, the vomit stench was replaced by the sweet fragrance of roses. This seemed a bit ridiculous. He checked for fraud. 'Okay, so what did they do? They put something in the vents, some perfume?' He looked around; nothing seemed amiss. The search for the cause of the smell led him to stop praying and then the puke stink returned. But every time he turned his attention towards God, the smell of the vomit disappeared. So, like a scientist, he tested it. Does connection with God actually change his sensory experience? He pivoted carefully back and forth between a focus on God and then allowing the more mundane smell of the vomit to fill his senses. It worked. 'I did it twice and I'll never forget … It smelled really like the most fantastic smell you've ever smelled in your entire life. It was just a total moment of things and I've never been able to explain that'. As he finished the story, he brought it back into the secular frame: 'I don't share it a lot because people think you're a nut job when you say this kind of stuff. It is exactly the kind of magical tale that a reasonable person would check multiple times. In the end, for Phil it is about fact, hard and solid, not emotion, and not fantasy. 'I can't justify your emotions. I can only justify what is fact for me, what I've felt'. For him, God's reality has been verified by his senses.

This kind of anxiety about the question of real and unreal becomes especially visible in the ways charismatic evangelical participants demand coherence of themselves and the world around them, even when their impulse towards supernaturalism makes this difficult. In a series of interviews aiming to understand how people think about the relationship between thoughts, feelings, spirits, and imagination, our initial questions centred on the idea of mental causation: that is, can anger, care, or envy affect another person if these feelings are not expressed outwardly? Charismatic evangelical subjects began by answering the questions in non-supernaturalist ways. They described a fully bounded mind, with no space for thoughts to leak out into the world so as to have effects. Yet, because they feel strongly that prayer can heal and also that curses can hurt, they later struggled to reconcile the closed system of their secular world-view with their evangelical impulses towards porosity. So, for instance, when asked if thoughts can travel and have an effect upon the world, they nearly all said 'never', often with the strong implication that this was a nutty idea. In other words, when asked if 'Martha' could change the world just by thinking kind or angry thoughts, they offered an emphatic 'no'. Then, as the interview progressed, it became clear to practitioners that prayer and cursing are somewhere in the general world of mental causation. This made them uncomfortable. Jean, a single mom and deeply religious, noticed the pattern when I began asking about envy. At this point, after questions about care and anger, she understood that the survey was testing whether the mind could affect the world and she could guess that I was about to ask if envious thoughts were any different from kind or angry ones. The problem was that at this moment, by abstracting the question, she also realized that I was trying to understand how things that are somewhat like thoughts travelled and she hit upon the idea that God's thoughts and spirits were in this same general category of the immaterial. 'Woah', she exclaimed, 'where is this going?' She had me pause and we talked through the difference between prayer and mental causation. She was anxious to clarify that she felt both that the mind was bounded and that thoughts could not travel except in story books, but also that there was a realm and a path through which other ephemeral things, like God's communications, could, and did, travel. Further, because she hadn't worked through this distinction previously, the sense that she might have hit upon an incoherence in her world-view made her uncomfortable. She was demonstrating a Western ontological anxiety tied to supernaturalism.

Conclusion

What is it like to try to reach God in a society in which a broad affinity for supernatural experience sits quite close to a strong sense that the real and the unreal are very clearly separate? I argue that for the US charismatic evangelicals I talked with, their local theory of mind builds directly from the US folk psychological theory of mind in which mind is viewed as supernaturally inert and bounded. They imagine their minds and selves as closely overlapped as well as solidly bounded by a wall – or buffer – which encloses the spiritually inactive interior of the mind-self. Yet, because evangelicals insist on the oft-present reality of the supernatural, the wall is viewed both as imposing but also as somewhat easily broken. This conception has an important relationship to the kinds of spiritual events that charismatics tend to notice, find compelling, and learn to experience. Encounters with God are often expressed through physically potent experiences which propel adherents though the secular buffer and into direct contact with the divine. These are experienced as completely transformative breakthroughs that come on spontaneously. In Luhrmann's (2012b) work on the Vineyard church, 'as-if', pretend, and playfulness provide tools for negotiating the bounds of US secularism or what I am calling anxious supernaturalism. In this essay, her approach is complemented by a set of tools that are in less playful registers, but that are also quite influential in the US charismatic evangelical world. I am talking about external materiality, and especially bodily rupture, in which the wall between the natural and the supernatural is breached by a blast of somatic energy – something so 'real' that it is nearly impossible to deny. In fact, multiple strategies, including speech, emotions, and pretending, are experienced as effective for crossing the barrier. In other words, charismatic spiritual experiences form in a dialogue both with their prayer practices and with a local theory of mind, which, together, have real effects on people's capacity for experience. As such, this essay contributes to an anthropological theory of mind by demonstrating that the local textures of mind, or, in this case, the bounds of the mind and self, have a relationship to the parameters of and possibilities for religious experience.

This essay thus suggests that an anthropological theory of mind could provide an important tool for viewing both cultural difference and change. Psychological anthropologists and cultural psychologists have shown that ideas about mind differ across contexts (Hollan 2000; Lillard 1998; Moore & Mathews 2001). Scholars of Christianity have also touched on the mind with their interest in interiority, sincerity, and propositional belief (Keane 2007; Robbins 2010). Our project continues this work while also responding to critiques of essentialism in the study of subjectivity (Good, Hyde, Pinto & Good 2008). By looking at the mind among Christians across cultures and through cultural encounter, we portray models of the mind as ever-changing products of historical and cultural negotiation, not fixed pre-existing entities. It helps that our exploration of a local theory of mind relies on a ground-up, experience-near, phenomenological approach which accesses the mind via the senses. Instead of studying adepts or official discourses and theorizations, and while recognizing that language mediates all experience, we study the sensory forms enacted by everyday practitioners that emerge from their local somatic modes of attention, learning, and experience (Csordas 1993; Meyer 2010). From a vantage point that begins with the sensory, we are less likely to fall immediately into the secular model of seeing the mind as independent of the body.

When Rita Astuti (2001) asks if we are all natural dualists, I take this to suggest that conceptualizing a division between mind and body is something that all people can and do do, at least at times. It seems likely that this is correct. But intuitions about either the separation of mind and body or about their interconnectedness are shaped by cultural invitations that push us in various directions. In the United States, our culture invites us to imagine the mind and body as starkly separated. That separation becomes crucial for evangelicals trying to access the supernatural. The body and other external material then provide evidence of the real. When evangelicals talk about their certainty that God is present, they explain that this is no fantasy of the mind. Instead, this is real, concrete, sensory experience. And not just any sensory experience, but something so powerful that it cannot be ignored, cannot be some mind-generated fake, and therefore is very likely to be God. Similarly, there are moments in which prayer and speech become embodied actions experienced as external to the mind which enable evangelicals to cross the buffer. In each of the cases discussed in this essay – speech, prayer, bodily rupture, and smell – the body and its actions are key both to the evangelical understanding of the strong separation between mind and/or self and the world and to the ways in which some people can break across to access the spiritual realm.

NOTES

I would like to acknowledge the support of Tanya Luhrmann, Felicity Aulino, Emily Ng, Rachel Smith, John Dulin, Vivian Dzokoto, Kara Weissman, Nikki Ross-Zehnder, Cristine Legare, Michael Lifshitz, Jon Bialecki, Jim Clifford, Susan Harding, Barbara Epstein, and Marilyn Westerkamp, as well as express tremendous appreciation to all of my evangelical interlocutors, especially Pastors Tim and Beiser for their generosity and willingness to engage with science. And to Michelle Glowa for her loving patience as I drove all over California searching out experiences of the Holy Spirit.

[1] All interviewees' names are pseudonyms.

[2] This paragraph is based on a description drafted collectively by the Mind and Spirit team and used to illustrate the joint nature of the research.

[3] This essay is not primarily about comparison. It focuses on a small group of evangelicals in central California. Yet the method used to develop these insights was deeply comparative. Over two years, our team of researchers spent months sharing and comparing insights from our fieldwork. And this made a difference. Without the Methodists, for instance, the unusual focus on high arousal rhythms in evangelical worship was less obvious. Even more striking, without the Thai comfort with plural ontologies (Aulino, this volume), US ontological anxiety would be nigh invisible, at least to my eyes.

REFERENCES

ALLEN, R. 1927. *The spontaneous expansion of the church: and the causes which hinder it.* London: World Dominion Press.

APPADURAI, A. 1996. *Modernity at large: cultural dimensions of globalization.* Minneapolis: University of Minnesota Press.

ASTUTI, R. 2001. Are we all natural dualists? A cognitive developmental approach. *Journal of the Royal Anthropological Institute* (N.S.) 7, 429-47.

AUSTIN, J.L. 1962. *How to do things with words.* London: Oxford University Press.

BIALECKI, J. 2015. The Third Wave and the Third World: C. Peter Wagner, John Wimber, and the pedagogy of global renewal in the late twentieth century. *Pneuma* **37**, 177-200.

BRAHINSKY, J. 2012. Pentecostal body logics: cultivating a modern sensorium. *Cultural Anthropology* **27**, 215-38.

——— 2013. Cultivating discontinuity: Pentecostal pedagogies of yielding and control. *Anthropology & Education Quarterly* **44**, 399-422.

COX, H. 1995. *Fire from heaven: the rise of Pentecostal spirituality and the reshaping of religion in the twenty-first century*. Reading, Mass.: Addison-Wesley.

CSORDAS, T.J. 1993. Somatic modes of attention. *Cultural Anthropology* **8**, 135-56.

GOOD, M.-J.D., S.T. HYDE, S. PINTO & B.J. GOOD (eds) 2008. *Postcolonial disorders*. Berkeley: University of California Press.

HOLLAN, D. 2000. Constructivist models of mind, contemporary psychoanalysis, and the development of culture theory. *American Anthropologist* **102**, 538-50.

JOHNSON, P.E. 1978. *A shopkeeper's millennium: society and revivals in Rochester, New York, 1815-1837*. New York: Hill & Wang.

KAZIN, M. 1995. *The populist persuasion: an American history*. New York: Basic Books.

KEANE, W. 2007. *Christian moderns: freedom and fetish in the mission encounter*. Berkeley: University of California Press.

KNOX, R.A. 2000 [1950]. *Enthusiasm: a chapter in the history of religion: with special reference to the XVII and XVIII centuries*. Oxford: Clarendon Press.

LILLARD, A. 1998. Ethnopsychologies: cultural variations in theories of mind. *Psychological Bulletin* **123**, 3-32.

LORD, A. 2005. *Spirit-shaped mission: a holistic charismatic missiology*. Milton Keynes: Paternoster.

LUHRMANN, T.M. 2011. Toward an anthropological theory of mind: overview. *Journal of the Finnish Anthropological Society* **36**: 4, 5-13.

——— 2012*a*. A hyperreal God and modern belief: toward an anthropological theory of mind. *Current Anthropology* **53**, 371-95.

——— 2012*b*. *When God talks back: understanding the American evangelical relationship with God*. New York: Knopf.

McCLUNG, G. 1984. Readings in the Church growth dynamics of the missionary expansion of the Pentecostal movement. Th.M. thesis, Fuller Theological Seminary of World Mission.

MACGAVRAN, D., J. HUEGEL, J. TAYLOR & H.W. YODER 1963. *Church growth in Mexico*. Grand Rapids, Mich.: Eerdmans.

MARSDEN, G. 2006. *Fundamentalism and American culture: the shaping of twentieth-century evangelicalism, 1870-1925*. Oxford: University Press.

MEYER, B. 2010. Aesthetics of persuasion: global Christianity and Pentecostalism's sensational forms. *South Atlantic Quarterly* **109**, 741-63.

MOORE, C.C. & H.F. MATHEWS 2001. *The psychology of cultural experience*. Cambridge: University Press.

PEW RESEARCH CENTER 2018. When Americans say they believe in God, what do they mean? 25 April (available online: *https://www.pewforum.org/2018/04/25/when-americans-say-they-believe-in-god-what-do-they-mean/*, accessed 13 January 2020).

POMERVILLE, P. 1985. *The third force in missions: a Pentecostal contribution to contemporary mission theology*. Peabody, Mass.: Hendrickson.

ROBBINS, J. 2003. On the paradoxes of global Pentecostalism and the perils of continuity thinking. *Religion* **33**, 221-31.

——— 2010. Anthropology, Pentecostalism, and the new Paul: conversion, event, and social transformation. *South Atlantic Quarterly* **109**, 633-52.

SAMARIN, W.J. 1972. *Tongues of men and angels: the religious language of Pentecostalism*. New York: Macmillan.

SCHMIDT, L.E. 2000. *Hearing things: religion, illusion, and the American Enlightenment*. Cambridge, Mass.: Harvard University Press.

SPITTLER, R.P. 1988. Implicit values in Pentecostal missions. *Missiology: An International Review* **16**, 409-24.

TAVES, A. 1999. *Fits, trances, and visions: experiencing religion and explaining experience from Wesley to James*. Princeton: University Press.

TAYLOR, C. 2007. *A secular age*. Cambridge, Mass.: Belknap Press of Harvard University Press.

WAGNER, C.P. 1989. Third Wave. In *Dictionary of Pentecostal and charismatic movements* (eds) S.M. Burgess & G.B. McGee, 843-44. Grand Rapids, Mich.: Zondervan.

——— 1996. *Confronting the Powers: how the New Testament church experienced the power of strategic-level spiritual warfare*. Ventura, Calif.: Regal Books.

Wigger, J.H. 1998. *Taking heaven by storm: Methodism and the rise of popular Christianity in America*. Oxford: University Press.

Franchir la zone tampon : anxiété ontologique chez les évangéliques étasuniens et théorie anthropologique de l'esprit

Résumé

Les universitaires décrivent le modèle dominant de l'esprit aux Etats-Unis comme un modèle séculier : l'esprit est délimité, privé, sans activité surnaturelle, c'est le lieu où l'on situe son Moi et son identité. L'auteur avance que les évangéliques charismatiques étasuniens ressentent dans leur vie séculière l'existence d'une frontière apparemment immuable entre leur Moi spirituel immatériel et le monde matériel (ce que Charles Taylor appellerait *boundedness*), mais que dans le même temps, leur volonté d'établir un lien avec le surnaturel leur fait imaginer que cette frontière peut, dans certaines circonstances, être poreuse, formant une zone tampon fragile et friable entre le naturel et le surnaturel. Pour rendre possible cette porosité, les charismatiques mettent au point des stratégies pour franchir la zone tampon : prière à haute voix, émotions fortes, manières ludiques de « faire semblant » et rupture corporelle ou « effraction » du divin. Ces stratégies apportent la preuve que le surnaturel existe, mais ceux qui les pratiquent restent inquiets de la relation entre leurs expériences surnaturelles et le scepticisme qui les entoure. Cette « inquiétude ontologique » se manifeste de trois manières : premièrement, les charismatiques entretiennent des sensations physiques intenses qui démontrent la réalité de Dieu. Deuxièmement, ils décrivent leur vécu avec un réalisme « de bon sens ». Enfin, ils sont perturbés par la discordance entre leurs penchants évangéliques et séculiers sur la possibilité d'action mentale.

3

Vulnerable minds, bodily thoughts, and sensory spirits: local theory of mind and spiritual experience in Ghana

JOHN DULIN *Utah Valley University*

This essay looks at the resonances between common cultural models of the mind in the central region of Ghana and patterns of spiritual experience among charismatic evangelical Christians and practitioners of southern Ghana's indigenous religion, known as traditionalists. In particular, I examine the resonance between the model of the mind that construes it as porous, as vulnerable to forcible take-over by hostile entities, and experiences of divine beings insistently pushing people to do their will. It is also relatively common for people in Ghana to report seeing the divine with their eyes and hearing it with their ears. I argue that this experience resonates with, and is perhaps facilitated by, a tendency of local models of mind in Ghana to blend sense and percept.

Neuroscientist Antonio Damasio (2000) lives in a society permeated by mind-body dualism, so he can write a book arguing that bodily feeling is a crucial part of consciousness and claim it as a major intervention. In less dualistic societies, this would appear self-evident. For example, in addressing Damasio's work, anthropologist Kathryn Geurts (2005) noted that the Anlo-Ewe of Ghana tend to meld mind and body, including sense perception and mental perception, into a single gestalt. She gives Damasio credit for moving beyond mind-body dualism, but adds that he still has much to learn about human psychology from the Anlo-Ewe. For example, she writes, he claimed that bodily feeling creates a sense of 'self-proprietorship' and that consciousness entails that there is an 'I' that belongs to 'me'. Geurts points out that this assumes that 'one body' has 'one self' (2005: 170) – and yet many societies claim that many selves can inhabit one body in the experience of spirit possession (cf. Lambek 1981). Of course, she is talking about a different level of explanation than Damasio, and of course taking this claim too far has its own problems (Spiro 1993). My point here is that Geurts uses ethnographic data to argue that the Anlo-Ewe draw lines around experience differently than Damasio, and differently than the Euro-American social milieu that serves as the backdrop for his research. More specifically, she suggests that where Western models draw explicit lines – like those between mind and body or between self and other – the Anlo-Ewe highlight the links (Geurts 2005: 165; see also Ameka 2002). Or, to use linguist Felix Ameka's term, Ewe language tends to 'bundle' processes like sensation, perception, and cognition (2002: 44-5), whereas many Euro-American discourses tend to emphasize distinctions between these domains. The goal of this essay is to explore culturally specific models of mental domains in postcolonial Ghana and their impact on experience.

My claim is that a cultural tendency in understanding mental events may give rise to an experiential tendency in the phenomenology of spiritual experience (Cassaniti & Luhrmann 2014). I do not mean to argue that local theories of mind in Ghana cause spiritual experience directly, the way one billiard ball knocks into another and causes it to move (see Latour 2005). Instead, I want to suggest that these implicit models may create conditions that are favourable to, and resonate with, certain patterns of spiritual experience. In our work in Cape Coast, Ghana, we identified two facets of the local theory of mind that seem likely to condition spiritual experience: the bundling of mind and body, and the bundling of self-mind and other-mind. I argue that the bundling of self-mind and other-mind resonates with an experience of the divine as persistent, immanent in the body, and difficult-to-resist. The bundling of mind and body resonates with experience of the divine as external, as seeable with the eyes and hearable with the ears.

Charismatic Christianity and traditionalism

The research in this article comes out of the Mind and Spirit project. The Mind and Spirit project is a Templeton-funded, Stanford-based comparative and interdisciplinary project under the direction of T.M. Luhrmann (PI), drawing on the expertise of anthropologists, psychologists, historians, and philosophers. The project asks whether different understandings of 'mind', broadly construed, might shape or be related to the ways that people attend to and interpret experiences they deem spiritual or supernatural. We took a mixed-method, multi-phase approach, combining participant observation, long-form semi-structured interviews, quantitative surveys among the general population and local undergraduates, and experimental research with children and adults. We worked in five different countries: China, Ghana, Thailand, Vanuatu, and the United States, with some work in Ecuadorian Amazonia. In each country, we included a focus on an urban charismatic evangelical church, with additional work in a rural charismatic evangelical church, and in another urban and rural religious setting of local importance.[1] I conducted my research with urban charismatic evangelicals and urban 'traditionalists', those who practise the indigenous religion of Ghana.

My portion of the research took place in Cape Coast, a city along the coast of southern Ghana. The residents of Cape Coast are mostly from the Fante subgroup of the Akan language family. The Fante share much in common with other Akan, including historical matriliny and similar indigenous religious practices. The Fante in particular are known to be well acclimatized to Europeans, given that, as a port city, they have had more sustained contact with European colonizers than have people of the interior. These interactions included business transactions, administrative functions, and intermarriage (Holsey 2008). Cape Coast is home to a famous colonial castle with dungeons that served as a holding area for men and women sold into the transatlantic slave trade. This is a history that, according to Bayo Holsey (2008), many local Fante prefer to forget because they see their ancestors as complicit, even though many were not given much of a choice. Also connected to its long contact with Europeans, Cape Coast is known as a national centre of Methodism and is presently home to a

Journal of the Royal Anthropological Institute (N.S.), 61-76
© Royal Anthropological Institute 2020

deluge of Mainline, African Independent, Classic Pentecostal, and New Charismatic churches (Meyer 2004).

My focus in Cape Coast was the on the city-dwellers; Vivian Dzokoto (this volume) focused on the Fante-speaking rural subjects. We chose as our urban Christian site the Lighthouse Chapel International, a vibrant, growing member of a new wave of charismatic churches. These new churches play contemporary worship music and cater to young, upwardly mobile professionals while still affirming faith in the gifts of the Holy Spirit (Asamoah-Gyadu 2004; Daswani 2015; Gifford 2004). They are like the 'third-wave' charismatic evangelical churches in the United States that emerged after the 1960s and made the older, more formal Pentecostal practices more accessible to the youthful middle class (Bialecki 2017). The Lighthouse Chapel Church in Cape Coast has architecture reminiscent of neighbouring colonial castles and is one of the most striking, well-maintained buildings in the area. The church has its share of well-to-do professionals, as the line-up of cars parked in the compound every Sunday makes clear (the church's website displays this line-up), though many young, non-car-owning college graduates also attend. These young people are always dressed well and filled with hopes of getting ahead, but they struggle to rise above a state of precarity that seems indefinitely prolonged.

At the Lighthouse, tongues, boisterous prayers, and collapsed shaking bodies overcome with the Holy Spirit are standard fare; so are smartphones, social media accounts, and pastoral exhortations for members to be technologically savvy (Reinhardt 2014). Like many charismatic evangelical services in Ghana, those at Lighthouse emphasize spiritual warfare: the assumption that Christians are intimately and actively involved in a supernatural battle between the soldiers of God and his demonic opponents, who are present and active in their everyday world. Congregants fight demonic influence through prayer and blessing, and they overlay these practices with a shiny, modern surface. The loudest, most aggressive declarations of spiritual war are reserved for all-night prayer services, which, unlike the Sunday meetings, are not broadcast over the Internet. Most importantly, Lighthouse members believe that God is active in the world, responding to prayers and communicating with Christians, the way one person might respond to another. These were the characteristics we sought in our urban churches. I interviewed twenty congregants whom we identified as 'committed Christians': adults who attended church often more than once a week between the ages of 20 and 50, half of them men, and half women. The majority of the charismatic Christians were Fante-speakers, but the sample also included speakers of Twi, Ewe, and one Ga-speaker. For this essay, I will focus primarily on the Fante context as a stand-in for Akan culture. I will reference secondary literature on Ewe peoples to show the salience of certain patterns in both Akan and Ewe contexts. While I recognize that there are important variations between and within these categories, for the sake of this essay, I will focus on common patterns that cross-cut different ethno-linguistic groups in southern Ghana.[2]

Our comparison religious group were those likely to be targets of that spiritual warfare, practitioners of the indigenous Akan religion (see Meyer 1999), whom the Ghanaian census and local English-language parlance refer to as 'traditionalists'. Marleen de Witte (2012) notes that 'neo-traditionalists' in Ghana compete with charismatic Christians in the public sphere. In doing so, many have adopted worship forms that mirror those of charismatic Christians, such as their use of a holy book, and their use of radio, television, and billboards to promote indigenous religion. By contrast, the traditionalists in our sample primarily attend to 'state' deities, which are connected to local chiefs, and have a relatively muted presence in the public religious marketplace. Because they do not seek to promote traditionalism as a religion-*qua*-religion, they resemble charismatic Christians less than do their neo-traditionalist counterparts. However, like charismatic Christians, these traditionalists see divine powers as active in everyday human affairs: the divine punishes, blesses, and, most importantly for this essay, *communicates* with humans (Field 1969). These communications do not come from the high God, Onyame, who in major Akan schemes is a distant and uninvolved supreme deity (Gyekye 1987), but from the *abosom*, the 'lesser gods'.

Some see the *abosom* as realizing the will of the high God on earth, though each god has his or her own idiosyncratic demands and taboos, and some *abosom* do things, like murdering innocents, that even traditionalists would call evil. Traditionalists worship, pray to, feed, and observe the taboos of these lesser deities. Their priests and priestesses are called *okomfo* in Akan, or *abosomfo* if they work primarily with the gods from the dry northern plains. They serve as mediums for the gods when people seek out the gods' assistance. The gods normally possess the *okomfo* during the consults, taking full control of them, so the client can interact with the god directly (Ephirim-Donkor 2008). Once the god leaves, the *okomfo* usually cannot remember anything that transpired while possessed. Unlike members of the Lighthouse, the *okomfo* tend to lack English proficiency. Some Ghanaians of a higher social strata describe them as poor, unrefined, and hygienically compromised – and yet many Christians in Cape Coast seek out the gods on occasion for help with specific problems, like witchcraft, illness, and other misfortune. These priests and priestesses of the gods compare with charismatic Christians in the intensity and regularity with which they pray to, listen to, and attempt to merge with their deities. Again, we interviewed twenty people. Half were male, half female, and all were between the ages of 20 and 50. All the individuals in the traditionalist sample were Fante, with the exception of one Ewe priestess who spoke Fante as a second language.

Despite differences of class, education, and religion, I found that Christians and *okomfo* shared similar understandings of the mind. Here I claim that their shared cultural context influences the phenomenological shape of their religious experiences in similar ways.

Porous minds and persistent gods

In this section, I will discuss the ways my interlocutors described a model of the mind as porous, as vulnerable to external entities that can insert into one's mind alien thoughts, desires, motivations, and perceptions. This is very similar to Charles Taylor's concept of a 'porous self', which 'is vulnerable, to spirits, demons, cosmic forces' (2007: 38) and 'emerges … in the various kinds of "possession", all the way from a full taking over of the person, as with a medium, to various kinds of domination by, or partial fusion with, a spirit or God' (2007: 39). For Taylor, the opposite of the porous self is the buffered self, which entails a clear separation of the inner world from the outer world. A buffered self does not have to worry about spiritual invasion, and can take for granted that all thoughts and motivations originate in human minds, confined to bone-encased brains. Thus, the buffered 'can see itself invulnerable, as master of the meanings of things for it' (2007: 38). The distinction between a porous and buffered mind-self is consistent with other distinctions anthropologists often make, between models of humans as bounded, individualistic, and self-sufficient, on the one hand, and porous, partible, and dependent, on the other (Geertz 1974; Shweder & LeVine 1984; Spiro 1993; Strathern 1988). The difference here is that my treatment is more focused on the domain that roughly corresponds to 'the mind' in many Euro-American discourses. Also, our comparison of five sites allows us to consider a more nuanced set of differences than that which often emerges in typical distinctions between 'Western' and 'non-Western' models of self/person/mind (see the Introduction). Like many essays in this volume, I am discussing a porous model of mind that looks something like Taylor describes, but it takes on a historically particular form in contemporary Ghana.

Let me begin to build my account of porosity by observing that vulnerability to malicious others is highly salient to my participants. Glenn Adams (2005), a cross-cultural psychologist, claimed that the prominence of what he calls 'enemyship' in West Africa arises in part from the fact that social networks are highly interdependent and relatively difficult to escape from. He defines enemyship as a 'personal relationship of hatred and malice in which one person desires another person's downfall or attempts to sabotage another person's progress' (2005: 948). A majority of my charismatic and traditionalist interlocutors told me that someone in their life was secretly plotting against them; hence, one must be careful about telling people one's plans for progressing in life, lest your enemy get wind of them and try to sabotage your ambitions – often through backbiting or malicious magic (*juju*). The prayers and blessings of both charismatic Christians and traditionalists often focus on destroying enemies or, at least, forestalling their machinations. I was interacting with a possessed *okomfo* at his shrine, when, speaking with the authoritative voice of his deity, he declared that my enemy 'will die on a hot afternoon'. Anthropologists have not taken up the term 'enemyship', but anthropological treatments of sorcery and witchcraft in West Africa have demonstrated the salience of malicious others in common social imaginaries (e.g. Geschiere 2013).

Early anthropological writings on the subject defined a witch as a person who attacks another person by 'eating' their vitality. The witch identity is contained within the person, often in the form of a physical substance (Evans-Pritchard 1937). This is distinguished from sorcery, a mystical attack carried out through a formula, not necessarily as an inherent attribute of the person (Stewart & Strathern 2004). This distinction does not hold up cross-culturally, but it does in Ghana, in the distinction between *eyan* (witch) and *juju* (sorcery). In Ghana and west Africa more generally, the witches with sufficient access to harm you tend to be close family members (Geschiere 2013). Many of our Ghanaian interlocutors claimed that there was a witch in every family. Birgit Meyer notes that in southern Ghana diverse malevolent figures in Ga, Akan, and Ewe contexts have been 'lumped together' and translated into a single English word: 'witchcraft' (2015: 200). Consistent with this observation, our interlocutors tended to treat witchcraft in Ga, Ewe, and Akan contexts as more or less the same phenomena. Moreover, as the literature on witchcraft in southern Ghana predicts (Onyinah 2002), the witch figure in our interlocutors' accounts tended to be aunts, grandmothers, even mothers – women who stand in a hierarchical relationship to others, who can claim obligation and deference from subordinates. The malice of witches spills out into the world when the witch's spirit leaves their body and attacks their family members in the spirit realm, wreaking havoc in their lives, often by manipulating the thoughts and perceptions of others. Besiwa,[3] a heavy-set charismatic Christian woman with a graduate degree, reported that her aunt had brought economic ruin upon her parents with her witchcraft powers. They had once had a thriving book and stationery shop in town, but then one day the customers stopped coming. People told her that they could

Journal of the Royal Anthropological Institute (N.S.), 61-76
© Royal Anthropological Institute 2020

not see the shop and they just kept passing it by. God revealed to Besiwa that her aunt was a witch and she had planted a black spiritual tree in the shop, which warped the perception of potential customers, making the shop essentially invisible.

Generally, malevolent magic from non-kin can cause harm if the assailant finds an entry point into people's bodies. Food and sex are common trojan horses of malevolent magic (Onyinah 2002: 69-75), enabling a sorcerer or witch to invade another person's intentional locus, and control their thoughts, desires, sense-perception, and character.[4] Once when a traditionalist priest consulted his god on my behalf, the god instructed me to avoid food offered by strangers lest I be poisoned, or suffer the dangers of magic that would force me to do things against my will, like give money away. When an elderly traditionalist priestess invited me to eat at her home, my charismatic Christian friends urged me refuse her food for fear that I might fall in love with her. My mind would become so clouded, they told me, I would not recognize my wife. The prospect that I might eat the wrong thing, then forget my wife, and fall in love with an 80-year-old woman only has a hint of plausibility if you see your mind as potentially not your own, if you see it as vulnerable to hostile invasion by an outside force. Eating the wrong thing has the potential to change you into an entirely different person, even a witch: the embodiment of evil, the epitome of a 'bad mind' (see Dzokoto, this volume).[5] One of our interlocutors told of a time she experienced her spirit leave her body at night, which, for some, is a tell-tale sign of a witch. 'I think I'm a witch', she told her mother in the morning. Her mother asked her if she ate anything, like a bullfrog, while she was in the spirit realm and she said no; so, she was safe, but had she eaten something she would have had reason to worry. Another interlocutor told of a time a friend offered her young nephew candy at school. He accepted it and kept it in his backpack for a few days. When he went to retrieve it, he found it had transformed into a human finger. If he had eaten the candy, she told me, he would have become a witch. I asked many of my interlocutors about these stories, and most insisted that these kinds of things happen. Similarly, in the early to mid-twentieth century, Margaret Field (1960; 1961) documented that many people in rural Ga and Assante contexts visited shrines convinced that they had unwittingly transformed into witches. They hoped that the religious specialists at the shrines could help reverse their condition.

In common Akan conceptions, the transmission of witchcraft is akin to possession. However, although in the case of normative possession the spirit and vessel remain separable entities, when one falls victim to witchcraft possession the evil spirit becomes intimately fused with the vessel so that it is hard to distinguish between the possessed person and the spirit that possesses (Bannerman-Richter 1982: 46). Echoing this idea, one of our charismatic interlocutors stated that a witch is not merely possessed by an evil spirit but 'she has embraced the spirit with her soul, so now the soul is corrupt'. As the stories above illustrate, this potential *permanent* loss of one's fate (which can include mind, behaviour, personality) to witchcraft is a real and terrifying prospect for many of the people we interviewed. Also, vulnerability to the influence of spirits and other malevolent forces was a powerful reason many people turned to Christianity. This is what Birgit Meyer argues in her work. In a book chapter that engages with Charles Taylor, she claims the Ewe possess an 'idea of the person as being subject to being inhabited ... by different kinds of spirits', which, she claims 'points toward an understanding of the person as permeable and open, organically linked to the world around it' (2012: 94). She argues that the appeal of Christianity was that the Holy Spirit, a new kind of spirit, could fill people and could protect them from the 'different kinds of spirits' pining to inhabit them. The Holy Spirit 'affected a kind of closure' and prayer acts as a 'spiritual hedge' against malicious spiritual forces. She further claims that this closure is in 'certain respects quite close to Taylor's notion of a "buffered self", but that among the Ewe 'the buffered self is in constant need of being secured by powerful prayer and vigilance' (2012: 94). The intense work that must go into buffering presupposes a self that is, at base, porous and vulnerable to hostile invasion. As Brahinsky shows in this volume, many charismatics in the United States work to shatter the buffer, not create it.

Ewe and Akan models of the person are not identical, but the logic of buffers and porousness in relation to the Holy Spirit is quite similar among charismatic evangelical Christians in both contexts. The sermons of the Lighthouse church I attended often warned against the prospect of having one's mind and will taken over by hostile forces. The pastor one Sunday told a story of a man who almost ate bread containing love magic served to him by his scheming secretary. Luckily, 'his wife was a prayerful woman'. The man became angered by a phone call at just the right time and threw the bread out of the window before eating it. A 'mad man' found the enchanted bread, ate it, and ended up stalking the woman, following her impulsively as if guided by a 'GPS'. In public prayers, the leader would frequently say things like, 'Delivering you from demons, delivering you from evil spirits, and any door that will let evil spirits into your life'. The pastor often quoted a scripture from Matthew about possession:

> When an unclean spirit goes out of a man, he goes through dry places, seeking rest, and finds none. Then he says, 'I will return to my house from which I came'. And when he comes, he finds it empty, swept, and put in order. Then he goes and takes with him seven other spirits more wicked than himself, and they enter and dwell there; and the last state of that man is worse than the first (Matthew 12: 43-5).

This verse makes clear the need for continued protection to prevent repeated possession. One must maintain 'benevolent' possession from the Holy Spirit so demons do not find an empty, hospitable house. When I asked charismatics why they spoke in tongues, they usually justified it in terms of this kind of selective porosity that has a protective function – what one could call protective porosity. On the one hand, speaking in tongues prevents the devil from hearing the content of one's prayer. On the other hand, when one prays in tongues, the Holy Spirit provides the content, taking over one's mind and speech, ensuring that one prays for the right thing. The Holy Spirit-authored content of glossolalia is transparent to God and determined by him, but often remains opaque to the believer who animates the prayer. This protective porosity shields one from conspiring evil spirits. It is a *kind* of buffer, as Meyer claimed, but one that is not presupposed like Taylor's secular buffer and those of Brahinsky's interlocutors. It must be secured through the right kind of porosity, in which one merges with the Holy Spirit (as opposed to unholy spirits) in a benevolent divine-human protective hierarchy (Dulin forthcoming).

This emphasis on porosity in thinking about thinking likely shapes the spiritual experiences people report. In particular, it seems to dispose people to experience moments when God speaks inside the mind as more forceful, insistently pushing them to do his will, giving them an 'urge' in the body, which contrasts starkly with the subtlety of typical North American charismatic experiences of God speaking to their thoughts. Generally, charismatic evangelical Christianity invites people to experience God as speaking to them inside their minds. As US author Mark Virkler describes the process, 'God's voice normally sounds like a flow of spontaneous thoughts, rather than an audible voice. I have since discovered certain characteristics of God's interjected thoughts which help me to recognize them' (Virkler & Virkler 1986: 29). People who join these churches learn to pick out thoughts they might once have experienced as their own, and attribute them to God. When Luhrmann (2012) described the process among charismatic evangelical Christians in the United States, she saw that congregants trained their minds to notice the signals God is always transmitting, whether we listen or not. These transmissions could be missed amid the endless babble of human-authored thought. Likewise, while some of Brahinsky's charismatic evangelical Christian interlocutors talk about strong experiences, or nagging thoughts that come from God, on the whole, many experiences of God speaking to their thoughts were subtle and amorphous.

In Ghana, this was different. When we asked Christians if God ever spoke to their 'minds', their answers sometimes resembled those of charismatic evangelical Christians in the United States. They described subtle 'promptings', a calm voice in the mind, as well as intuitions that seemed like infusions of information without any describable thought form. Many of these descriptions varied, but there was one pattern the vast majority of our interlocutors held in common: they described God speaking to them in the form of some kind of difficult-to-resist pressure. Godwin, a soft-spoken, middle-aged medical entrepreneur whom I saw at every church event, recalled a time he set out to give a church lesson that he had prepared, when an intrusive thought came into his head, telling him to teach something different. He tried to put it aside but it persisted. He described it as 'like being put under duress to do something': 'you intend not to do it' but 'there is no way you can free yourself' from doing it (Dulin forthcoming). Another charismatic Christian man described a time God was 'disturbing me "in quotes"' to pray. He said 'in quotes' because he thought it was not polite to say God was disturbing him, but it was the best word he could think of to describe the experience. Others would describe God giving them an 'urge' felt in the body, which fills them with anxiety until they stop resisting it. As one charismatic man described it, 'The urge was just there, coming, coming . . . something like pressure to do it' (Dulin forthcoming). In some of the charismatic Christian accounts, it is almost like God is controlling their actions. For example, one charismatic Christian woman said that sometimes when the bishop asks for an offering of 100 cedi (about $25), she impulsively gives 200 cedis: 'I don't seem to be in control of it. I just felt like I should give this'.

Signature encounters the *okomfo* have with their gods mirror the charismatic experience of divine insistence. Arguably, common experiences of *okomfo* represent an intensified iteration of this otherworldly push. First of all, the gods of my traditionalist interlocutors often initially make themselves known to their future mediums through disruptive possession experiences (Field 1969). Eric, a muscular, cheeky *okomfo* in his mid-twenties, just blacked out one day while at school. Apparently, he had been uncontrollable and maybe dangerous during possession, because he woke up to find his hands tied. Others, like Albert, a short thin, even-tempered *okomfo*, experienced more gradual, incremental possession. As he tells it, he had always been shy at school until one day he found himself overwhelmingly hyperactive, so much so that he could not function in class. This turned into an ongoing problem. He wanted to study but could not remain seated. Outside of class, his hands and body involuntarily shook when anyone around him quarrelled or played music. These were signs that 'maybe the gods wanted to possess me'. I would call these partial possessions, as he was still conscious during these events, even if he was not fully in control. One day, when Albert returned to his hometown after spending time away, 'the [god] revealed himself' and he finally blacked out. When he regained consciousness, his body was wet and a large number of people stood, staring at him. It was obvious to everyone he had been possessed by the god. They even brought out drums and played them in an attempt to get him to dance. A kind of 'partial possession' was not limited to the pre-possession period. Some of our traditionalist informants described direction from the gods coming in the form of a volitional push, something like a midway point between dissociative possession and full self-control. They described receiving 'urges' to, for example, avoid a river, phone someone, or return home from a friend's house. In describing these 'urges', the traditionalists used the Fante phrase '*csoso me do*', 'the urge fell upon me'. This phrase can refer to an experience of an urge or impulse in the body, including sexual urges. It can also refer to something like intuition, including intuition experienced as a push to act. Our Fante translators interpreted the phrase as describing a physical urge or impulse *combined with* a transmission of intuition-like knowledge from the gods (E. Aseidu, pers. comm., 24 June 2017): *intuition + bodily urge*. The English-language charismatic Christian accounts of divine 'urges' discussed earlier carry both of these connotations.

Generally, for both my charismatic evangelical Christian and traditionalist interlocutors, divine communication was often experienced as a volitional shift felt in the body, pushing the recipient towards a specific course of action. Usually, the outcome was positive and the motivation benevolent. Even so, they reported experiencing this benevolent message as an overwhelming 'disturbance', 'urge', or 'pressure' from an invisible other – like their mind and will were close to being taken over, like they could almost not refuse the push. One could say that the model of the mind as porous, and the experience of the divine insistently overriding one's intent, are mutually reinforcing, each amplifying the plausibility of the other.

The *ho-tse* dimension of mind

The examples I have given of mental porosity – being transformed into a witch, being forced to fall in love, or being unable to see a shop – are not seen first and foremost as *mental* phenomena. If I were to describe a love spell as 'mind control', my interlocutors would not disagree with me. However, they are just as likely to talk about it as control of the body or control of action. This is because among my interlocutors there is a relative de-emphasis on the mind as a discrete domain, which may be a feature of some porous models of the mind, at least the kind that limit the formation of a buffered identity. According to Taylor (2007), the mind becomes very important for a buffered self because, according to this model, the mind is the primary generator of 'meaning'. By contrast, in Ghana, the mental, as a discrete domain, appears de-emphasized when juxtaposed with hyper-mind-focused contexts like the United States (see Dzokoto, Opare-Henaku & Kpobi 2013) and urban China (at least the urban Chinese Ng describes in this volume). Likewise, what I call 'the bundling of mind and body' describes a tendency that only comes into focus when juxtaposed with active mind-body splitting in other contexts. In this section, I argue that this bundling of mind-stuff and body-stuff resonates with an experience of the divine that feels unmediated by the mind: the divine is presented directly to the ears and the eyes.

The language of bundling will only get us so far in understanding this less dualistic model of mind. Akan languages are more adequate to this task than English. For example, the Fante greeting '*Wɔ ho tze dɛñ?*' could translate as 'How are you?', but an alternative rendering would be 'How do you sense-perceive your body-self?' '*Wɔ ho*' could translate as 'you', or, more literally, as 'your body', but to ask about the '*ho*' is not only to ask about one's bodily health. It is also an inquiry into one's general well-being, including psychological well-being. Hence, I would render *ho* 'body-self'. The word '*tze*' in this context could translate as 'are', but, more literally, I would translate it as 'sense-perceive'. There are not different words in Fante for sense and perceive: *tze* captures both processes at once. *Tze* is also the word used in Fante for feel, taste, hear, listen, and touch (cf. Agyekum 2002). Therefore, in one of their most common social interactions, Fante people ask each other, 'How do you sense-perceive your body-self?' It is true that, in some major Akan schemes, the spirit (*sunsum*) and the soul (*kra*) are important elements of the self, but they do not exhaust it, given that one's soul and spirit can leave one's *ho*, yet one's *ho* remains animate with some semblance of one's former self, though transformed in some way (Gyekye 1987). Soul loss, for example, is evident in depression and spirit loss can lead to dullness, a diminished capacity for personal excellence.

I am tempted to call the conceptual collapse (from a North American perspective) of dualisms of mind and body, sense and percept, the *ho-tse* theory of mind: a model in which mind-stuff – thinking, believing, intending, etc. – is not imagined as sharply separate from body-stuff, but is rather imagined as a mutually constituting, inseparable mash of body-mind-world connections. This is all consistent with Geurts's (2003; 2005) work on the Ewe 'sensorium', which she noticed did not split up cognition and the senses in the way these elements of experience are often parsed out in the United States and elsewhere. Granted, Fante does have a word that translates as mind-thought, *adwen*, but it does not designate an autonomous domain of perception, introspection, and meaning-making per se. As Dzokoto notes in this volume, the word *adwen* tends to refer to thinking involved in planning and executing action. That is one reason why the mind has moral salience in Ghana: if one has a 'bad mind', one will surely make evil plans to act in a socially damaging way. I did not hear many people talk about practising personal introspection to learn if they have a bad mind or not, or attempting to decipher their own true intentions. It appeared that people saw the moral status of their minds as transparent in their behaviour. In one of the interviews, we asked our interlocutors if it was important to think about their thoughts. Those who said yes tended to focus not on self-knowledge, but on the need to pay attention to thoughts in order to 'plan' and act judiciously. A large portion said it was a waste of time to think about one's thoughts. Indeed, the Fante word for anxiety is *adwen-dwen*, 'thinking-thinking': thinking directed at the mind in a way that is unrelated to action leads to an undesirably anxious emotional state.

The strong link between thinking and action was highlighted when I asked our interlocutors to give examples of thoughts associated with particular emotions. When I asked for an example of an envious thought, a common answer was 'backbiting'; when I asked for an example of an angry thought, a common answer was 'hitting someone'; when I asked for an example of a caring thought, a common answer was 'helping someone'. By giving an unqualified description of actions as examples of thoughts, these answers illustrate a de-emphasis on thought as internal representation and an emphasis on its role as a driver of action. This collapse of thought into action – a collapse that points to a de-emphasis on mental representation as an autonomous domain of meaning-making – dovetails well with the blending of mind and body in what I have called the *ho-tze* theory of mind. The categories of *tze-ho* (sense-perceive body-self) and *adwen* (mind-thought-action) both blend mind and body, though one might say they blend distinct slices of mind-body. Generally, the conceptual collapse of mind into body-action also resonates with how both charismatic Christians and traditionalists described God pushing them to action, which was often felt as an 'urge' in the body – a God-thought that is also an action-push.

I argue here that the inattention to mental perception as distinct from the bodily senses resonates with a greater tendency to both perceive *and* sense the invisible other – or, to phrase it negatively, it resonates with a diminished tendency to mentally perceive God without also seeing or hearing God in a concrete way with one's eyes and ears. When we asked people to describe what it is like when God speaks to their minds, some charismatic Christians described a voice that was distinctively mental and clearly non-sensory. Yet about a quarter of them blurred the line between a voice heard in the mind and a voice heard with the ears. Comfort, a serious, no-frills charismatic Christian administrative assistant, struggled to describe the experience of God speaking to her mind, then suddenly told me that sometimes she feels God's breath on her ears and hears him audibly whispering. I also asked Delali – a woman who recently completed a graduate degree in finance and comes to church dressed like a businesswoman – to explain the experience of God speaking to her mind, and she described an experience that came off as more than just mental. She said God's voice sounds like 'flowing waters', and added 'you virtually hear it'. What she described sounded auditory, so I asked her if she heard it with her ears. She said yes, but then wondered, 'Do I hear it with my ears or not my ears?' She finally concluded, 'I think physically you hear it with your ears', 'but', she added, 'If it is a spiritual thing it should be [in] the mind and your heart . . . [the mind and heart] should be in tune' (Dulin forthcoming). It was as if she had not until that moment cared to attend to the question of whether the voice was inside or outside the mind, though other kinds of internality were important to her, like inner 'attunement' of the heart and mind. Compared to traditionalists, the charismatic Christians gave significant attention to the quality of internal experience. They described experiences of inner calm and intuition, but when there was a phenomenological overlap between a sensory and mental experience (e.g. mental/sensory image, mental/sensory voice), they often defaulted to a sensory interpretation of what happened to them.

These accounts suggest that attention, or a lack thereof, to the distinction between mental and sensory makes a difference in the way people experience God speaking. The account that one of our charismatic Christian research assistants gave of her experience with God's voice shows that one's understanding of one's experience can change once one learns to pay attention to the percept-sense distinction. She initially reported that God spoke to her ears daily. However, after conducting many interviews for us that asked people whether God spoke to their mind or their thoughts, she realized she was actually hearing God speak in her mind. Careful attention to the mental as a distinct domain may be something one must learn – to some extent. Paying attention to internal experience is not the same as drawing attention to the boundary between the thoughts and the senses. Luhrmann (2012) found that her US charismatic evangelical subjects were so hesitant to imagine an external being in their interior mental space that they struggled to break down the boundary the secular model of the mind had established. This struggle was less apparent in Ghana.

I also found that Christianity made a difference. Our traditionalist interlocutors gave less attention to the qualities of their internal experience than charismatics did. While six of the twenty charismatic Christians described the divine voice as unambiguously mental, not one of the traditionalists described their experience as an unequivocal mental voice – if the gods spoke to them with a voice, they heard them with their ears.[6] Some descriptions of hearing with ears have details that suggest they experienced the voice as outside their heads. See, for example, the following account by a traditional priestess:

> I was pregnant, so not knowing that the man for which I was pregnant had a girlfriend and the girlfriend had cursed me and I did not know. So, I was there one day and I heard a voice say 'eih, so you will not help yourself that you are going to die?' and I got frightened ... I could hear the voice from afar. And I was wondering who was talking because I was in my room alone. So, I got up and went to fetch water and I took my bath. So, it was the god that told me to go and buy full water [a solution used on dead bodies] and put it in my bathing water all the time.

The priestess said the god told her of an enemy, a woman who had reason to attempt to kill her through an unspecified spiritual means. The god specified that a bath in 'full water' would protect her. Its voice had a concrete location in the world: she heard it from far away. At first, she thought a person was talking, but because she was alone she concluded it was her god. Many charismatic Christians and traditionalists who hear voices report being surprised and turning their head to see who was speaking.[7] Most are comfortable saying whether the voice was heard a half meter from their ears, up close like a whisper, or inside the ears, as if they were wearing earphones. More charismatic Christians in Ghana's urban sample reported hearing God with their ears than among the urban charismatic samples in the four other countries.

There is a similar bias towards the sensory in Ghanaian charismatic and traditionalist accounts of divine communication through imagery and visions. In our main interview about spiritual experience, we asked our participants if the divine had ever communicated with them by placing an image in their minds. Much like the question about God *speaking* to their minds, the answers of both charismatics and traditionalists suggest they do not attend very closely to the boundary between mental and sensory images. When asked about mental images, many charismatic Christians claimed that God had indeed given them a mental image, but then upon further questioning, they disclosed that the experience was also sensory. For example, when I asked Edmund, an earnest Bible student at the Lighthouse, if God ever put a picture in his mind, he told of a time he was lying down and he saw a figure hand him some keys. This dramatized a Bible verse he had just read. I asked him if he had seen this with his mind or his eyes, and he defaulted to the sensory: '*with my eyes*', he said confidently. In an answer to the same question about God putting an image in his mind, another charismatic Christian said that he saw an image of the future. After probes, he insisted that he saw the image with his eyes. Edem – a charismatic Christian hairstylist who worried that ancestral gods were bothering her family – gave a striking example of a blurred line between the sensory and the mental. She told of seeing an *abottia* (dwarf), a short, mischievous spirit, relaxing in her home. At first, she said she saw it in her mind, but then insisted it was outside her head. Yet she only saw it when she closed her eyes. When she opened her eyes, she could not see the dwarf. However, because she believed she was seeing something that was actually there, she claimed it as a visual, not mental, experience. A few others were quite clear that an experience was mental. God showed one charismatic Christian woman pictures of people to whom she needed to give a message, 'like passport' photos, but she described it as clearly mental. She said, 'I saw it with my mind ... I did not see it in front of my eyes like this piece of paper'.[8] However, these were in the minority: an insistence that one was seeing with one's eyes was the norm.

Many traditionalists also talk about seeing physical, external visions from the gods. Taken as a whole, the traditionalists describe their visual experiences as more clearly non-mental, as more unambiguous in their direct presentation to the retina. When the gods first started showing interest in one little girl (who would grow up to be a priestess), she was shown an image of a man and woman on the wall while she was lying in bed. As she told the story, she added these details: 'the man had shaved off his hair and the woman had plaited her hair'. She kept staring and staring at this image on her wall. It was so real to her that she eventually woke her mother and tried to show her, but 'she said she couldn't see it'. Another priestess was undergoing arduous training to become an *okomfo* in typical institutionalized isolation. When experiencing sadness at being away from her children, her god comforted her with a vision, 'I could be lying down in the afternoons thinking about my children when the ... [god] ... it was like a mirror and it would show the images of all of my children. I could sit and cry for a while and the ... [god] would tell me not to cry'. Many of these accounts describe visual experiences in physical ways: 'on the wall', 'like a mirror'. By describing these experiences in such concrete ways, they were not attempting to find metaphors for a mental experience; they were attempting to communicate the experiences' external, sensory quality. They were emphatic: they saw these visions with their eyes, not in their minds.

Conclusion

The resonances between cultural models of mind and patterns of spiritual experience described in this essay support the classic anthropological contention that culture-specific conceptions are more than just window dressing. They are often embedded in subjective experience in profound ways. There are a few ways to conceptualize the relationship between cultural models of mind and spiritual experience that emerge here. At the very least, we can see representations of mind – present in discourses and the structure of language – and first-person phenomenological descriptions as manifesting a similar pattern that cross-cuts different scales and dimensions of life. Finding resonances between models of mind and detailed descriptions of experience provides one response to the kind of scepticism Maurice Bloch (1977) raised about non-linear models of time, or the objections Melford Spiro (1993) raised about diverse models of the self: that they are cultural representations with social, and sometimes political, importance, but that they do not necessarily reflect quotidian experience of time and self. By contrast, the findings discussed here support the claim that patterns reflected in models of mind have a presence in the phenomenological shape of first-person experience.

A second way of conceptualizing this relationship is a bit more tentative, but not implausible. We can see cultural models of mind not just as reflecting, but as structuring people's consciousness on a deep level. The models of mind here would be conceptualized as preceding spiritual experience and playing a large part in generating it. This way of conceiving the experience is consistent with a constructivist side of a debate in the study of spiritual experience in fields of psychology and religious studies. To gloss this argument, the claim is that religious or cultural schemes do not only shape the interpretation of experience, but they also help constitute the experience itself. In response to theorists who claim there is something *sui generis* about religious experience, strong constructivists argue, essentially, that religious experience per se would not exist without religious and cultural explanatory schemes that constitute it (see Proudfoot 1985: 156-216; Taves 2009: 90-4). I am not suggesting that porous and *tse-ho* models

Journal of the Royal Anthropological Institute (N.S.), 61-76
© Royal Anthropological Institute 2020

of the mind constitute the religious experience writ large, but that they may form part of composite schematic structures (which include religious schemas) that process phenomena and set expectations, and hence help give experience, including spiritual experience, a particular phenomenal shape. I have shown that, in our Ghana data on spiritual experience and models of mind, we find the kinds of resonances we would expect if there were this kind of confluence between the model and the experience. If one has an 'urge' to act that seems to come out of nowhere, there is a model of mental porosity ready-made to interpret it as an external spiritual force. This is a model of the mind that frames one's thoughts and desires as easily supplanted, which could supply one with inferences that amplify the subjective strength and seeming unavoidability of the God-push. If one experiences a vivid voice/image that could potentially be mental or sensory, the sense-percept-blending *tse-ho* model of the mind may reduce the tendency to relegate the phenomena to the status of *either* externally sensed *or* mentally perceived. Indeed, the model may enable the subject to, with relative ease, just let the experience rest as a sensed-perceived voice or image. In conclusion, it is plausible that these models of the mind frame and structure experience, and thus contribute significantly to a cultural ecology that makes sensory encounters with the divine, and the experience of divine insistence and pressure, more likely.

NOTES

This essay would not have been possible without numerous interlocutors and research assistants in the field, but special thanks are due to Eunice Otoo for handling so many facets of data collection and participating in useful conversations throughout the research process. Appreciations are due to Tanya Luhrmann, Vivian Dzokoto, Emily Ng, Felicity Aulino, Joshua Brahinsky, Rachel Smith, and Rita Astuti for reading earlier versions of the draft and providing valuable feedback. I would also like to thank the two anonymous reviewers for responses to the manuscript that significantly improved the essay.

[1] This paragraph is based on a description drafted collectively by the Mind and Spirit team and used to illustrate the joint nature of the research.

[2] Most charismatics were English-speakers and preferred to answer questions in English, though they had the opportunity to switch to Fante if they needed. All non-English language interviews were conducted in Fante. All interviews with people from other ethno-linguistic groups were conducted in English. All the local terms from the primary research that have been translated into English are translated from Fante.

[3] All names used are pseudonyms to protect confidentiality.

[4] In a similar vein, Kofi Busia (1951) notes that in Ashanti, the kinds of incompetence that have historically led to chiefs being de-stooled are often attributed to witchcraft.

[5] Some have documented an Akan concept that witchcraft can be used for good, pro-social purposes (Onyinah 2002: 66). This idea is familiar to my interlocutors. They would often make comments about how 'whites' use witchcraft to make computers, and so on. However, when they talked about witchcraft contagion, it was always of the malevolent, soul-destroying kind.

[6] There were few times when a voice was not identified as mental or sensory, and one traditionalist said that an inexperienced person might hear the gods only with their minds, but an experienced *okomfo* hears with their ears (Dulin forthcoming).

[7] There was a probe in the interview that asked those who said they had heard a voice, 'Did you turn your head to see who was speaking?'

[8] Some charismatic Christians described seeing visions with 'spiritual eyes' and hearing voices with 'spiritual ears'. When asked to clarify, these statements often refer to experiences that felt physical but were not visible to others. It could also refer to images and voices experienced as mental. The common element in different uses of the term was that the image or voice gave insight into a spiritual reality.

REFERENCES

ADAMS, G. 2005. The cultural grounding of personal relationship: enemyship in North American and West African worlds. *Journal of Personality and Social Psychology* **88**, 948-68.

AGYEKUM, K. 2002. Lexical polysemy and metaphorical extension of *te* 'hear' verb of perception in Akan. *Legon Journal of Humanities* **13**, 99-113.

AMEKA, F.K. 2002. Cultural scripting of body parts for emotions: on 'jealousy' and related emotions in Ewe. *Pragmatics and Cognition* **10**, 27-55.

ASAMOAH-GYADU, J. 2004. *African charismatics: current developments within independent indigenous Pentecostalism in Ghana.* Leiden: Brill.

BANNERMAN-RICHTER, G. 1982. *The practice of witchcraft in Ghana.* Sacramento, Calif: Gabari.

BIALECKI, J. 2017. *A diagram for fire: miracles and variation in an American charismatic movement.* Oakland: University of California Press.

BLOCH, M. 1977. The past and the present in the present. *Man* (N.S.) **12**, 278-92.

BUSIA, K. 1951. *The position of the chief in the modern political system of Ashanti: a study of the influence of contemporary social changes on Ashanti political institutions.* London: Oxford University Press.

CASSANITI, J.L. & T.M. LUHRMANN 2014. The cultural kindling of spiritual experiences. *Current Anthropology* **55**:S10, S333-43.

DAMASIO, A.R. 2000. *The feeling of what happens: body and emotion in the making of consciousness.* London: Heinemann.

DASWANI, G. 2015. *Looking back, moving forward: transformation and ethical practice in the Ghanaian Church of Pentecost.* Toronto: University Press.

DE WITTE, M. 2012. Neo-traditional religions. In *The Wiley-Blackwell companion to African religions* (ed.) E. Bongmba, 173-83. Oxford: Wiley-Blackwell.

DULIN, J. forthcoming. Charismatic Christianity's hard cultural forms and the local patterning of the divine voice in Ghana. *American Anthropologist.*

DZOKOTO, V.A., A. OPARE-HENAKU & L.A. KPOBI 2013. Somatic referencing and psychologisation in emotion narratives: a USA-Ghana comparison. *Psychology and Developing Societies* **25**, 311-31.

EPHIRIM-DONKOR, A. 2008. Akom: the ultimate mediumship experience among the Akan. *Journal of the American Academy of Religion* **76**, 54-81.

EVANS-PRITCHARD, E.E. 1937. *Witchcraft, oracles and magic among the Azande.* Oxford: Clarendon Press.

FIELD, M.J. 1960. *Search for security: an ethno-psychiatric study of rural Ghana.* London: Faber & Faber.

——— 1961. *Religion and medicine of the Gã people.* London: Oxford University Press.

——— 1969. Spirit possession in Ghana. In *Spirit mediumship and society in Africa* (eds) J. Beattie & J. Middleton, 3-13. London: Routledge & Kegan Paul.

GEERTZ, C. 1974. 'From the native's point of view': on the nature of anthropological understanding. *Bulletin of the American Academy of Arts and Sciences* **28**:1, 26-45.

GESCHIERE, P. 2013. *Witchcraft, intimacy, and trust: Africa in comparison.* Chicago: University Press.

GEURTS, K.L. 2003. *Culture and the senses: embodiment, identity, and well-being in an African community.* Berkeley: University of California Press.

——— 2005. Consciousness as 'feeling in the body': a West African theory of embodiment, emotion and the making of mind. In *Empire of the senses: the sensual culture reader* (ed.) D. Howes, 164-78. Oxford: Berg.

GIFFORD, P. 2004. *Ghana's new Christianity: Pentecostalism in a globalizing African economy.* Bloomington: Indiana University Press.

GYEKYE, K. 1987. *An essay on African philosophical thought: the Akan conceptual scheme.* Cambridge: University Press.

HOLSEY, B. 2008. *Routes of remembrance: refashioning the slave trade in Ghana.* Chicago: University Press.

LAMBEK, M. 1981. *Human spirits: a cultural account of trance in Mayotte.* Cambridge: University Press.

LATOUR, B. 2005. *Reassembling the social: an introduction to actor-network-theory.* Oxford: University Press.

LUHRMANN, T.M. 2012. *When God talks back: understanding the American evangelical relationship with God.* New York: Knopf.

MEYER, B. 1999. *Translating the devil.* Trenton, N.J.: Africa World.

——— 2004. Christianity in Africa: from African independent to Pentecostal-charismatic churches. In *The Wiley-Blackwell companion to African religions* (ed.) E. Bongmba, 153-70. Oxford: Wiley-Blackwell.

——— 2012. Religious and secular, 'spiritual' and 'physical' in Ghana. In *What matters? Ethnographies of value in a (not so) secular age* (eds) C. Bender & A. Taves, 86-118. New York: Columbia University Press.

——— 2015. *Sensational movies: video, vision, and Christianity in Ghana.* Berkeley: University of California Press.

ONYINAH, O. 2002. Akan witchcraft and the concept of exorcism in the Church of Pentecost. Ph.D. dissertation, University of Birmingham.

PROUDFOOT, W. 1985. *Religious experience.* Berkeley: University of California Press.

Reinhardt, B. 2014. Soaking in tapes: the haptic voice of global Pentecostal pedagogy in Ghana. *Journal of the Royal Anthropological Institute* (N.S.) **20**, 315-36.

Shweder, R.A. & R.A. LeVine 1984. *Culture theory: essays on mind, self, and emotion.* Cambridge: University Press.

Spiro, M.E. 1993. Is the Western conception of the self 'peculiar' within the context of the world cultures? *Ethos* **21**, 107-53.

Stewart, P.J. & A. Strathern 2004. *Witchcraft, sorcery, rumors, and gossip.* Cambridge: University Press.

Strathern, M. 1988. *The gender of the gift: problems with women and problems with society in Melanesia.* Berkeley: University of California Press.

Taves, A. 2009. *Religious experience reconsidered: a building-block approach to the study of religion and other spiritual things.* Princeton: University Press.

Taylor, C. 2007. *A secular age.* Cambridge, Mass.: Belknap Press of Harvard University Press.

Virkler, M. & P. Virkler 1986. *Dialogue with God.* Gainesville, Fla: Bridge-Logos.

Esprits vulnérables, pensées corporelles et esprits sensoriels : théorie locale de l'esprit et de l'expérience spirituelle au Ghana

Résumé

Cet essai s'intéresse aux résonances entre les modèles culturels communs de l'esprit dans le centre du Ghana et les schémas d'expérience spirituelle parmi les chrétiens évangéliques charismatiques, d'une part, et les « traditionalistes », praticiens de la religion autochtone du sud du pays, d'autre part. L'auteur examine en particulier la résonance entre le modèle qui considère que l'esprit est poreux, vulnérable à l'emprise d'entités hostiles, et l'expérience faite par des personnes d'être poussées par des êtres divins à faire leur volonté. Les Ghanéens racontent assez souvent qu'ils ont vu la divinité de leurs yeux et l'ont entendue de leurs oreilles. L'auteur affirme que cette expérience fait écho à une tendance des modèles locaux ghanéens de l'esprit à mêler sens et perceptions et est peut-être facilitée par celle-ci.

4

Adwenhoasem: an Akan theory of mind

VIVIAN AFI DZOKOTO *Virginia Commonwealth University*

This essay explores the way the domain of what English-speakers call the mind – believing, thinking, feeling, and other mental acts – is represented and mapped by Ghana's Akan ethno-linguistic group. It uses several sources of evidence: mind and mind-related words in Fante (an Akan language); the largest Akan (Twi) proverb compendium; longsemi-structured interviews with forty adult Christians and African traditional religion practitioners; and short-term ethnographic fieldwork by a Ghanaian scholar. The work finds four dimensions of what we might call an Akan theory of mind that seem to be shaped by local language and culture. First, the central function of the mind is planning – not identity. Second, one of the most salient qualities of the mind is its moral valence. The 'bad minds' of others are an ever-present potential threat to social harmony and personal well-being. Third, the mind is understood to be porous in nature. The minds of all people are vulnerable to supernatural influences, and some spiritually powerful people can exert supernatural power through mental action. Fourth and finally, some elements which English-speakers would imagine as part of the mind (like feeling) are instead identified with the body.

I come to this essay as a psychologist, born to Ghanaian parents, resident in southern Ghana for nearly two decades, and having conducted research in the country for more than twenty years. A large portion of my work to date has focused on the way feelings are represented, understood, and identified with the body in this social world (e.g. Dzokoto *et al.* 2018). The current work expands this focus to ask how Ghana's Akan ethno-linguistic group maps and understands the terrain of what English-speakers – particularly, middle-class Western-educated North Americans – would call the mind. I found an emphasis on *planning*. My Akan interlocutors represented the mind as the production centre for strategies to accomplish an individual's goals. Second, I saw that the *moral valence* of mind is highly salient. My Akan interlocutors understood the 'bad minds' of others as an ever-present potential threat. Third, I observed that they understood the mind to be *porous* in nature. All people are understood to be vulnerable to supernatural influences; some people – witches – can exert supernatural power through mental action. Prayer is thought both to enable benevolent spiritual forces to enter the mind and to keep malevolent spiritual forces outside. Fourth and finally, I found that the mind is represented as *deeply intertwined with the body*. In all these ways, Akan culture imagines mental life differently from the Enlightenment tradition.

Before I lay out the empirical observations that led us to these findings, let me unpack some of the challenges of thinking about mind in an African context.

Thinking about mind in Africa

The obvious difficulty in setting out a cultural representation of mind in any particular African tradition is that the very enterprise is steeped in racism and stigma. Many of the great European philosophers of the colonial era (including Voltaire, Hume, and Kant) took Africans to be both primitive and childlike, with an inability for sophisticated or complex thought production. The perspective dominated European imagination for well into the twentieth century. Furthermore, postcolonial theorists argue that iterations of such stereotypes were internalized by Africans with long-lasting effects that extended far beyond the duration of the colonial era (Abraham 2015; Maldonado-Torres 2007; Mungazi 1996; Ngũgĩ 1986). Consider, for example, the following remarks about 'the African mind' by the South African-born and British-trained ethnopsychiatrist John Colin Carothers:

> The African ... [is] lacking in spontaneity, foresight, tenacity, judgement, and humility; inapt for sound abstraction and logic; given to phantasy [*sic*] and fabrication; and, in general, [is] unstable, impulsive, unreliable, irresponsible, and living in the present without reflection or ambition (1953: 89).

> The psychology of the African is essentially the psychology of the African child ... [The African] type of consciousness ... correspond[s] to a prehypnotic state (1953: 109).

> The African is [characterized by] lack of sustained interest, with lack of drive and concentration; [he]can spend much of his life in dreams. (1953: 122).

To be fair, many Europeans disagreed. Robin Horton (1967) challenged the demeaning stereotypes explicitly by describing African thought as logical and rational in character, and treating witchcraft beliefs as equivalent to a scientific theory of reality. Nevertheless, this history haunts the study of mind in Africa. There is always the fear that to compare is to demean.

Malose Makhubela (2016) identifies this history as the reason that the attempt to study psychology in Africa is 'going nowhere slowly'. Sophisticated scholars in the postcolony are sceptical of the universal claims of psychology, seeing them as tainted by power and domination. Yet when they reject any claim to universalism, everything disappears into particularism. 'This new polemic has led to a narrow relativism, epistemic populism and the *in toto* rejection of all research-making claims of universality and western knowledge, where all things propounded by the subalternized are regarded to be valid' (Makhubela 2016: 4). The problem becomes that in creating a model that sets itself against a dominant Enlightenment representation, one creates a thing ('the African mind') that simply does not capture the diversity of the context and creates in turn its own problems of hegemony.

My approach is both/and: an approach towards studying human consciousness that accepts that all humans experience awareness – but also that social groups can represent that awareness differently. Here I agree with Augustine Nwoye's conception of what psychology in Africa should be:

> an inclusive psychology encompassing not only the study of African indigenous psychology but also the study of the human condition and culture and the life of the mind in contemporary Africa, as

well as the exploration and adoption, where necessary, of aspects of western psychology that appear relevant for enabling us to confront the challenges of our present African predicament (2015: 105).

I take this understanding of comparativism to be the point of the Mind and Spirit project. We are looking at particulars, but because we do so comparatively, we do not lapse into particularism and we can reach towards general theory.

I begin with the philosophical tradition within the Akan. In his 1738 treatise on *the art of sober and accurate philosophizing*, Wilhelm Anton Amo, a philosopher from what is now Ghana, set out an account of mentality, rationality, cognition, learning, and knowability. He purported to provide not an 'African' representation of the mind but a representation of mind itself. In 1987, Kwasi Wiredu, himself an Akan, took Amo's model, his deep understanding of Western philosophy, and his Oxford training to put forth what he explicitly took to be an Akan model of mind. That model was intricately linked with Akan cosmology. Wiredu conceptualized personhood with spiritual components (the *sunsum* and *ɔkra*) and a sense that the capacity to will emerges out of the acting human body: it is neither given nor automatically (developmentally) achieved. He observed that for the Akan, 'thoughts are not in the mind, but are of the mind' (Wiredu 1987: 159), and that these thoughts seem to be 'the mind in episodic action' (1987: 167). In short, Wiredu took mind – as understood by the Akan – to be as much a disposition to act as a repository of thought (see also Minkus 1980). In *An essay on African philosophical thought* Kwame Gyekye (1995) developed his views into a more general argument about Africa.

In this essay, I develop these philosophical observations with empirical findings. My work shares these authors' sense that there is specificity in African experiences that is not best defined as falling short of a Western one – or lumped together with all non-Western experiences. Indeed, I believe that as we come to understand the specificity of African experiences more deeply, we may come to rethink the presumptions of Western psychological models. In other words, as we come to appreciate the specificity of an Akan model of mind, we will come to appreciate that the standard representation of mental models in academic psychology is, in some ways, also a local and specific model of how thinking, feeling, and acting unfold. Like Wiredu, I observed an emphasis on an action-focused mind; *the mind enables one to do*. In particular, I observed that Akan narratives about mind represent it as outward-focused and quintessentially pragmatic. This action-orientation role of the mind leads to a sense that minds matter because of the actions – and the patterns of actions – that they produce and thus should be evaluated morally. I also observed an Akan narrative of consciousness that integrally includes the body, and the spiritual components *sunsum* and *ɔkra*. Like Gyekye (1996: 36), I observed that self is imagined as very much influenced by other members of one's social space. I also observed that for the Akan, mind is understood not as localized primarily to *headspace*, but as somehow more dispersed. It is not imagined as centred on the interior experiences of the individuated self. Rather, mind impacts and is impacted by other members of the social milieu. In addition, the mind is partly bodily focused in architecture and porous to spiritual forces in disposition.

I support these observations by drawing not only on fieldwork data, but also on two independent sources of evidence. These are the rich proverbs that are of such importance to the Akan, and the Akan lexicon. This has the advantage of providing an historical depth to my model that fieldwork does not always provide. This approach to research is known as 'data triangulation': the exploration of multiple, different sources of data for areas of possible empirical and/or conceptual convergence (Patton 1999). My goal is to develop and test bottom-up, transdisciplinary, culturally appropriate methods through which African perspectives can both engage with mainstream academic discourse and question its ontological assumptions about human nature.

Interviews

I begin with the interviews. My fieldsite was the southern and central parts of Central Region's Abura-Asebu-Kwamankese (AAK) district in Ghana. This area is predominantly rural. Adjacent to the Cape Coast Municipal District (Central Region's administrative capital district), it is estimated to have a population of 120,000. The economy of the AAK district focuses largely on agriculture: food crops – maize, cassava, peanuts, tiger nuts (*Cyperus esculentus*) – for local consumption and retail, and citrus for export. The residents in this area are predominantly Fante. I conducted interviews over a two-month period during the summer of 2017. In this period, I also attended church services, observed shrine consultations, and discussed my observations with John Dulin, who was in the field at the same time. These interviews thus were set within a rich ethnographic context.

The interviews formed part of a larger, multi-country research project about spiritual experiences and the mind. The Mind and Spirit project is a Templeton-funded, Stanford-based comparative and interdisciplinary project under the direction of T.M. Luhrmann (PI), drawing on the expertise of anthropologists, psychologists, historians, and philosophers. The project asks whether different understandings of 'mind', broadly construed, might shape or be related to the ways that people attend to and interpret experiences they deem spiritual or supernatural. We took a mixed-method, multi-phase approach, combining participant observation, long-form semi-structured interviews, quantitative surveys among the general population and local undergraduates, and psychological experiments with children and adults. We worked in five different countries: China, Ghana, Thailand, Vanuatu, and the United States, with some work in the Ecuadorian Amazon. In each country, we included a focus on an urban charismatic evangelical church, with additional work in a rural charismatic evangelical church, and in another urban and rural religious setting of local importance.[1]

My interview sample consisted of twenty adult charismatic Christians recruited from two church congregations in the rural study area, and twenty traditional priests (*akɔmfo*, *bosomfo*, and *nyisifo*), their assistants (*ɔbrafo*), and priests-in-training serving as assistants recruited from shrines in villages and small towns. These traditional priests, described in more detail by Dulin (this volume), are experts who interact with and are often possessed by the local gods. They often provide local medical care, but their primary purpose is to ward off malevolent forces for local clients. There were ten male and ten female participants in each subgroup, ranging in age from 26 to 79. The traditional priests were understood to interact with the many lower gods and nature spirits recognized by the traditional religion. Clients came to them for medical help and for protection against dangerous powers. Some of the priests (and their assistants) supplemented their income by farming (both men and women) or working in shops (women only). One woman served as traditional birth attendant in her community.[2] In contrast, the charismatic Christians worked in a variety of full-time occupations (farming, dressmaking, driving, carpentry, retail, and teaching). Their churches were small compared to the big charismatic Christians churches in the nearby city of Cape

Coast. The congregations ranged from 70 to 120 adults – typical for these rural village churches.

The relationship between the traditionalists and charismatic Christians was complicated. On the one hand, many pastors actively denounced traditional priests as devil-worshippers and many Christians described them as invoking evil powers. On the other hand, the traditionalists also served as local healers in their communities (as previously mentioned, one priestess served as a traditional birth attendant). Their services were more accessible and cheaper than clinics. Several of the traditionalists acknowledged the tension between the two groups, and expressed resentment at members of their profession being consulted by priests for spiritual help growing their congregations, and then being labelled as villains when the congregations flourished.

The in-depth semi-structured phenomenological interviews ranged in duration from three to ten hours per person (some people had much to say), at a location of the interviewee's choosing in one to three sessions. The interviews were conducted in Fante (and on a few occasions a mixture of Fante and English as some interviewees naturally switched between languages); audio-recorded with permission from each interviewee; and translated, transcribed, and checked for accuracy by research assistants.

I set out below what seem to me to be the dominant ways these interview participants described the general domain of thinking, believing, desiring, and other mental acts. I am reflecting here on the comments they made about the polysemous term '*adwen*' (pronounced *ah-jwin*, emphasis on the second syllable, same word for singular and plural) in the contexts in which it referred to 'mind' over the course of these long interviews. (I revisit the meaning of *adwen* in my discussion of the mind lexicon later in this essay.) Some comments were made in direct response to questions about *adwen*; some were made in passing. Four themes seemed to emerge again and again.

Theme 1: Planning

All my participants described planning and problem-solving for the future as the fundamental function of *adwen*. To be clear, planning was not something our interviews intended to explore. We asked explicit questions about whether people should share their thoughts and feelings, whether imagining things that could not come true was good, and so forth. Yet when asked such questions, both male and female participants, whether Christian or traditionalist, spoke about creating plans to achieve specific future goals such as starting or growing a business, building a house, and purchasing land. In short, my interviewees presented the mind as the tool responsible for creating a plan to achieve the specified goal, and did so with such effortlessness that it seemed clear that they were describing a widely held conception.

E.A., a '50+' year female traditionalist, explained:

> As for the *adwen* it is used for so many things. You use your *adwen* to plan [lit. take mind]. For example, I want to build a house and need money for it. My *adwen* will help me know what work I need to do to get the money … maybe go and sell this thing it will tell me no; go for fish or imported cloth to sell it will tell me yes. And then I can use the little money I get to lay blocks and start building the foundation.

J.L., a 25-year-old male Christian, stated:

> [*Adwen*] is something that God created as part of a person's life. It is like the light of a car. It is used to light the way. Or it can be like the engine of a car. Once the engine is started, the car can go anywhere you want to go because it controls the car to move anywhere. Let's assume I want to do something but

> I do not have enough skills and knowledge on it, the *adwen* will make me know that if I make a prayer
> request about it, I might have knowledge to do it well. Or that if I go to see a particular person, the
> person might give me enough information about that. Or that the plan will succeed if I do it this or
> that way. By thinking, our thoughts can provide us with accurate ways to do those things successfully,
> just like we expected.

It was clear from these interviews that to my participants, the most salient function of what English-speakers call the 'mind' was its utilitarian function. They talked about *adwen* as a tool. Of course, implicit in this idea of planning are a host of cognitive processes and capabilities: attention; encoding and retrieval of information; short-term and long-term memory; language processing; perception; problem-solving; option comparison; and thinking. However, these capacities were not part of the narratives my participants told. Only when specifically asked follow-up questions like 'What is the *adwen* used for in a school setting?' did they respond with an account of a container for the storage of information, or a processing centre for facts and ideas.

It seemed that my participants did not think about mind as a headspace-bound model of functioning that centres on the cognitive manipulation of abstract representations of the world, nor as the source of identity and selfhood. Instead, when they described the domain of thinking, feeling, and so forth, they focused on an individual's engagement with this world: his or her intentions, actions, and efficacy.

Here is an example of the way participants highlighted the importance of action-directed thought. K.O, a 54-year-old male traditional priest stated:

> The *adwen* is there, but before you will think, then it means you are doing it for a purpose. Even if
> you are thinking of evil, then it means that you are going to use the evil thoughts for a purpose. If you
> are thinking of a good thing, then it means you are going to use it for a purpose. If you always think
> of something and you are unable to use it for something, then it is not worthwhile. That will make
> you sick, those things often destroy people, it makes you go mad.

It seemed to me that people spoke of *adwen* as a tool for planning for *the future*. This observation is at odds with theories about African culture (e.g. TRIOS theory: Jones 2003) that describe temporal orientations in Africa as relaxed and contingent. People in Ghana and other African countries do tend to score lower on Hofstede's cultural dimension of long-term orientation compared to Western nations.[3] Yet, as my Fante participants spoke, it was clear that they thought deeply about the future and described *adwen* – thinking, feeling, planning – as what takes one into the future, helps one prepare for the future, and provides a blueprint for the future and the future self. The action orientation of *adwen* appears to be a way to assert – or at least to try to exert – some control over life; not only in the present, but also in the future. It was as if they imagined *adwen* as a sea captain charting a course and directing the ship's path through life's stormy and uncertain seas, rather than (as Charles Taylor [2007] describes, for example) an expression of identity. When my participants spoke of mind-like things, they spoke about how to be effective, not about who they were.

Theme 2: Moral valence

In these conversations, I was also struck by how often my participants spoke of *adwen* as 'bad' or 'good'. It is unclear to me whether this is because this is the most accessible or most obvious quality of the *adwen* (as Adams [2005] notes, the concern about enemies is pervasive in Ghana), or whether it is because our study also included a focus on spiritual experiences. For whichever reason, person after person gave accounts of *adwen* that were either 'good' or 'bad'. (As we shall see, 'good *adwen*' and 'bad *adwen*' 'are explicit Fante phrases.) The emphasis on a 'bad *adwen*' was particularly evident. J.G., a 28-year-old Christian male construction worker described the perception that bad minds lurk everywhere, even in one's household:

> Your household members can destroy your life. They can even turn you into a drunkard, you can smoke wee [marijuana] or you can even do things which are uncalled for so you should let God protect you against such things.

The notion that the social world inevitably includes individuals with bad intentions towards the self is commonplace in African epistemology. E.E. Evans-Pritchard (1937: 178) famously observed that witchcraft served as a common explanation for misfortune in everyday Azande activities. Hans Werner Debrunner (1961: 6) found an omnipresent fear of harmful witch activity in Ghana's Akan group, and Malcolm McLeod (1975: 108) reported that patronage of anti-witchcraft shrines was popular in colonial Asante. Many anthropologists note that witchcraft beliefs influence attributions of misfortune and, in some cases, wealth in contemporary African settings, both urban and rural (Comaroff & Comaroff 1993; Geschiere 2013; Parish 2000). Dulin (this volume) addresses the perceived relationship, in an urban Ghanaian setting, between specific food consumption and experiencing spiritual harm. For my participants, the existence of witches was taken for granted regardless of whether or not they had personally encountered one.

The striking feature of this observation that some people (including, but not limited to, witches) have bad *adwen* was how fixed my participants took this quality to be. They spoke as if good people had good *adwen* and bad people had bad *adwen*, as if goodness and badness was a kind of stuff the *adwen* had rather than a feature of some situation. Wiredu (1995: 131) also comments on the mind-dispositional attribution connection in his Akan model of the mind. The good/bad dichotomy was quite different from the way that people in other settings seemed to understand moral valence. Smith (this volume) observes that for the Ni-Vanuatu, there is a tendency to situate meaning and moral purpose as external to the mind. For them, people's moral qualities are always shifting, and always striving. No one is ever good enough; most bad people can change. Aulino (this volume) found that in Thailand, people spoke as if the mind were like a kaleidoscope: experience and even perceptions are ever-changing and contingent upon karma, conditioning, and mental components that can be organized in an infinite number of combinations. For my Akan participants, by contrast, what drives behaviour is dichotomous rather than kaleidoscopic: *adwen* was either good or bad, not both, and was largely assumed to be stable over time.

Theme 3: Porosity

Our team took the term 'porosity' from Charles Taylor (1992), who lays out a contrast between modern 'buffered' selves – in which there appear to be distinct boundaries between mind and body, self and other, physical and the cosmic – and a way of being in the world that is more fluid. In his account, 'porous' selves and minds are associated with a permeability, a bleeding into one another, such that the self and the other, the physical and the cosmic, and the mind and the body cross over into each other and influence each other, often with discernible phenomenological impact.

It seemed clear that to my participants, *adwen* was porous. For them, some people with bad minds were able to able to directly affect the physical world without physical mediation. They assumed that a witch can poison someone's food with nothing more than the thought of doing so and a look; that they could make someone fall ill, cause barenness and disruption in marriages, and cause businesses to fail by willing it. Witches and wizards can kill, as E.A. explained:

> As for a wizard, whatever you do he is a wizard. Whatever you do to him, no matter how you train him, because of the [wizardry] power that he has, he has done so many bad things that if he doesn't do that for one day, he is unsettled. He can use his own mind to do it [harm someone] ... He is a wizard and a wizard is scary. Wizardry is scary so he can do it [harm someone with his mind].

E.A.'s representation captures the potency and permanence of this particular type of *adwen*. Similarly, V.K., a 35-year-old female Christian, stated:

> People have different characters in them. There are people who will instantly make known their displeasure when somebody offends them, and after talking about it, forgive the person. But there are others, even when you have apologized to them they would still be angry. It then means that person has a spirit. It is either she is a witch or a certain spirit lives with her that uses her. So you even motivate her to cause more harm the moment you apologize. And so, there are some people when they do something to you, you don't have to motivate them because as you motivate them, their spirit grows. Maybe you might say something and she can use that to hurt you.

V.K. further explained that the mind of a non-witch has the power to affect the world if the bad-minded individual vocalizes an evil thought. She stated:

> If it is something she has in her *adwen*, and so she says it wherever she goes that she wishes that a bad thing will happen (for example, that Jane dies), there may be spirits hovering around at the time she said that and that spirit can make whatever she said come true. Cursing is not only about the use of water or going to a herbalist to 'do something'. When somebody offends you and you keep the pain in you, you will see that wherever you go you talk about it ... Those things can also harm people.

The porous nature of *adwen* allows not only for minds to act on the world, but also for forces and influences external to the self to seep into and influence (and in some cases take over) the *adwen*.

Meanwhile, good *adwen* can serve as vessels, as conduits for the Holy Spirit, which protects the *adwen* by filling it up so that bad forces cannot enter. For a traditionalist, a good *adwen* and the body to which it belongs can serve as a vessel for a god. For example, K.O., a 54-year-old male traditional priest, recounted a transformative experience in his youth when he drummed on the state drum (see Yankah 1995 for an overview of the role of the state drummer) to assemble the township without any knowledge or training on how to do so:

> The drummer who was supposed to go and play the drum for them [the community] to go was dead, they were not getting anyone to play [drums] ... The thought that came into my *adwen* to leave my mother's home to go and take the drum and play the drum that the community people should come and let's go ... I didn't know what I was saying [drumming] ... And when they came it was me ... They thought it was the [professional] drummer that they went to call, when they came it was me! And what is amazing is that I didn't already know how to play a drum from my childhood.

K.O. attributed this sudden know-how to possession by the god of the state drum:

> I was possessed by the god. Nobody took me to learn how to play any drum. Today I teach how to play every drum because the god is a drummer.

Deities are not the only spirit beings capable of controlling the *adwen*. Individuals can also get possessed by ghosts for brief periods. We saw this when a teenaged boy died unexpectedly in one of our fieldsites (the we here includes myself, John Dulin, and Kara Weisman, contributors to this volume, all of whom were in Ghana at the time). One of his relatives was possessed during the funeral activities and communicated a message from the dead boy about the cause of his death.

A further implication of the porous mind is that these minds are vulnerable to bewitchment (in which the *adwen* is temporarily taken over by a bad mind or spirit) and madness (in which the *adwen* is broken by a bad mind or spirit). When this happens, people can lose control of their *adwen*. Over the past decade and a half, this form of spirit-*adwen* interfacing has become particularly associated across Ghana with a crime called Sakawa. Here, unsuspecting individuals are said to be temporarily controlled by evil forces, which prevent them from engaging with the world normally, and make them susceptible to being duped by criminals: for example, through email scams. In such cases, evil-minded individuals reportedly seek spiritual help (from local deities via shrines) in order to gain the ability to exert the temporary mind control (Oduro-Frimpong 2014). In none of these cases do the victims willingly give up the control of their *adwen*. A.B. (a 50-year-old female traditionalist) recounted what she perceived as a narrow escape from such individuals as follows:

> I went to Accra about two months ago and two ladies tried to take my money. They use a charm to take people's money. My god told me that these ladies are thieves and I became alert. If my god wasn't with me, they would have taken all my money.

Dulin (this volume) similarly observes that his participants perceived the mind as vulnerable to invasion by an external spiritual force. He notes that minds are particularly vulnerable to invasion if their associated bodies make contact (through touch, food, or sex) with a person with malicious intent or an item that has been spiritually tainted. Invaded minds lose their role as the driver of action and intention, and the individual's thoughts and actions are instead controlled by the invader.

As a result, people needed protection for their vulnerable *adwen*. That was the reason many of them gave for membership in Christian organizations and engaging in spiritual practices. For example, J.G., a 28-year-old male Christian construction worker, stated:

> The reason I pray is that as a human being if you do not pray, whatever the enemy will plan against you, he will achieve it. If you pray and you worship God and you do whatever he wants, if the enemies plan something against you, God will not watch for that problem to befall you. He will take it off you. Yes, I pray for protection. God will protect you, he will deliver you at all times. And whatever you will put before him, he will do it for you.

Traditional priests and priestesses agreed. K.O. explained the need for spiritual protection as follows:

> When we seek spiritual protection, we do so to prevent spiritual misfortunes. Sickness can happen to anybody, however; the one which is spiritual that can give you problems will go back [to the sender] when it comes to meet that 'spiritual security'.

Traditionalist interviewees emphasized the importance of being obedient to their gods (by giving sacrifices as required, and observing dietary and other taboos) as a way of ensuring that they fall under deiform protection. Christian interviewees emphasized the importance of church attendance, fasting, private prayer – in particular invoking the blood of Jesus – tithing, and participating in church-organized prayer meetings as a way of ensuring that they were under God's protection.

K.D. (a male traditionalist who was unclear about his age) gave an idea of the form such protection might take in his account of what happened after he 'called his gods' as he was being mugged by a group of people on an isolated road.

> I called upon my gods to come to my aid . . . I used my hand to hit him [one of the assailants], then he fell on the ground and the rest ran away. So I called upon them [the gods] and they truly came to my rescue. The guy fell behaving like a crocodile or like a fish. He was just crawling on the floor like that . . . So I realized truly there is a god.

F.E., a 38-year-old female charismatic Christian, gave an account of God's protection taking public transportation out of town thus:

> I was the one who stopped [the] vehicle, but after stopping it something told me, 'Don't go' . . . so even the mate [conductor] got angry a little but I told him that I had forgotten something so I wouldn't go . . . [I took another vehicle, and we passed the first. It had been in an accident] and there were people who were injured inside it! So I told the mate of the [vehicle] I was sitting in . . . And he said it means God loves you, God loves you.

The implication is clear: a good *adwen* by itself is not sufficient to provide complete protection against misfortune. It neither eliminates feelings such as envy and jealousy from the minds of others, nor thwarts other dangerous motivations from others.

Theme 4: Body

I was struck by how physical spiritual and supernatural experiences were for my participants. These experiences were in some sense presented as 'mental'. God entered the *adwen* or spoke to their mind. Yet the account of that event was often quite body-centred. Here a traditionalist, K.O., explains possession:

> It enters from your heart into your *adwen*. Before I had this calling, I did not know that was what was going to happen. So sometimes I got startled, when it happened like that then I would feel dizzy. So it is from your soul, sometimes when the spirit is like that you will realize that the person will be shaking. The shaking comes from his soul to his feet, it does not start from his feet to his head. That is how it is in life. The spirit gets to your *adwen* through your soul then passes through the body to [get to] the *adwen*.

Charismatic Christians everywhere describe people who can experience prophecy, when the spirit of God temporarily controls the mind in order to convey a message to an audience or an individual. They can be overcome by a song, or fall to the ground in an experience known as being 'slain in the spirit' (see Brahinsky, this volume). These more bodily expressions of worship were strongly embraced by my Christian participants, and seemingly less so in some other settings (Thailand [Aulino, this volume]; urban China [Ng, this volume]; and in ambivalent, comparable ways in the United States [Brahinsky, this volume]). K.B., a 30-year-old female teacher, illustrated her corporeal spiritual experience as follows:

> Last week, . . . Pastor asked us to pray about our destiny. What I saw was that all of a sudden I was down rolling on the floor. I felt that was the Spirit of God. [This kind of thing] happens anytime God wants to deliver me.

Here the phenomenology described by the Christians and traditionalists differed somewhat. Traditionalists regularly experienced possession experiences. In these, their gods took over their entire bodies to engage in particular motions (e.g. dancing, walking). The Christian whole-body experiences, on the other hand, tended to involve falling and motionlessness. Both groups of participants reported a variety of physical sensations such as feeling hot and trembling during encounters with the supernatural.

The Fante lexicon for 'mind'

While in the field, I set out to create a Fante lexicon of the mind to see if the themes I saw emerging in the interviews would occur within it. Fante is an Akan language that has a significant degree of overlap with Ashanti Twi (the latter is the language on which the limited published work on mind from Ghana is based). Similar to Ashanti Twi (the most widely spoken Akan language), the same word (*adwen* in Fante, *adwene* in Twi) is used as a linguistic label for mind, thought, idea, and opinion. The specific referent word is determined in use via the accompanying linguistic context.

In consultation with bilingual research assistants, cultural linguistic experts (individuals fluent in Fante with a minimum of forty years of Fante as one of their primary languages, and able to discuss and explain Fante language nuances and patterns), and some interviewees, I generated a list of all Fante mind-related words and expressions, and their literal and non-literal meanings. This was an iterative process, starting prior to the interviews, and continuing after the study's main interviews were complete. I found evidence that the themes that seemed to emerge from the interviews were also present in the lexicon.

Theme 1: Planning

The verbs 'to think' and 'to worry' are derivatives of *adwen*: *dwen* and *adwendwen*, respectively. In Fante, an individual can be asked to *dwen ho* (think about something specific), *fa adwen* (literally take mind; decide), *kyerɛ w'adwen* (literally show your mind; show what's in your mind, voice an opinion), *si w'adwen piw* (make up your mind firmly), and *sor w'adwen hwɛ* (test your mind and see/turn on [focus] your mind). These expressions suggest that *adwen* is indeed understood as the engagement of one's mental faculties in a specific manner for a specific purpose.

Theme 2: Moral valence

An individual is often said to have either a good mind (*adwen pa*) or a bad mind (*adwen bon*). Even though the Fante label *adwen* also captures thoughts, ideas, or opinions (depending on context), these phrases specifically refer to general mental faculties. Thoughts, ideas, and opinions can be also be bad. However, it is the badness of the mind as a whole – rather than bad thoughts, ideas, or opinions – that features prominently in linguistic expressions within the lexicon. Moreover, the lexicon also suggests that goodness or badness of the mind appears to be considered a constant, or at least long-lasting, quality of the mind and its products. A bad mind is behind a bad person, one who deliberately seeks in some way the downfall of others. Proverbs such as 'If a head is bad, when you cut it off and put it in the shade, it jumps into the sunshine' (i.e. if someone is determined to misbehave, they will do so at all times) speak to the inevitability of bad minds engaging in bad behaviour. I discuss proverbs in more detail below.

Theme 3: Porosity

In the Fante mind lexicon, references to the mind's vulnerability to external forces and influences are present and represented by metaphors of spoilage and control. One such referent is the broken/spoilt mind '*adwen asɛi*'. This communicates the existence of a level of functionality that the broken mind, owing to its *sɛi* (broken-ness), is unable to achieve. Also functioning as an insult, the notion of a mind that is broken conveys an understanding that something has been done to the mind. In other words, in contrast to planning, where the mind is the agent, broken functionality is not a result of the agency of the mind. It is neither something that the mind does to itself, nor is it viewed as the result of decay. The responsible agent is an external influence.

A second expression conveys a similar sentiment: *afa n'adwen* ('It has taken his/her mind'). While the cultural narrative includes chemical agents (e.g. marijuana), the spirit world can 'take' the mind. The phrase implies that people lose long-term control of their minds because of a spiritually mediated punishment or curse. The phrase is also used for mental illness. For this reason, people with psychotic symptoms, and even diagnoses of schizophrenia, seek out spiritual help as a pathway to healing (see, e.g., Opare-Henaku & Utsey 2017; Read 2012).

Theme 4: Body
While many words for mind-related actions include the Fante mind root word (*adwen*), not all do. For example, the words for remember (*kae*), wisdom (*nyansa*), and knowledge (*nyimdzi*) do not include the *adwen* stem. Some of these words which do not use the *adwen* stem appear to be lexically located in and associated with the body. For instance, self/impulse control (*ahohyedo*; literally self/body control/suppress) contains a stem (*ho*) which can include the physical body. In contrast, the Fante word for forgetfulness, *awerɛfir*, does not include a reference to the body (*a* denotes noun status; *werɛ* = soul – or soul mouthpiece/linguist, according to an *okomfo* interviewee; and the meaning of *fir* is unclear, possibly a derivative of *firi*, to leave). However, a variant expression of forgetfulness – *ne werɛfir no ho* – involves both the soul and the self/body. In other words, some words that English-speakers associate with the mind are also associated with the body in Fante.

Words used for emotions and general subjective well-being are also linguistically associated with the general human body (e.g. *ahowoyaw*, self/body/skin pain [envy]) and its specific parts (e.g. the stomach in *ayemhyehye* [literally stomach-burn; anxiety]). As such, the Fante representation of mind includes more than the word does in a Euro-American setting. It is not restricted to headspace (*itsir bɔɔba*), but rather is distributed across many aspects of the person. Kofi Agyekum (2016) noted a similar pattern in Twi: in the most widely spoken Akan language, he observes that expressions involving the body (*ho*) are pervasive and used as metaphors for emotions and character traits.

Proverbs about the mind
I now want to extend these linguistic reflections by examining proverbs, which many Africanist scholars and philosophers describe as a long-standing cultural practice that captures cultural values (Brookman-Amissah 1986; Gyekye 1995; 1996). John Mbiti (1969) describes them as storing the oldest forms of African and religious philosophical insights. Using a compendium of 7,015 Akan proverbs compiled by Peggy Appiah, Kwame Anthony Appiah, and Ivor Agyeman-Duah over two generations (2007), which is to date the largest published collection of Ghanaian proverbs (twice as long as its 1879 predecessor by Johann Gottlieb Christaller), I explored themes relevant to *adwen*. I also asked interviewees to nominate proverbs they knew concerning the mind, but owing to the exhaustiveness of the compendium (which was collected over decades, and thus much longer than the fieldwork period), they did not come up with any that were additional. While the proverbs in the compendium were in Ashanti Twi, not in Fante, which was used for the interviews and the generated lexicon, the themes noted in the interviews and lexicon were present in the proverbs, suggesting that the observations

were common across the two Akan dialects. Two bilingual (Fante and English) research assistants went through the proverb compendium and identified proverbs that met at least one of the following inclusion criteria:

i. The proverb made direct reference to mind (*adwene*): e.g. '*The mind is like palm oil; when it lies still, we heat it up*'.
ii. The proverb made an indirect reference to mind: e.g. by referencing mental activity and qualities such as wisdom (*nyansa*), thought (*dwen*), or worry (*adwendwen*). For instance, the proverb '*Poverty makes the poor man sell his wisdom to the rich man*' refers to wisdom, and not directly to the mind.
iii. The *manifest meaning* of the proverb (provided by the compendium authors in English) was related to mind, mental qualities, or mental activity. For example, a proverb which translates into English as '*Whether it is to him who buys on credit or to him who pays on the spot, the owner says he will no longer sell*' is 'used when someone has decided not to do something and no amount of persuasion will change their mind (manifest meaning)'. Since the manifest meaning contains mind, it is included in the list.

This approach resulted in a set of 268 proverbs which either directly or implicitly referred to the mind or mental activity. Of these, 144 addressed wisdom, 47 mentioned thought, and 15 contained mind. Other cognitive themes included judgement (11), intelligence (7), and concentration (3). In addition, given the divergence observed in the interviews between Fante representations of mind and the representation familiar to me from my psychological training in the United States, I explored themes of interiority by revisiting a subset of proverbs containing emotion themes (discussed in detail in Dzokoto *et al*. 2018). While there is certainly much more to say about this collection, and linguists might find this analytic approach dissatisfyingly elementary, here I merely wish to report that the themes identified above were also expressed in proverbs.

Theme 1: Planning
Thirteen proverbs included messages about the need for planning to precede successful action. '*The hornblowers say: if you prepare before action, you succeed*' (i.e. if you plan before you act, you are more likely to succeed) addresses this theme directly. In contrast, '*One does not smoke the whole carcass over the fire*' (i.e. you must consider in depth before coming to a decision) does so using food preparation imagery. Another proverb drawing on food preparation imagery is '*Chew, chew, chew, fufu mathematics, we work it in the mortar*' (i.e. every activity has its own area of planning).

Theme 2: Moral valence
Akan mind-referencing proverbs tend to present dichotomies: *child* versus *adult*, *foolish* versus *wise*, *dull* versus *active*, *broken* versus *in working order*, *unfocused* versus *focused*, and, as found in the interviews, *bad* mind versus *good* mind (in each case the second component is preferred). In general, these dichotomies do not include an in-between, grey area.
    The existence of good and bad minds and the need to be wary of the latter can be seen in eight proverbs, including: '*It may happen one day that a bad man is rare*' (i.e. don't indulge in wishful thinking in the present even if you think that things will be better in the future). Proverbs such as these suggest a world-view in which bad minds

are an inevitable part of the social world. The valuing of good thoughts and the negative consequences of bad thoughts are captured by proverbs such as 'If you think good thoughts, you will achieve good things. If you think bad thoughts, then evil entangles you'. *Good thoughts* may also have some intrinsic protective power, as the following proverb suggests: '*If your thoughts are pure [lit. what is in your head is white], the Ntuamoa does not kill you*' (i.e. the powerful fetish priest protects the virtuous).

Theme 3: Porosity

Some Akan proverbs refer to supernatural influences active in the social world, and associated vulnerabilities of the mind. Mensah Adinkrah (2015: 159) reviewed thirty-four Akan proverbs that explicitly mentioned a witch or witchcraft. I found five mind-focused proverbs referring to porosity. '*Possession amounts to explanation*' (i.e. what has been said enables one to have insight into the situation) refers to the possession of the minds of traditionalists by local deities. Spirit possession often features in divination and (according to the traditionalists interviewed for this project) can result in the provision or generation of explanations of misfortune, solutions to problems, and cures for diseases. '*We don't use our mouth to drive away witchcraft*' (i.e. you must use adequate means to ward off danger; mere talking is not enough) refers to the powerful nature of a particular group of people with dangerous supernatural powers, and the seriousness with which this potential threat to well-being should be addressed.

Theme 4: Body

Some proverbs used the body and its parts as metaphors to communicate maxims related to the mind. For example, the body is used to illustrate the actions of a foolish mind in proverbs such as '*If a stupid person is developing a swollen body, he says he is going to be fat*' (i.e. a fool cannot recognize the truth). Nineteen mind proverbs mentioned the head, seven the mouth, four the nose, and one each referred to the hands, foot, and ear. Take, for example, the proverb: '*It is the hare that has ears, let us call him so that he can explain things to us*' (i.e. if you are doubtful about something, call on the elders to explain it, for after all they have spent so much time listening to wisdom). It communicates that wisdom enters the mind through the ears and the act of listening. In other work (e.g. Dzokoto *et al.* 2018), I have examined emotion-focused proverbs. Some of these, such as '*The skin splits where it is softest*' (i.e. everything or every society has its vulnerable point), use body referents to communicate emotion themes (in this case, emotional vulnerability). While these do not locate the mind in the body, proverbs such as these use the body as a means to describe the mind and associated internal experiences.

Different ways of feeling

These observations resonate with my earlier work on affect in contemporary Ghana. I have previously argued, in a similar vein to Csordas's work on culturally shaped somatic modes of attention (1993), that in West African settings, including those in which the Akan live and work, people report experiencing and engaging in the world in more somatic and contextual ways than is typical of North American settings. One might think that this may be nothing more than a function of language. More Fante emotion words contain body parts in their literal translations than English ones do (Dzokoto & Okazaki 2006). However, the somatic focus (in comparison to an interiority focus) emerged again and again in my studies, even when the participants were

English-speakers and completed the tasks in English. For example, in one study undergraduates in Accra and in the midwestern United States filled out questionnaires which asked them about the attention they paid to their emotions and somatic experiences. The Americans scored more highly on the emotion questions, and the Ghanaians more highly on the body ones (Dzokoto 2010). In another study, Americans used more emotion words to describe important events than did Ghanaians (Dzokoto, Opare-Henaku & Kpobi 2013). In another study, this one about Ga and Ewe emotion lexica (two southern Ghanaian languages), we found a focus on body and social context (Dzokoto, Senft, Kpobi & Washington-Nortey 2016). This work is consistent with that of anthropologists and linguists (Agykeum 2016; Ameka 2002; Ansah 2013; Geurts 2009) who see in Ghana a pattern of selective awareness away from 'headspace' and towards somatic and social contexts in a variety of settings. This position argues neither that cognition is unimportant, nor that abstract thought has no place. Instead, it makes the case that elaborations of 'headspace' are not salient in Akan and other West African settings.

Conclusion

I do not mean to imply that all Akans (past, present, and future) necessarily agree with this model of mind. Neither do I mean to imply that this account of a local theory about the mind is exhaustive. Indeed, this study is informed by Fante and Asante Twi, only two of the nine (or sixteen, depending on which linguistic grouping one observes) Akan languages in existence. However, like Wiredu and Gyekye, I do think that my observations capture the important dimensions of the local theory of mind. I argue here that the Akan cultural context fosters a representation of mental action – thinking, feeling, believing, etc. – that has minimal focus on the inner 'psychological' self, and an elaborated focus on other aspects of the self (such as the body) and the social milieu within which the self is located. This is not to say that inward-focused cognition is irrelevant to, absent from, or completely unimportant in the Akan. (There is published work on Akan knowing [Harvey 2015], Akan truth [Wiredu 2004], Akan rationality [Majeed 2013], and Akan conceptual schemes [Gyekye 1995].) I simply suggest that the relative salience of non-headspace components of mind, such as the body, and other aspects of the self may markedly overshadow interiority.

This matters because the local theory of mind I see at work in Akan culture helps to explain behaviours which seem so puzzling to Western observers, who may assume that Charles Taylor's notion of the modern, firmly bounded mind is not a folk theory but simply a true description of human minds. The porosity of *adwen* helps explain why witchcraft beliefs are taken seriously, and why interpersonal interactions and spiritual practices are so central to Akan identity. *Adwen*'s moral valence helps to explain why Akan identity may be based not on what one thinks one is, but on what one does. Because *adwen* extends beyond headspace, perhaps belief/meaning-making/knowing may not be contingent only on thought, but also include the body. It may be that Taylor's model of the 'modern' mind – where thought is private and supernaturally inert, where individuals feel the need to say what is in their mind because what they think makes them who they are – makes more sense in a pluralistic, predictable world. The Akan model of mind, with its de-emphasis on privacy and interiority and its sharp awareness of dangerous others, may make more sense in an unpredictable environment and a face-to-face society.

Journal of the Royal Anthropological Institute (N.S.), 77-94
© Royal Anthropological Institute 2020

This representational emphasis may help to explain the markedly vivid spiritual experiences described by my interviewees. As Dulin (this volume) illustrates, and as was the experience for many of my interviewees, even when these intrusions did not completely take over the mind, they could be very forceful, taking the form of repeated and often very specific naggings, promptings, or thoughts that experiencers described as impossible to ignore. Experiences of the spiritual/supernatural were strikingly sensory and body-centred. It may indeed be that, as Luhrmann's work suggests (2011 and this volume), people's enculturated models of mind may shape the way they perceive, interpret, and respond to their physical worlds, and what they take to be evidence of invisible others. These differences in attention may alter what they 'deem' spiritual (Taves 2009).

I conclude with my participant K.O.'s words:

The human body is empty, and then the spirit enters it and gives life to the heart and the head ... It is like a starter, traffic indicator and a gear. They have their independent functions to play. The starter is the soul, the traffic indicator is the heart and the gear is your mind. That is what changes and controls everything – the eye, ear, nose and mouth. The mind controls it. The starter sends signals to the traffic indicator then the traffic indicator pumps the gears to control everything. That is their difference, they all have their functions to play.

NOTES

I am very grateful to Tanya Luhrmann, the anonymous reviewers, and the Editor of the *JRAI* for their detailed feedback on drafts. I would also like to thank Chioke I'Anson for feedback on an earlier draft of this essay. Many thanks to the entire Mind and Spirit research team, project advisors, and project manager (Nicole Ross-Zehnder). A big thank you to Joseph Ansah, Eunice Otoo, The Great Mossi, Jojo Lewis, Mohammed Bosu, Nana Ansua Peterson, and Comfort Turkson for recruitment assistance, logistical support, and research assistance during the fieldwork period. Finally, I am grateful to my interlocutors for their openness and patience.

[1] This paragraph is based on a description drafted collectively by the Mind and Spirit team and used to illustrate the joint nature of the research

[2] For more information about traditionalists, see Dulin's account in this volume.

[3] See the Hofstede Insights Database (*https://www.hofstede-insights.com/product/compare-countries/*).

REFERENCES

ABRAHAM, W.E. 2015. *The mind of Africa*. Legon-Accra: Sub-Saharan Publishers.

ADAMS, G. 2005. The cultural grounding of personal relationship: enemyship in North American and West African worlds. *Journal of Personality and Social Psychology* **88**, 948-68.

ADINKRAH, M. 2015. *Witchcraft, witches and violence in Ghana*. New York: Berghahn Books.

AGYEKUM, K. 2016. Bodily state and metaphors relating to ho, 'body', in Akan. *Metaphor and the Social World* **6**, 326-44.

AMEKA, F. 2002. Cultural scripting of body parts for emotions: on 'jealousy' and related emotions in Ewe. *Pragmatics and Cognition* **10**, 27-58.

AMO, W.A. 1738. *De arte sobrie et accurate philosophandi* [The art of sober and accurate philosophizing]. Halle.

ANSAH, G.N. 2013. Culture in embodiment: evidence from conceptual metaphors/metonymies of anger in Akan and English. In *Compendium of cognitive linguistics research*, vol. **2** (ed.) T.F. Li, 63-82. New York: Nova Science Publishers.

APPIAH, P., A. APPIAH & I. AGYEMAN-DUAH 2007. *Bu me be: proverbs of the Akans* (Second edition). Banbury, Oxon: Ayebia Clarke Publishing.

BROOKMAN-AMISSAH, J. 1986. Akan proverbs about death. *Anthropos* **81**: 1/3, 75-85.

CAROTHERS, J.C. 1953. *The African mind in health and disease: a study in ethnopsychiatry*. Geneva: World Health Organization.

COMAROFF, J. & J.L. COMAROFF 1993. Introduction. In *Modernity and its malcontents: ritual and power in postcolonial Africa* (eds) J. Comaroff & J.L. Comaroff, ix-xxxvii. Chicago: University Press.

Journal of the Royal Anthropological Institute (N.S.), 77-94
© Royal Anthropological Institute 2020

CSORDAS, T. 1993. Somatic modes of attention. *Cultural Anthropology* **8**, 135-56.

DEBRUNNER, H.W. 1961. *Witchcraft in Ghana: a study on the belief in destructive witches and its effect on the Akan tribes.* Accra: Presbyterian Book Depot.

DZOKOTO, V. 2010. Different ways of feeling: emotion and somatic awareness in Ghanaians and Euro-Americans. *Journal of Social, Evolutionary, and Cultural Psychology* **4**: 2, 68-78.

——— & S. OKAZAKI 2006. Happiness in the eye and the heart: somatic referencing in West African emotion lexica. *Journal of Black Psychology* **32**: 2, 17-140.

———, A. OPARE-HENAKU & L. KPOBI 2013. Somatic referencing and psychologisation in emotion narratives: a USA-Ghana comparison. *Psychology and Developing Societies* **25**, 311-31.

———, A. OSEI-TUTU, J. KYEI, M. TWUM-ASANTE, D. ATTAH & D. AHORSU 2018. Emotion norms, display rules, and regulation in the Akan society of Ghana: an exploration using proverbs. *Frontiers in Psychology* **9** (available online: *https://www.frontiersin.org/articles/10.3389/fpsyg.2018.01916/full*, accessed 16 January 2020).

———, N. SENFT, L. KPOBI & P.M. WASHINGTON-NORTEY 2016. Their hands have lost their bones: exploring cultural scripts in two West African affect lexica. *Journal of Psycholinguistic Research* **45**, 1473-97.

EVANS-PRITCHARD, E.E. 1937. *Witchcraft, oracles and magic among the Azande.* Oxford: University Press.

GESCHIERE, P. 2013. *Witchcraft, intimacy, and trust.* Chicago: University Press.

GEURTS, K. 2009. *Culture and the senses.* Berkeley: University of California Press.

GYEKYE, K. 1995. *An essay on African philosophical thought: the Akan conceptual scheme* (Revised edition). Philadelphia: Temple University Press.

——— 1996. *African cultural values: an introduction.* Philadelphia: Sankofa.

HARVEY, M. 2015. Medial deities and relational meanings: tracing elements of an Akan grammar of knowing. *Journal of Africana Religions* **3**, 397-441.

HORTON, R. 1967. African traditional thought and Western science. Part I: From tradition to science. *Africa: Journal of the International African Institute* **37**, 50-71.

JONES, J.M. 2003. TRIOS: a psychological theory of the African legacy in American culture. *Journal of Social Issues* **59**, 217-42.

LUHRMANN, T.M. 2011. Towards an anthropological theory of mind: overview. *Journal of the Finnish Anthropological Association* **36**: 4, 5-13.

MCLEOD, M. 1975. On the spread of anti-witchcraft cults in modern Asante. In *Changing social structure in Ghana* (ed.) J. Goody, 107-18. London: International African Institute.

MAJEED, H.M. 2013. A critique of the concept of quasi-physicalism in Akan philosophy. *African Studies Quarterly* **14**: 1/2, 23-33.

MAKHUBELA, M. 2016. 'From psychology in Africa to African psychology': going nowhere slowly. *Psychology in Society [PINS]* **5**, 1-18.

MALDONADO-TORRES, N. 2007. On the coloniality of being: contributions to the development of a concept. *Cultural Studies* **21**, 240-70.

MBITI, J. 1969. *African religions and philosophy.* New York: Doubleday.

MINKUS, H. 1980. The concept of spirit in Akwapim Akan philosophy. *Africa: Journal of the International African Institute* **50**, 182-92.

MUNGAZI, D.A. 1996. *The mind of black Africa.* New York: Praeger.

NGŨGĨ WA THIONG'O 1986. *Decolonising the mind: the politics of language in African literature.* London: James Currey.

NWOYE, A. 2015. What is African psychology the psychology of? *Theory & Psychology* **25**, 96-116.

ODURO-FRIMPONG, J. 2014. 'Not a cedi tied to their names': Sakawa rituals and cyberfraud in Ghanaian popular video movies. *African Studies Review* **57**, 131-47.

OPARE-HENAKU, A. & S.O. UTSEY 2017. Culturally prescribed beliefs about mental illness among the Akan of Ghana. *Transcultural Psychiatry* **54**, 502-22.

PARISH, J. 2000. From the body to the wallet: conceptualizing Akan witchcraft at home and abroad. *Journal of the Royal Anthropological Institute* (N.S.) **6**, 487-500.

PATTON, M.Q. 1999. Enhancing the quality and credibility of qualitative analysis. *Health Services Research* **34**, 1189-208.

READ, U. 2012. 'I want the one that will heal me completely so it won't come back again': the limits of antipsychotic medication in rural Ghana. *Transcultural Psychiatry* **49**, 438-60.

TAVES, A. 2009. *Religious experience reconsidered.* Princeton: University Press.

TAYLOR, C. 1992. *Sources of the self: the making of the modern identity.* Cambridge: University Press.

——— 2007. *A secular age.* Cambridge, Mass: Belknap Press of Harvard University Press.

Wiredu, K. 1987. The concept of mind with particular reference to the language and thought of the Akans. In *Contemporary philosophy: a new survey*, vol. **5** (ed.) G. Fløistad, 153-79. Dordrecht: Springer.

——— 1995. The concept of mind with particular reference to the language and thought of the Akans. In *Readings in African philosophy: an Akan collection* (ed.) K. Safro, 123-53. Lanham, Md: University Press of America.

——— 2004. Truth and an African language. In *African philosophy: new and traditional perspectives* (ed.) L.M. Brown, 35-50. Oxford: University Press.

Yankah, K. 1995. *Speaking for the chief: Okyeame and the politics of Akan royal oratory*. Bloomington: Indiana University Press.

Adwenhoasem : une théorie de l'esprit chez les Akans

Résumé

Le présent essai explore la manière dont ce que les anglophones appellent *mind* (traduit par *esprit* : croyance, pensée, sentiments et autres actes mentaux) est représenté et situé par les membres du groupe ethnolinguistique akan du Ghana. Il s'appuie sur plusieurs sources de données : les mots de l'esprit et apparentés en fante, une langue du groupe akan, le plus grand recueil de proverbes akan (en twi), de longs entretiens semi-structurés avec quarante adultes, chrétiens et praticiens de la religion traditionnelle, et une courte enquête ethnographique menée par un universitaire ghanéen. Ce travail identifie quatre dimensions de ce que l'on pourrait appeler une théorie akan de l'esprit, qui semble modelée par la langue et la culture locales. Pour commencer, la fonction centrale de l'esprit est la planification, et non l'identité. Deuxièmement, l'une des qualités saillantes de l'esprit est sa valence morale : le « mauvais esprit » d'autrui est une menace potentielle qui plane sur l'harmonie sociale et le bien-être personnel. Troisièmement, l'esprit est conçu comme poreux par nature. Les esprits de tous sont vulnérables aux influences surnaturelles et certaines personnes possédant un esprit puissant peuvent exercer un pouvoir surnaturel par leur action mentale. Quatrièmement, certains éléments que les anglophones incluent dans la notion de *mind* (comme les sentiments) sont plutôt situées dans le corps.

5

The mind and the Devil: porosity and discernment in two Chinese charismatic-style churches

EMILY NG *University of Amsterdam*

This essay explores otherworldly encounters and notions of mind across two charismatic-style churches in China. In Zhao Village Church in rural Henan province, Christian congregants more often approached the mind as porous to the Devil's corruption. In Living Church in Shanghai, congregants were more influenced by bounded, psychological notions of the mind as an entity; although the mind was also held to be permeable to spiritual personae, its interior workings stood as the central hindrance to discernment, rather than the externality of the Devil. And while those in Shanghai stressed a gradual, retroactive verification of potential spiritual signs, those in Henan strove for a rhythm of immediate response. Meanwhile, Shanghai congregants described fewer sensory and embodied encounters with divine voice, pain, and healing than congregants in Henan. Such divergent theories of mind, virtuous rhythms, and distributions within the Christian spiritual sensorium might be understood in part through styles of engagement accentuated at these churches, and in part through the uneven unfolding of religious abolition and revival in China, including the heightened urban presence of psychotherapeutic genres and the rural presence of spirit mediumship in recent decades. These variations in personhood and otherworldly encounter, including deeply porous ones, were thus co-present in an atheist secular milieu, after what have been seen as some of the most thorough secularization campaigns conducted by a modern state.

'The problem with so-called "charismatics"', Pastor Chen mused, 'is that they see meaning in everything and anything. Any coincidence'. It was a casual dinner with a group of congregants in central Shanghai, where struggles and contradictions in the practice of Christianity were often hashed out. Pastor Chen continued. He critiqued the over-eagerness to see meaning only because he sympathized with it. He himself was once of this sort, finding divine significance in every coincidence. But over time, he realized that this was also a form of superstition – that Christianity too could come to resemble idolatry. Seen from without – from the eyes of mainline Chinese churches, for instance – Chen's commentary may seem paradoxical, given that Living Church could in some sense be considered an emblematic charismatic house church, one that encourages a

Journal of the Royal Anthropological Institute (N.S.), 95-113

direct, experiential relationship with God.[1] Yet it was precisely through the continuous undoing of easy surety that those at the church learned to discern whether any given experience was indeed from God. Pastor Chen's critique of 'so-called "charismatics"' was part of a long-standing discussion at the church surrounding 'caution' (*jinshen*) towards the interpretation of potential spiritual encounters.

The importance of caution arose in part from what Pastor Chen and the congregants took as a central hindrance to discernment: the human mind. For those at Living Church, the difficulty of knowing God stemmed in large part from the pernicious presence of the mind and the self; humans are wont to mistake their own desire and rationale for divine will.[2]

Meanwhile, at Zhao Village Church in rural Henan province, concerns with discernment were as pressing as they were in Shanghai. Yet while troubles of human desire were also contended with, the mind was not the central figure leading one astray – it was the Devil.

'The Devil tells lies and leads you to believe falsely', Pastor Zhao explained as we discussed the possibility of mistakenly taking an experience to be from God. The Devil may mislead through several means, he continued: by direct influence and the instillation of temptation, or by entry through a breach opened in the human heart-mind owing to the impurity of one's desire. Moreover, the Devil can exploit such human emotions as anger, fuelling the fire to ignite a murderous rage. For Pastor Zhao and congregants at Zhao Village Church, 'corruption' (*baihuai*) by the Devil must be contended with day to day, through practices of confession and repentance. While evocations of human intention were by no means absent, danger arose by way of infiltration: being entered by the Devil in place of being entered by God.

The avoidance of corruption and the need for caution signalled two distinct approaches to the mind. In Zhao Village, the mind posed a spiritual risk owing more to its fundamental permeability to demonic influence, and less to its tendency towards excessive interpretation. Conversely, congregants in Shanghai explicitly denounced excessive ascriptions of immoral and spiritually mistaken thoughts to the Devil, and turned their concern towards the dangerous self-certainty of the human mind. While discussing the misrecognition of divine messages at Living Church with Mei, a former industrial designer in her late twenties, I asked her if such errors originated in the Devil. 'No', she shook her head, 'it's from yourself, because you have the freedom of will ... In fact, it's you yourself making the choice ... one might mistakenly take oneself to be God'.

As part of this special issue on theories of mind and spiritual kindling, this essay describes styles of charismatic Christian engagement across two churches in China, with relation to porous and buffered notions of the mind and self. Expanding theory of mind from its usage in developmental psychology, anthropologists have used the term to describe cultural variations in how mental states are apprehended, with consequences for how one operates in the world (Keane 2015; Luhrmann *et al.* 2011; Robbins & Rumsey 2008). Here, I approach porosity and bufferedness as a dimension of mind, linked to such other dimensions as epistemic stance and relational responsibility (Luhrmann *et al.* 2011).

In *A secular age*, Charles Taylor (2007) describes two senses of religious selfhood. The porous self, for Taylor, is one open and vulnerable to spirits and other supernatural forces. Meaning, including thoughts, feelings, and spiritual forces, does not merely reside within the mind, but can reside fully outside the mind – coming from without, including the presence of spirits, possession, and charged objects. By contrast, for the

Journal of the Royal Anthropological Institute (N.S.), 95-113

buffered (or bounded) self, exemplified by modern Christianity in secular contexts, the interiority of the human mind becomes the site for spiritualities. Meaning is turned inwards towards a sense of mental depth. Boundaries harden between mind and world, mind and body, interior and exterior. Taylor brackets out Pentecostalism as a counter-movement external to more 'in the head' versions of 'official Christianity' (2007: 555). Here, by approaching porosity and bufferedness through styles and variations, I take Taylor's concepts as a point of departure, to illustrate tensions and potentialities internal to Christianity (Bialecki 2017; Reinhardt 2015).

My encounters in Shanghai and Henan province suggest that any theory of mind in China today must be approached vis-à-vis distinct landscapes of historical inheritance and religious revival. Twentieth-century translations of Western psychology and recent urban proliferations of psychological discourses, transmitted in part through schooling and urban sociality, may have provided conditions for more self-consciously 'buffered' notions of mind in discernment practices among middle-class congregants I met in Shanghai. In Zhao Village, concepts of direct otherworldly transmission common in rural revivals of temple rituals and spirit mediumship, along with a more distributed sense of personhood, were echoed in more 'porous' notions of mind in discernment among congregants I met. These two approaches to the mind were accompanied by divergent styles of spiritual engagement. Those at Zhao Village Church described more sensory and corporeal encounters with the divine and demonic, and strove for a virtuous rhythm of immediacy, while experiences of God through thought, inspiration, and beyond-coincidental events were more common at Living Church, accompanied by a spiritual emphasis on gradual verification.

These theories of mind were thus linked to particular sensational forms that mediated possible modes of relation with the otherworldly (Meyer 2010). Such 'distributions of the sensible' (Rancière 2004) varied without being entirely distinct, given their shared Chinese Protestant sources. Within the overlapping yet non-identical semiotic ideologies at the two churches, the mind held a different place in 'the sorting out of proper relations among, and boundaries between, words, things, and subjects' (Keane 2007: 4). The human mind mapped differently onto which (and how commonly) particular objects and sensations were considered divine or demonic, what (and in what contexts) genres of religious speech were considered legitimate, and which (and under what circumstances) spiritual personae were considered agentic.

Such distinctions were by no means absolute, and the rural-urban divide does not fully account for questions of difference – a wide array of churches exist in cities and in villages. Even within a single congregation, Christianity can be taken up and actualized differently (Bialecki 2017). The portraits of the mind, the senses, and temporality I sketch in this essay foreground contrasts rather than similarities, in part because the presence of sensory spiritual encounters between the city and village was more marked in China than in other sites of this collaborative project. I thus use these distinctions to consider multiple modes of Christian engagement in China today, after a lengthy history of secularization campaigns. Attending to critical responses to Taylor's account of the secular – particularly his spatial and temporal relegation of porousness to the world of 'our ancestors' and 'almost all other [non-Western] contemporary societies' (2007: 1, 42) – I show how buffered and porous engagements are co-present and variously manifest within a contemporary atheist secular nation-state.[3]

Journal of the Royal Anthropological Institute (N.S.), 95-113
© 2020 The Authors. *Journal of the Royal Anthropological Institute* published by John Wiley & Sons Ltd on behalf of the Royal Anthropological Institute

Christianity in China

China holds the world's seventh largest Christian population despite Christianity's minority status in the country, estimated at around 5 per cent (Pew Research Center 2011).[4] According to some projections, it is slated to become the largest Christian nation within a matter of decades (Micklethwait & Wooldridge 2009). Following anti-superstition campaigns across the twentieth century and the official abolition of religion during the Cultural Revolution (1966-76), Christianity – Protestantism in particular – has 'returned' amid broader scenes of religious revival since the 1980s (Bays 2012). While most Chinese churches have remained non-denominational since severing their ties with foreign missions in the 1950s, scholars have suggested that many are 'Pentecostal by default' in their styles of worship, even when the churches themselves reject being identified as Pentecostal or charismatic (Y. Liu 2017; Oblau 2011; F. Yang, Tong & Anderson 2017). Given the rise of Pentecostal and charismatic Christianity across the globe since the 1970s (Jenkins 2002), China offers a lens into how Christianity manifests and transforms in the contemporary world, particularly in contexts of secular governance.

Beyond numbers, the history of Protestantism in China is entangled, not unlike elsewhere, with that of secularization. Prior to missionary efforts to define Chinese religion for purposes of conversion, the concept of religion as a distinct domain did not exist in there (Goossaert & Palmer 2011). By the nineteenth century, in the face of military, political, and economic threats from British, Japanese, French, and other forces, modern religion – exemplified by Protestantism – was seen as both an agent of foreign imperialism and a potential resource for anti-imperial efforts, given its associations with military-political brawn. By contrast, temple networks and ritual practices were often seen as ineffectual in securing national sovereignty despite their cultural-spiritual value, and were variously placed on the other side of the Protestant conceptual divide as outmoded superstition. Such concepts had profound consequences; whether a temple was kept or displaced depended on its categorization (Nedostup 2010). By introducing religion as a modern concept, Protestant missions simultaneously offered categories for its governance. Following the victory of the atheist Communist Party over the comparatively Protestant-friendly Nationalist Party in 1949, all religion would come under suspicion, including Christianity. As noted above, religious suppression reached its heights during the Cultural Revolution, when all practices were officially banned. After the ban was partially lifted in the post-Mao economic reform era, Protestant churches were still placed in two state-designated categories: illegal, unregistered 'house churches' and legal churches registered with the Three Self Patriotic Movement.

Christianity in China today must thus be understood through its formal abolition and revival, which varied by context.[5] In much of rural China, Protestant congregations had been devastated since the 1950s, with churches shut down as property was redistributed during Land Reform. Yet subsequent enforcement varied with shifts in political atmosphere, and in some cases the persecution of religious authorities inadvertently drove the underground growth of experiential, charismatic-style religiosity (Kao 2009; Lian 2010). With the legalization of religion following Mao's death, the 1980s saw a 'rural decade' of Protestant revival (Bays 2012). Given the concurrent rebuilding of Buddhist, Daoist, and Confucian temples and the return of ritual and spirit mediumship in villages, Protestant concepts once again commingled with Chinese 'popular' religious concepts, from eschatological themes to petitioning the divine for healing (Dean 2003; Lian 2010).

Journal of the Royal Anthropological Institute (N.S.), 95-113
© 2020 The Authors. *Journal of the Royal Anthropological Institute* published by John Wiley & Sons Ltd on behalf of the Royal Anthropological Institute

In the cities, modern police forces established in the early 1900s enabled more thorough enforcement of anti-superstition campaigns than in rural regions, though Christianity was treated separately, protected by extra-territoriality rights under which foreign missionaries were not subject to Chinese law (Goossaert & Palmer 2011). Such laws lost their effect with the end of the Second World War, and by the start of the Cultural Revolution, all churches were officially closed (Lian 2010). While Protestantism first flourished in rural regions upon religious re-legalization in the 1980s, by the 1990s, Christian growth gained speed in the cities. White-collar converts and entrepreneurial 'boss Christians' grew in parallel with an intellectual scene of 'cultural Christians': academics at elite secular universities seeking Western 'lessons' from Christianity on such themes as civil society and capitalistic development, regardless of their own faith (Bays 2012; Cao 2011). Meanwhile, psychological discourses were also on the rise in cities. Variously adopted and spurned historically, psychotherapeutic ideas, practices, and institutions have seen an explosive growth in urban China, particularly since the early 2000s (H.-Y. Huang 2015; J. Yang 2015; Zhang 2017). Paralleling privatization and middle-class consumerism, academic psychology and psychiatry, private sector psychotherapy training, and popular psychological media have flourished in cities like Shanghai. These psychological discourses, I suggest below, have also influenced urban Christianity.

Such rural-urban distinctions are by no means total, and the urbanization of rural towns and massive rural-urban labour migrations since the 1980s continually blur and remake such conceptual boundaries (Kipnis 2016). Nonetheless, regional histories make various modes of engagement more or less available across religious landscapes. Rural and urban congregants have differed in their socioeconomic worlds and general familiarity with Christian doctrines, with rural churches marked by tendencies toward charismatic engagements and pragmatic dimensions of conversion (Bays 2003). In his work at a rural migrant Protestant church in Beijing, Jianbo Huang (2014) writes that while urban Chinese Christians tend to emphasize intellectual and text-centred approaches, rural migrant Christians tend emphasize charismatic-style experience and emotional worship. Liping Liang (2012) finds that while urban Protestants often convert after learning about Christian doctrines and values, rural Christians tend to do the reverse, converting first, then learning of Christian values. I suggest that in the urban and rural churches where I worked, distinct theories of mind were linked to particular rhythms and modes of spiritual experience.

Two churches

The work presented here draws on eight months of fieldwork, undertaken as part of the collaborative, multi-sited Mind and Spirit project. The Mind and Spirit project is a Templeton-funded, Stanford-based comparative and interdisciplinary project under the direction of T.M. Luhrmann (PI), drawing on the expertise of anthropologists, psychologists, historians, and philosophers. The project asks whether different understandings of 'mind', broadly construed, might shape or be related to the ways that people attend to and interpret experiences they deem spiritual or supernatural. We took a mixed-method, multi-phase approach, combining participant observation, long-form semi-structured interviews, quantitative surveys among the general population and local undergraduates, and psychological experiments with children and adults. We worked in five different countries: China, Ghana, Thailand, Vanuatu, and the United States, with some work in the Ecuadorian Amazon. In

Journal of the Royal Anthropological Institute (N.S.), 95-113
© 2020 The Authors. *Journal of the Royal Anthropological Institute* published by John Wiley & Sons Ltd on behalf of the Royal Anthropological Institute

each country, we included a focus on an urban charismatic evangelical church, with additional work in a rural charismatic evangelical church, and in another urban and rural religious setting of local importance.[6] In China, I worked in a charismatic church in Shanghai and a charismatic-style church in rural Henan province, and among Buddhist cultivators in Shanghai and those who practise spirit mediumship and possession in rural Henan. In this essay, I focus on the two churches, drawing on my work in non-Christian settings only when exploring contrasts and mutual influences.

The first church I turn to below is situated in Zhao Village, a village of several thousand in Nanyang County of Henan province. Termed by some as the 'Galilee of China', Henan province holds China's largest and fastest-growing Christian population (Hattaway 2009). Zhao Village Church was a state-sanctioned Three Self church. It was founded following a revelation received by Pastor Zhao's wife in the mid-1990s, after which they applied for an official permit and built the church on their own land. Himself a first-generation convert, Pastor Zhao represents the sixth generation of Christians locally since the nineteenth-century arrival of Norwegian Lutheran missionaries. Around sixty to eighty congregants attended the church on Sundays, though I was told that during national holidays, when younger villagers return home from work in the cities, attendance reached over a hundred. When I first arrived there, I was struck by the ever-present accounts of revelations, gifts, and miraculous healing. Yet it is important to note that Pastor Zhao and most congregants explicitly condemned 'charismatic' (ling'en) Christianity, a term that carried intensely negative connotations at the time of my stay, owing in part to the state's association of charismatic Christianity with 'evil cults' (xiejiao) and thus the risk of legal persecution.

The second church I describe below, Living Church in Shanghai, was a church of similar size but the reverse of Zhao Village Church on paper. It was an unregistered house church outside of the state-sanctioned system, and explicitly drew influence from transnational charismatic movements. Alongside contemporary charismatic scenes in Korea, Taiwan, the United States, and beyond, the pastor and congregants were also influenced by Pentecostal-inflected Chinese theologies and an eclectic range of spiritual sources across geographies and histories – from Chinese theologian Watchman Nee to Spanish mystic Miguel de Molinos. But despite their status as a charismatic house church, as we will see, congregants in Shanghai described fewer encounters with embodied experiences often associated with charismatic movements than those at the state-sanctioned, explicitly anti-charismatic Zhao Village Church. This thus complicates conventional depictions of fiery underground house churches and staid state-sanctioned churches.

The Devil and the moralized intensification of porosity: Zhao Village Church

When I first arrived at Zhao Village Church, I was quickly brought into a world in which the self and the mind were intensely porous to external otherworldly influences. One's own morally loaded thoughts, affects, and actions were often said to originate from or be propelled by God or the Devil; the human mind was by no means autonomous. As Xiu Li, the 60-year-old hymn leader put it:

> Anger is from the Devil. God causes people to love one another, causes people to be harmonious. When demonic spirits arrive, they come to corrupt people, causing competition and slander ... If the Devil assaults me, my heart-mind feels a sense of unpeace.

Journal of the Royal Anthropological Institute (N.S.), 95-113
© 2020 The Authors. *Journal of the Royal Anthropological Institute* published by John Wiley & Sons Ltd on behalf of the Royal Anthropological Institute

The Devil (*mogui*) – often used interchangeably with demons (*xieling*) – could also escalate otherwise negligible affects, until the human fails to be self-contained. In the words of Xiao Fang, a congregant in her mid-thirties who worked at the village credit union:

> For instance, when one is angry, demons corrupt you and drive you to strike your child ... [At first] you are just a little angry ... Demons will borrow this and aggravate you through your children, making it so that you must hit them and sin. Those imprisoned for murder ... that's all the Devil. They end up killing someone over something very minor.

This particular articulation of porosity, wherein the demonic acts through the intensification of affect, was resonant with non-Christian accounts of spirit possession and mediumship practices I encountered in rural Henan. Although congregants at Zhao Village Church strongly condemned such practices, many had paid visits to temples and spirit mediums prior to conversion, or had family members who did, and were likely familiar with these concepts of spiritual action. As Birgit Meyer (1999) found in her work in Ghana, the power of non-Christian spirits was reformulated into a Christian image of the Devil and remained a real force to be contended with. Here, Buddhist, Daoist, and other regional deities and spirits were relegated to a language of 'fake gods' (*jiashen*) and collapsed into a monotheistic concept of the Devil.

In Zhao Village, the Christian emphasis on good and evil not only sustained but also intensified the sense of porosity to ongoing demonic influence. Rather than the emphasis on good and bad minds in both Christian and non-Christian settings in Ghana, where evil intention to harm others took central stage in ideas of witchcraft (see Dulin and Dzokoto, this volume), the non-Christian mediums I met in rural Henan presented spirits as driven not always by evil, but also by coincidence, rightful desire (including anger and revenge), and personal greed. For the most part in non-Christian settings, only dedicated spirit mediums struggled directly with the spirit world day to day, and not, for instance, those who engaged more broadly in common temple rituals and visited mediums as supplicants. Moreover, troubling encounters with ghosts and spirits were not always linked with the wrongdoing of the affected human. By contrast, when such spirits were deemed demonic at Zhao Village Church, and engaged through a constant monitoring of individual good and evil, encounters with spiritual entities became ongoing for regular congregants, not just for pastors and preachers. Porosity was thus moralized and intensified, and distributed more broadly across the church community instead of engaged regularly by the select few as in the case of mediumship. As Smith (this volume) shows for Vanuatu, Christianity seemed to have polarized and interiorized the battle between good and evil, escalating a sense of moralized self-reflection and attention towards individual sin. And like in Vanuatu, an increased focus on interiority did not diminish material experiences of the otherworldly.

For those at Zhao Village Church, human minds and bodies, along with one's material surroundings, were rarely considered spiritually inert. The village temple, homes of non-Christian villagers, and objects deemed idolatrous exuded demonic potency. Moreover, influence by the Devil was transparent to God, evoking his immediate displeasure. This ever-present porosity to the divine and demonic was linked to an ethics of immediacy and a grammar of the body.

Journal of the Royal Anthropological Institute (N.S.), 95-113
© 2020 The Authors. *Journal of the Royal Anthropological Institute* published by John Wiley & Sons Ltd on behalf of the Royal Anthropological Institute

Corporeal discernment, acute pain, and the virtuous rhythm of immediacy

Among the range of spiritual experiences that the Mind and Spirit project explored, those of direct revelation through hearing the voice of God, internal visions, and dreams were strikingly common in Zhao Village. More congregants in Zhao Village described more of these particular experiences than in most other charismatic Christian sites in this collaborative project. Yet, despite the presence of such sensorial spiritual encounters as an audible voice from God, accounts of voice and visions were often deemed 'small' testimonies in Zhao Village. The term 'big testimony' tended to be reserved for miraculous healing. Alongside healing, the body was central to discernment day to day, particularly in the form of acute pain.

Xiu Li, the hymn leader, spoke of her own gift of discernment. When someone arrived to speak with her, if it was in accordance with God's grace, she received a pulsating headache on the right side. If the person was sent by Satan (*sadan*), she received the same headache, but on the left side. The pulsing pain allowed her to recognize whether a given person was affected by demons.

While Xiu Li stood out for the consistency and specificity of her localized headaches, discernment through pain was familiar to most congregants I met at Zhao Village Church. Acute pain served as a crucial sign for recognizing the presence of evil and sin, inextricably linked to God's displeasure. Lian, a congregant in her mid-thirties, spoke of visiting a neighbour, a member of Eastern Lightning, a self-identified Christian group outlawed as a cult by the state and deemed heretical by many Christian communities. Upon entering her neighbour's home, Lian recalled,

> My head felt the pain of being pricked and pricked (*zha*, as in stung by a needle) again and again. I knew in my heart-mind, this is the same feeling as when I think of something not in line with God's intention – my head will also hurt as if it's being pricked again and again.

This style of discernment through acute pain appeared to be absent across other sites of this collaboration, including Shanghai, while resonating with similar accounts of pain among spirit mediums I met in rural Henan. For the spirit mediums, tutelary spirits often communicated their desires and displeasures through signals of the human body, particularly pain and other forms of corporeal torment. Pain, within such collective repertoires, can be transformed into or experienced as a form of virtuous comportment (Throop 2010).

The significance of pain, embodiment, and otherworldly transmission here can in part be understood in relation to rich renderings of body and illness in China historically, from demonological medicines to medicines of cosmic correspondence (Unschuld 1985). While no single theory of the mind or body would capture these schools of Chinese thought, the body often held sociomoral and cosmological significance, and the dualist divide between mind and matter often did not provide the central conceptual tension or point of interest (Jullien 1995). With the twentieth-century scramble for Western scientific solutions, Chinese medical thought and practice saw dramatic changes amid efforts to 'get on track with the world', and became more engaged with Western medical and psychological concepts (L.H. Liu 1995; Zhan 2009). Nonetheless, the body remained a salient site of social and political signification thereafter, continuing to register shifting histories (Farquhar 2002; Kleinman 1986).

Pain and other bodily sensations were centrally important in contemporary Christian spiritual practice in Zhao Village. Not unlike the moral torment of internalized sin introduced by Christianity elsewhere (Robbins 2004), congregants in Zhao Village articulated daily worries over individual evil. But this sense of interiority, often associated with Protestant mentalization, did not exclude the body. Indeed, congregants seemed to use corporeal signals as one of the primary means for detecting sin. Moreover, the sensational form of the embodied experience tended to operate as a seemingly self-sufficient or nearly self-sufficient method for distinguishing between godly, demonic, and other influences – what I am calling here corporeal discernment. This is in contrast to modes of discernment that emphasize, for instance, the use of reason or other forms of verification beyond the legible form of embodiment, even if bodily signs are engaged. This is a distinction of degrees and variations rather than in kind, particularly in charismatic settings in which bodily techniques are common, but may be linked variously to other modalities.

More generally, what might be called an ethics of immediacy was ever-present at Zhao Village Church. Discernment, whether through acute pain or other modalities, was often presented as an instant, direct gnosis – 'I simply knew' (wo jiu zhidao), 'I knew in an instant' (wo yixia jiu zhidao). A perceived sign should be taken up, judged as a manifestation of the godly or the demonic, and acted upon quickly – the truly faithful reacts fast, and delay may be punished. While this might appear unremarkable considering the centrality of immediacy in charismatic Christianity at large, it was a virtuous rhythm different from (even if at times co-present with) one of gradual verification, emphasized at Living Church in Shanghai below.

By virtuous rhythm, I am referring to recurrent temporal aspects of one's comportment and disposition that constitute and signal the good, situated within a shared repertoire. Such temporal aspects form a constellation, explicitly and implicitly, with other concepts and embodiments. In the case of charismatic and Pentecostal movements, for instance, immediacy points at once to the temporality of instantaneousness, spontaneity, and rupture, as well as the ideal lack of mediation between the faithful and the divine. Such spontaneity and immediacy may coexist, if tacitly, with other temporal engagements, and might themselves be seen as cultivated forms (Bialecki 2017; Brahinsky 2013). In Zhao Village, this more broadly shared charismatic-style emphasis on immediacy was enmeshed, for instance, with more specific corporeal genres of pain, bringing together rhythmic and sensorial forms that together provide the contours of how one ought (and ought not) to live. The weaving of bodily encodings and rhythms conditions the entire field of religious experience (de Abreu 2008).

On one occasion, Pastor Zhao relayed the case of a congregant whose leg had been struck with inexplicable pain for several days. It turned out that he had knelt at a funeral without realizing this was considered sinful of worship of the dead. According to Pastor Zhao, the congregant then confessed and repented, and his leg pain was alleviated immediately. The risk of delay was also central in the founding story of the church. One day, Pastor Zhao's wife heard God's voice: 'Give your house over and build a church'. She hesitated, as the family would have no other place to live. In the days that followed, her son, who suffered from haemophilia, began bleeding day and night, reaching the brink of death. In fear of losing him, she agreed to the request. 'After offering the place to God, this fulfilled God's entire desire . . . [my son] stopped bleeding'.

Aside from discernment and proper response, the pronouncement of faith also reflected this ethics of immediacy. The most dignified form of conversion was a speedy utterance of 'I believe', without full or even partial understanding, often accompanied by instant miraculous healing. The ethics of immediacy in Zhao Village may thus help illuminate the link between charismatic-style experiences among rural migrant congregants (J. Huang 2014) and the tendency in rural regions to convert before learning the tenets of Christianity (Liang 2012). The implicit form of the divine pact across the conversion narratives and testimonies I heard in Zhao Village seemed to be that of immediate loyalty accompanied by immediate effects. While the general theme of immediacy is common to charismatic Christianity at large far beyond China, and the rhythmic sensibility described here may of course be taken up in settings beyond the so-called 'rural', the religious logics implied by this ethics of immediacy came to be an explicit source of contention across rural-urban and intergenerational divides.

Flesh of the immaterial: discernment and the entification of mind at Living Church

In Shanghai, those I met at Living Church often denounced what they called a superstitious 'exchange-style faith' (*jiaohuanxing de xinyang*).[7] In these denunciations, offering one's faith for the gift of God's healing – the ideal mode of conversion and subsequent engagements in Zhao Village – became a paradigm case for flawed faith. As Pastor Chen put it during a sermon: 'Many people go to church, asking God for this or that, asking for God to heal this and that illness. Once they're healed, then it's "Amen! Thank the Lord! I believe!" This is much too elementary!' This mode of engagement was often associated with the 'traditional' Christianity of villagers and older congregants.

One reason for repugnance towards this so-called 'exchange-style faith', at times implicitly and at times explicitly, was its resemblance to what those at Living Church called traditional Chinese religion or Buddhism, where the petitioning of gods and bodhisattvas for health and fortune in exchange for ritual offerings, they suggested, was a central motif.[8] Christians, by contrast, should not be grounding their faith in the hedging of bets, but rather out of desire for the love of God and for serving him. Those at Living Church insisted on a radical asymmetry between creator and created, against the sense that God could be manipulated by human action (cf. Miyazaki 2000). The critique of material exchange and ritualization in Christian practice was also paired with a focus on a sincere spiritual attitude. As many have suggested, Protestant sincerity is often built on critiques of ritual efficacy in colonial and postcolonial worlds, even if the objects of such critiques are wide-ranging (Engelke 2007; Handman 2015; Keane 2007). The denunciations launched at Living Church similarly inherit China's semi-colonial legacies and historical missionary attacks on Chinese religion (Reinders 2004).

Moreover, at Living Church, sincerity and the critique of material exchange were paired with concerns over the perils of the mind. Compared with the sense of permeability and ongoing back-and-forth with the divine and demonic in Zhao Village, congregants in Shanghai articulated what Taylor (2007) would term a more buffered sense of self and mind, particularly in relation to the Devil, even while inhabiting a sense of self far more porous to spirited presence than the non-charismatic Christians and self-described atheists around them. Recall Pastor Chen's musing from the opening: that charismatics were at risk of spiritual error given their tendency to see meaning in anything and everything. Despite a co-present sense of partial porosity to the otherworldly, human interpretation – routed through the mind – was seen as a central hindrance to spiritual engagement in Shanghai.

When describing their own spiritual encounters, many congregants at Living Church, as noted, relayed an attitude of caution. Facing potential instances of divine encounter, they aimed for a simultaneous stance of suspended disbelief and suspended belief, owing to the fundamentally flawed mediation of the mind. This dual suspension is reminiscent of T.M. Luhrmann's (2012*b*) descriptions of the 'epistemological double register' in US neo-charismatic settings such as the Vineyard. In particular, a 'self-conscious combination of reification and qualification' was similarly taken up by those in Shanghai (2012*a*: 380).

Yet, unlike the light-hearted uses of imagination at the Vineyard, where God was described as real while one's own direct spiritual experience was often marked in part as play, the double movement of faith and suspension marked the serious effort of spiritual verification at Living Church. One suspends scepticism towards potential divine manifestation to remain porous to divine encounter, while suspending conviction towards one's own interpretation of spiritual occurrences until certainty can be reached regarding its divine status. This is not to say that engagements with God could not be playful in tone; they were at times for many. But rather than simply treating potential spiritual experiences as 'deeply satisfying daydreams', as at the Vineyard, most congregants I met at Living Church would consider a mere satisfying daydream to be a failed instance of discernment, to be discarded (albeit at times reluctantly) in the patient anticipation of a verified instance of divine encounter.

Li, a congregant in her mid-thirties known at the church as among the most enthusiastically engaged with direct spiritual experiences, spoke of her past interpretative errors.

> When I went to my first church back in 2013 . . . I erred on many things. At the time I felt, 'This is so spiritual! It's so great!' But after verifying (*yinzheng*), [the signs] turned out to be incorrect . . . I then concluded that *I myself* wanted some particular things, and packaged it in a façade of 'loving God'. I gave people the impression that these things came from God, when [in fact] the origin was my own desire.

When I asked her if the Devil was the source of these errors, she responded: 'We cannot blame the Devil for everything, because the Devil is very busy . . . the problem is also with ourselves'.

Rather than daily concerns with demonic influence, as in Zhao Village, congregants in Shanghai much more commonly cited human misinterpretation as a hindrance to spiritual life. While the Devil was also considered a dangerously powerful entity, he was assumed to maintain a distance from their daily affairs.

This focus on the mind in Shanghai may be linked to the longer history and recent boom of psychotherapeutic practices in urban China, and also specifically the influence the church draws from twentieth-century Chinese theologian Watchman Nee. Following Nee, those at Living Church emphasized not a dualist distinction of body and soul or flesh and spirit, but a triad of spirit, soul, and body (*ling, hun, ti*), where the soul was equated with modern Western psychological notions of mind. As Wu, a technological investor in his mid-forties, put it:

> Spirit, soul, body; spirit, mind, body, three strata. Sometimes people confuse the soul and the spirit. Thoughts, the will, and emotions are more of the soul. Spirit is level of the spiritual, higher than the level of the soul. [Spirit] is the level of faith and the supernatural.

For Watchman Nee, the body allows for what he calls 'world-consciousness', through which one comes into contact with the material world. The soul, in turn, is responsible for self-consciousness, including such faculties as volition, intellect, and emotion, and is explicitly linked with what's addressed in modern psychology. The spirit, by contrast, is the portion of the human that communes with God directly and is capable of

Journal of the Royal Anthropological Institute (N.S.), 95-113
© 2020 The Authors. *Journal of the Royal Anthropological Institute* published by John Wiley & Sons Ltd on behalf of the Royal Anthropological Institute

God-consciousness: 'God dwells in the spirit, self dwells in the soul, while senses dwell in the body' (Nee 1968: vol. 1, 26). In coming to know God, although the soul can be deployed to help 'activate' spirit in prayer practice, it is 'never a substitute for the spirit', and is instead the source of much error and human 'folly' (1968: vol. 2, 170; 1968: vol. 1, 167-71). The 'soulish' tendencies of humans, for Nee, can be seen in the self-centred desire to take pleasure in spiritual sensations, erroneously taken to be in the service of God. Nonetheless, Nee emphasizes, the soul – and by extension the self and the mind – is the most prominent aspect of humans, thus an entity to be reckoned with. Nee's writings can be considered alongside a lengthy history of debates on tripartite versus bipartite biblical formulations of spirit, soul, and body, from early Christian apologists through the Reformation (e.g. Delitzsch 1867 [1855]). Here, what interests me is the way this trichotomy made theological space for secularized concepts of mind in Shanghai.

For those at Living Church, what Watchman Nee terms the soul – seen as interchangeable with the psychological mind – became the main hindrance to discernment. The mind-soul, as Pastor Chen once put it, is 'the flesh of the immaterial', the non-material site of sin. In contrast to the externality of the Devil in Zhao Village, one's own mind was the central locus for thoughts and actions not in accordance with God's wishes.

Watchman Nee first came to prominence in China when such neologisms as the 'self' were imported for rethinking a new national subject (L.H. Liu 1995). Inheriting the historical encounter between Protestantism, Chinese anti-imperialism, and Western psychological sciences, the equivalence Nee drew between the Christian soul and secularized articulations of mind offered a theological language for those at Living Church nearly a century later, resonant with an urban culture saturated by psychological discourses.[9]

Thus, while part of a broader apparatus of secularization, psychological concepts also deeply influenced modern religious texts and contemplative practices through which Shanghai congregants accessed the divine. Notions of the soul continued to find new elaborations alongside notions of the psyche, opening up new theological spaces for encounter (see Pandolfo 2018). Many congregants were familiar with psychological theories, and some attended psychotherapeutic workshops in their spare time. By gaining a deeper understanding of the mind, they hoped to better identify and thereby cast aside their own psychic barriers for the sake of true discernment. These more buffered, psychology-inflected notions of the mind were linked to tempos and textures of spiritual experience that differed from the ethics of immediacy accompanying more porous renderings of the mind in Zhao Village.

Caution, verification, retroaction
At Living Church, critiques of so-called 'exchange-style faith' implied a distaste for the rapid rhythm of a tit-for-tat relation with God. If those in Zhao Village Church abided by an ethics of quick response, Pastor Chen often reminded congregants of the patient, expansive temporality of the divine. God, he would say, is not that stingy. God doesn't fuss over your minor infractions and niceties day to day, but rather awaits the unfolding of your faith and orientation towards him across your lifetime. In place of frequent confession and repentance, Pastor Chen emphasized congregants' attitude and stance towards God. A rightful attitude involved the desire to know God, and such knowing could include 'porous' spiritual encounters: hearing from God, receiving visions and

dreams, feeling the tingle of the Holy Spirit. Yet, while Pastor Chen encouraged openness towards such experiences, he also stressed the need for caution in discernment owing to the unreliable instrument of the human mind.

Many I met at Living Church yearned for an immediate, direct knowledge of God, including through sensory and embodied experiences. Yet, compared with congregants in Zhao Village, those at Living Church described far fewer encounters of this sort. Much more common were the sense of God guiding them through thoughts in their mind, inspiration in the spirit, and contextual circumstances that moved beyond coincidence. Moreover, spiritual encounters of any modality were subject to retroactive confirmation; their status often stood tentative until verified. As Sheng, a 30-year-old corporate trainer and Bible study leader, put it:

> In general, people don't realize at the moment [that they're being guided by God] … Usually it's *after* an event has passed that one realizes in retrospect. The problem is, many believers in fact have some degree of selfish desire in their own heart-mind. They will *say* that God is guiding me this way [when he is not] … This is quite horrifying.

Given that the mind was deemed a significant barrier to discernment, signs that appear to be divine were prone to human error; spiritual lucidity entailed the test of time.

Like many I spoke with at Living Church, Sheng's own encounters with the divine often came in the form of beyond-coincidental events, thoughts from God, and a sense of inspiration. His eyes widened as he described a form of sudden and intense inspiration during his painstaking preparations for Bible study. 'At times I would have no inspiration while examining scripture, then … I suddenly have a thought, and realize this passage could be interpreted in this way … it's an indescribable feeling'. Although such instances were exhilarating in the moment, Sheng was hesitant to tether discernment to the time of the experience. 'Even though you might say that this is inspiration from God, from the angle of caution, you need to conduct more textual research to confirm'.

Sheng was considered among the more cautious at Living Church, a self-described rationalist 'without many experiences'. But even those, like Li above, who were more disposed towards embodied and gnostic modalities abided by an emphasis on caution, requiring a virtuous rhythm of gradual, retroactive verification. Like congregants at Zhao Village Church, those at Living Church also held that direct, immediate discernment was possible (by way of the spirit, as it is the spirit that discerns the status of an embodied sensation). Yet, in contrast to the ethics of immediacy so prominent in Zhao Village, in which delayed interpretation and response to a potential divine sign signalled one's weakness of faith and corruption by the Devil, a protracted period of substantiation was seen as testament to one's spiritual maturity, even if one revelled in experiential gifts. Given the fallible mediation of the human mind, even the most potent sensations could not be taken as self-evident, as the potentiality of the sign awaits its subsequent confirmation.

Porosity after secularism

Recent discussions of religion and secularity have turned their attention to how secularism takes shape not only through institutional transformations, but also through attendant shifts in how the human mind and sensorium are conceptualized and inhabited (Asad 2003; Descola 2013; Hirschkind 2006; Meyer 2010).[10] One influential, if contentious, account, as noted, has been Charles Taylor's description of porous and buffered selves, wherein the buffered self is produced by the specificities of a secular context. Beyond the institutional compartmentalization of the religious sphere and the sense of disenchantment, secularism for Taylor importantly involves a third dimension: a distinct *condition of belief.* Whereas belief in the otherworldly, according to Taylor, is 'unchallenged, and indeed, unproblematic' in non-secular worlds, under secular conditions, belief comes to be 'understood to be one option among others, and frequently not the easiest to embrace' (2007: 3, 19). This account of secular selfhood, located largely in the modern West, is often defined by Taylor against what some have seen as an oversimplified mapping of the past and the non-West (Mahmood 2010).

In Taylor's rendering, what produces the sense of a spiritually inert mind closed to supernatural influence is in part the awareness of others' doubt. Knowing that one's neighbours abide by a humanist, spiritless universe, one's own religious selfhood is reconfigured. By this definition, my Christian interlocutors in both Shanghai and Zhao Village would be well suited for speaking to such secular conditions. Following violent secularization campaigns – the desecration of religious infrastructure, the arrest and punishment of religious leaders – across the twentieth century in Chinese cities and villages, these two churches would on no account be considered sites of 'never-secular Christianity' (Luhrmann 2012a). Congregants at both churches declared that while the world around them is brimming with atheists and Buddhists, Christians choose to bear the burden of the cross against an unbelieving majority. Indeed, 77 per cent of those surveyed in China identify as atheist or non-religious (WIN-Gallup International 2012). Yet, despite both holding a strong sense that belief in God was but one option among many, the sense of porosity and bufferedness in discernment practices varied considerably.

At Zhao Village Church, congregants held a relatively porous notion of the mind under constant influence from God and the Devil, and described many more sensorial and embodied experiences of the otherworldly than those in Shanghai (and in some modalities more than many other sites of the collaborative project). At Living Church in Shanghai, congregants held a comparatively buffered, psychology-inflected notion of the mind; repeated calls to bypass the mind in spiritual practice simultaneously reified it as an entity. With this sense of the mind as a bounded entity, those in Shanghai also described far fewer sensorial and corporeal encounters with the otherworldly than those in Zhao Village (and most other sites of the project). Whereas three-quarters of those I interviewed at Zhao Village Church described having experienced the externally audible voice of God, for instance – the sensory modality that offered the initial impetus and design for this project for T.M. Luhrmann – only one-quarter of those at Living Church did. It is a divergence greater than any cross-church comparison within any other national context of the project.

Given that congregants at both churches were well aware of the overwhelming presence of exclusive humanism around them – from that of the Communist state to that of their atheist kin – it seems that at least in the case of China, the differential presence of porous and buffered elements cannot be understood simply through the cognizance of others' doubt or lack thereof. The question of porosity thus cannot be taken, to evoke Jeanne Favret-Saada (1980), as one of the credulous subject, non-Western, non-modern, non-urban, or otherwise. Here, the salience of porous and buffered renderings is better understood through divergent modes and contexts of post-secular religiosity, and their attendant notions of mind and selfhood. At the same time, partly in line with Taylor's suggestion, ever-present elaborations of a self-sufficient

Journal of the Royal Anthropological Institute (N.S.), 95-113
© 2020 The Authors. *Journal of the Royal Anthropological Institute* published by John Wiley & Sons Ltd on behalf of the Royal Anthropological Institute

humanist mind through the urban rise of psychology may have contributed to this contrast.

As described above, cities in China have seen a proliferation of psychological discourses in recent decades. Psychotherapeutic practices were much less prevalent in Zhao Village, and psychological languages held less sway. While the rise of individualism has deeply affected both urban and rural China across Maoist and post-Reform eras (Yan 2010), rural life might be considered more relationally enmeshed with neighbours and kin when contrasted with the heightened sense of atomism in major cities, where, as many in Shanghai relayed, one often did not know one's neighbours. Notions of freedom, autonomy, and self-reliance – echoed in congregants' evocations of free will in Shanghai – were central to neoliberal discourses that saturated cities and special economic zones amid post-Reform labour migration (Zhang & Ong 2008). In Zhao Village Church, by contrast, concepts of otherworldly porosity and distributed personhood implicitly shared with non-Christian revivals of spirit possession and mediumship seemed to be of stronger influence than psychological theories of self. But in their Christian rearticulations, such concepts were differently moralized and diabolized.

These divergences in concepts of mind and person may also have been influenced in part by immersion in secularized theories of the human through state-run schooling. Most congregants at Living Church were college-educated. By contrast, most congregants I met in Zhao Village had spent much less time in formal education. Most had never attended high school; many had not completed elementary school. Indeed, a few younger preachers in Zhao Village who had undertaken more formal schooling, including state-sanctioned seminary training, described some hesitation towards the quick interpretation and constant engagement with spiritual experiences, particularly among the older generation. The contrasts I draw between the two churches is thus by no means stable or tied simply to rurality and urbanity, but also tied to ongoing productions of difference across an array of social schisms and imaginaries. I foreground the rural-urban distinction to consider one axis of variation in spite of a shared (if uneven) history of secularization campaigns, and the notable rural-urban contrast in China when compared to other sites of the project.

At the same time, the two churches also held qualities in common when juxtaposed with other sites. While congregants I met in both Shanghai and Zhao Village, like those in the United States, were reaching for God in contexts often considered intensely secularized, their concerns clustered less around what Brahinsky (this volume), in the United States, called 'ontological anxiety' and the need to repeatedly demonstrate the reality of God. Although practices of verification were as important in Shanghai as they were in San Francisco, unlike their US counterparts, congregants I met in Shanghai rarely qualified their spiritual encounters as 'crazy' (see Luhrmann 2012b). And while embodied encounters with God, as in the United States, were considered crucial in Zhao Village, accounts of these encounters – save those for the purposes of evangelizing – were rarely used to re-confirm God's existence. Instead, in both Shanghai and Zhao Village, discernment centred on *what God wants* from oneself, and the avoidance of God's displeasure. After the initial process of conversion, congregants focused their doubt more on their alignment with the desire of the divine other – more of a sense of 'relational concern', if you will, than a sense of ontological anxiety regarding the realness of God.

This divergence from the United States might be considered through religious-philosophical inheritances from various strands of Chinese thought; in particular,

Journal of the Royal Anthropological Institute (N.S.), 95-113
© 2020 The Authors. *Journal of the Royal Anthropological Institute* published by John Wiley & Sons Ltd on behalf of the Royal Anthropological Institute

the still-salient concerns with kinship and filial piety in spite of modern ruptures, and the historical focus on moral and cosmological analogy rather than ontological distinctions (Hall & Ames 1998; Jullien 1995). Some congregants, particularly those who were previously Buddhists or temple-goers, also shared an implicit sense of 'ontological pluralism', as described by Aulino (this volume) of Thailand, before their conversion. Although Christianity radically transformed this sense of multiplicity, the implicit need for ongoing demonstrations of ontological consistency did not seem as pressing as in the United States, where a history of philosophical and scientific interest in securing and purifying ontological categories (Descola 2013; Latour 1993) – in part inherited from Christianity – might inflect contemporary charismatic anxieties.

Such contrasts and parallels, whether within or beyond China, suggest that theories of mind present across histories and geographies – which entail different construals of reality and materiality – are deeply intertwined with the spiritual world and sensorium. Critical responses to Taylor's mapping and periodization of porous and buffered selves have suggested that disenchantment through the absence of spirits must be disentangled from both institutional secularism and unidirectional temporal claims, as the presence of spirits can also intensify in contexts of explicitly secular governance (Meyer 2012; Warner, VanAntwerpen & Calhoun 2010). The present essay shows that porous and buffered selves do not map neatly onto geopolitical borders. To understand construals of mind after secularism, at least in the case of China, one must attend to uneven landscapes and myriad styles of religious revival, which inherit and take up overlapping yet divergent histories of transformation, and are manifest through the most intimate sites of spiritual encounter. Deeply porous modes of personhood may be co-present with more bounded ones, even after what's been seen as some of the most thorough secularization campaigns conducted by a modern state.

NOTES

Many thanks go to all those in China who made this work possible, whom I will not name here for the sake of anonymity. I am grateful for this dynamic collaboration with Tanya Luhrmann, Cristine Legare, Felicity Aulino, Josh Brahinsky, John Dulin, Vivian Dzokoto, Rachel Smith, Nikki Ross-Zehnder, and Kara Weisman. Thanks also go to Jon Bialecki, Samuele Collu, and the two anonymous reviewers for their incisive feedback, and Nick Long, Justin Dyer, and the staff at the JRAI for their editorial support. Funding for the Mind and Spirit project was generously provided by the John Templeton Foundation (#55427). Final revisions were completed with support of the project Imagining the Rural in a Globalizing World (RURALIMAGINATIONS, 2018–23), which received funding from the European Research Council (ERC) under the European Union's Horizon 2020 research and innovation programme (#772436). Open Access was supported by the University of Amsterdam.

[1] Given the wavering political status and continued persecution of Christianity and other religious engagements in China, Living Church, Zhao Village, Zhao Village Church, and all interlocutors' names are pseudonyms.

[2] To note, Pastor Chen and congregants evoked an array of terms when speaking of discernment, including 'self' (ziji), 'heart-mind' (xin), and xueqi – literally blood-breath – referring to human tempers. Despite formal conceptual distinctions (described below), many Chinese linguistic-conceptual inheritances do not carry the post-Enlightenment mind-body dualism that the English 'mind' connotes. Moreover, the word xin refers to both the English 'heart' and 'mind' (hence the gloss 'heart-mind'). In this essay, I use 'mind' as a heuristic in dialogue with the other contributions to this special issue, letting its connotations unfold through my interlocutors' accounts.

[3] I am drawing on Ngo and Quijada's (2015) description of atheist secularism in communist and post-communist worlds, distinct from Protestant-inflected secularisms.

[4] Numbers only offer a general picture. Reliable estimates on religion are notoriously difficult to secure in China. The lowest estimates suggest 1 per cent, while church membership reports suggest 8 per cent (Pew Research Center 2011).

Journal of the Royal Anthropological Institute (N.S.), 95-113
© 2020 The Authors. *Journal of the Royal Anthropological Institute* published by John Wiley & Sons Ltd on behalf of the Royal Anthropological Institute

[5] See M.M.-H. Yang (2008) and Goossaert & Palmer (2011) for accounts of how national policies were variously deployed and eluded. Here, I highlight some urban-rural differences.

[6] This paragraph is based on a description drafted collectively by the Mind and Spirit team and used to illustrate the joint nature of the research.

[7] I heard this phrasing at several churches across Shanghai. In Zhao Village, this sentiment was mentioned by several younger, seminary-trained preachers, partly as a critique of the older generation, but it was not a prominent concern overall.

[8] Yet many white-collar Buddhists I met in Shanghai similarly condemned such exchange-like relations with bodhisattvas as 'superstitious'. Protestant-inflected critiques are thus taken up in contemporary religious engagements beyond Protestantism proper.

[9] Of course, Protestant concepts were themselves precursors of psychological discourses (Foucault 2006 [1961]). And, Nee was popular not only in urban regions (Lian 2010), though elements of his thought may be emphasized with different aims across contexts.

[10] Psychological anthropologists, of course, have long been exploring religion through embodiment and the psyche (Csordas 1997; Hollan 2000). But concerns with secularism in this manner were less central until more recently.

REFERENCES

ASAD, T. 2003. *Formations of the secular: Christianity, Islam, modernity.* Stanford: University Press.

BAYS, D.H. 2003. Chinese Protestant Christianity today. *The China Quarterly* **174**, 488-504.

——— 2012. *A new history of Christianity in China.* Malden, Mass.: Wiley-Blackwell.

BIALECKI, J. 2017. *A diagram for fire: miracles and variation in an American charismatic movement.* Oakland: University of California Press.

BRAHINSKY, J. 2013. Cultivating discontinuity: Pentecostal pedagogies of yielding and control. *Anthropology & Education Quarterly* **44**, 399-422.

CAO, N. 2011. *Constructing China's Jerusalem: Christians, power, and place in contemporary Wenzhou.* Stanford: University Press.

CSORDAS, T.J. 1997. *The sacred self: a cultural phenomenology of charismatic healing.* Berkeley: University of California Press.

DE ABREU, M.J.A. 2008. Goose bumps all over: breath, media, and tremor. *Social Text* **26**: 3, 59-78.

DEAN, K. 2003. Local communal religion in contemporary south-east China. *The China Quarterly* **174**, 338-58.

DELITZSCH, F. 1867 [1855]. *A system of biblical psychology* (trans. R.E. Wallis). Edinburgh: T. & T. Clark.

DESCOLA, P. 2013. *Beyond nature and culture* (trans. J. Lloyd). Chicago: University Press.

ENGELKE, M. 2007. *A problem of presence: beyond scripture in an African church.* Berkeley: University of California Press.

FARQUHAR, J. 2002. *Appetites: food and sex in post-socialist China.* Durham, N.C.: Duke University Press.

FAVRET-SAADA, J. 1980. *Deadly words: witchcraft in the Bocage* (trans. C. Cullen). New York: Cambridge University Press.

FOUCAULT, M. 2006 [1961]. *History of madness* (trans. J. Murphy). New York: Routledge.

GOOSSAERT, V. & D. PALMER 2011. *The religious question in modern China.* Chicago: University Press.

HALL, D.L. & R.T. AMES 1998. *Thinking from the Han: self, truth, and transcendence in Chinese and Western culture.* Albany: SUNY Press.

HANDMAN, C. 2015. *Critical Christianity: translation and denominational conflict in Papua New Guinea.* Oakland: University of California Press.

HATTAWAY, P. 2009. *Henan: the Galilee of China.* Carlisle: Piquant.

HIRSCHKIND, C. 2006. *The ethical soundscape: cassette sermons and Islamic counterpublics.* New York: Columbia University Press.

HOLLAN, D. 2000. Culture and dissociation in Toraja. *Transcultural Psychiatry* **37**, 545-59.

HUANG, H.-Y. 2015. From psychotherapy to psycho-boom: a historical overview of psychotherapy in China. *Psychoanalysis and Psychotherapy in China* **1**, 1-30.

HUANG, J. 2014. Being Christians in urbanizing China: the epistemological tensions of the rural churches in the city. *Current Anthropology* **55**: S10, S238-47.

JENKINS, P. 2002. *The next Christendom: the coming of global Christianity.* Oxford: University Press.

JULLIEN, F. 1995. *The propensity of things: toward a history of efficacy in China.* New York: Zone Books.

KAO, C.-Y. 2009. The Cultural Revolution and the emergence of Pentecostal-style Protestantism in China. *Journal of Contemporary Religion* **24**, 171-88.

Journal of the Royal Anthropological Institute (N.S.), 95-113
© 2020 The Authors. *Journal of the Royal Anthropological Institute* published by John Wiley & Sons Ltd on behalf of the Royal Anthropological Institute

KEANE, W. 2007. *Christian moderns: freedom and fetish in the mission encounter.* Berkeley: University of California Press.

———— 2015. *Ethical life: its natural and social histories.* Princeton: University Press.

KIPNIS, A.B. 2016. *From village to city: social transformation in a Chinese county seat.* Oakland: University of California Press.

KLEINMAN, A. 1986. *Social origins of distress and disease: depression, neurasthenia, and pain in modern China.* New Haven: Yale University Press.

LATOUR, B. 1993. *We have never been modern* (trans. C. Porter). Cambridge, Mass.: Harvard University Press.

LIAN, X. 2010. *Redeemed by fire: The rise of popular Christianity in modern China.* New Haven: Yale University Press.

LIANG, L. 2012. Multiple variations: perspectives on the religious psychology of Buddhist and Christian converts in the People's Republic of China. *Pastoral Psychology* **61**, 865-77.

LIU, L.H. 1995. *Translingual practice: literature, national culture, and translated modernity – China, 1900-1937.* Stanford: University Press.

LIU, Y. 2017. The 'Galilee of China': Pentecostals without Pentecostalism. In *Global Chinese Pentecostal and charismatic Christianity* (eds) F. Yang, J.K.C. Tong & A.H. Anderson, 200-16. Boston: Brill.

LUHRMANN, T.M. 2012a. A hyperreal God and modern belief: toward an anthropological theory of mind. *Current Anthropology* **53**, 371-95.

———— 2012b. *When God talks back: understanding the American evangelical relationship with God.* New York: Knopf.

————, R. ASTUTI, J. ROBBINS, *et al.* 2011. Towards an anthropological theory of mind. Position papers from the Lemelson Conference [includes introduction, individual essay and edited collection]. *Journal of the Finnish Anthropological Association* **36**: 4, 5-69.

MAHMOOD, S. 2010. Can secularism be other-wise? In *Varieties of secularism in a secular age* (eds) M. Warner, J. VanAntwerpen & C. Calhoun, 282-99. Cambridge, Mass.: Harvard University Press.

MEYER, B. 1999. *Translating the Devil: religion and modernity among the Ewe in Ghana.* Edinburgh: University Press.

———— 2010. Aesthetics of persuasion: global Christianity and Pentecostalism's sensational forms. *South Atlantic Quarterly* **109**, 741-63.

———— 2012. Religious and secular, 'spiritual' and 'physical' in Ghana. In *What matters? Ethnographies of value in a not so secular age* (eds) C. Bender & A. Taves, 86-118. New York: Columbia University Press.

MICKLETHWAIT, J. & A. WOOLDRIDGE 2009. *God is back: how the global revival of faith is changing the world.* New York: Penguin.

MIYAZAKI, H. 2000. Faith and its fulfillment: agency, exchange, and the Fijian aesthetics of completion. *American Ethnologist* **27**, 31-51.

NEDOSTUP, R. 2010. *Superstitious regimes: religion and the politics of Chinese modernity.* Cambridge, Mass.: Harvard University Asia Center.

NEE, W. 1968. *The spiritual man: in three volumes.* New York: Christian Fellowship Publishers.

NGO, T.T.T. & J.B. QUIJADA (eds) 2015. *Atheist secularism and its discontents: a comparative study of religion and Communism in Eurasia.* New York: Palgrave Macmillan.

OBLAU, G. 2011. Pentecostals by default? Contemporary Christianity in China. In *Asian and Pentecostal: The charismatic face of Christianity in Asia* (eds) A. Anderson & E. Tang, 411-36. Eugene, Ore.: Wipf and Stock.

PANDOLFO, S. 2018. *Knot of the soul: madness, psychoanalysis, Islam.* Chicago: University Press.

PEW RESEARCH CENTER 2011. Global Christianity: a report on the size and distribution of the world's Christian population (available online: *https://www.pewforum.org/2011/12/19/global-christianity-exec/*, accessed 17 January 2020).

RANCIÈRE, J. 2004. *The politics of aesthetics: the distribution of the sensible* (trans. G. Rockhill). New York: Bloomsbury.

REINDERS, E.R. 2004. *Borrowed gods and foreign bodies: Christian missionaries imagine Chinese religion.* Berkeley: University of California Press.

REINHARDT, B. 2015. A Christian plane of immanence? Contrapuntal reflections on Deleuze and Pentecostal spirituality. *HAU: Journal of Ethnographic Theory* **5**: 1, 405-36.

ROBBINS, J. 2004. *Becoming sinners: Christianity and moral torment in a Papua New Guinea society.* Berkeley: University of California Press.

———— & A. RUMSEY 2008. Introduction: Cultural and linguistic anthropology and the opacity of other minds. *Anthropological Quarterly* **81**, 407-20.

TAYLOR, C. 2007. *A secular age.* Cambridge, Mass.: Belknap Press of Harvard University Press.

Journal of the Royal Anthropological Institute (N.S.), 95-113

© 2020 The Authors. *Journal of the Royal Anthropological Institute* published by John Wiley & Sons Ltd on behalf of the Royal Anthropological Institute

THROOP, C.J. 2010. *Suffering and sentiment: exploring the vicissitudes of experience and pain in Yap*. Berkeley: University of California Press.

UNSCHULD, P.U. 1985. *Medicine in China: a history of ideas*. Berkeley: University of California Press.

WARNER, M., J. VANANTWERPEN & C. CALHOUN (eds) 2010. *Varieties of secularism in a secular age*. Cambridge, Mass.: Harvard University Press.

WIN-GALLUP INTERNATIONAL 2012. Global index of religiosity and atheism (available online: *https://sidmennt.is/wp-content/uploads/Gallup-International-um-tr%C3%BA-og-tr%C3%BAleysi-2012.pdf*, accessed 17 January 2020).

YAN, Y. 2010. The Chinese path to individualization. *British Journal of Sociology* **61**, 489-512.

YANG, F., J.K.C. TONG & A.H. ANDERSON (eds) 2017. *Global Chinese Pentecostal and charismatic Christianity*. Boston: Brill.

YANG, J. 2015. *Unknotting the heart: unemployment and therapeutic governance in China*. Ithaca, N.Y.: Cornell University Press.

YANG, M.M.-H. (ed.) 2008. *Chinese religiosities: afflictions of modernity and state formation*. Berkeley: University of California Press.

ZHAN, M. 2009. *Other-worldly: making Chinese medicine through transnational frames*. Durham, N.C.: Duke University Press.

ZHANG, L. 2017. The rise of therapeutic governing in postsocialist China. *Medical Anthropology* **36**, 6-18.

——— & A. ONG (eds) 2008. *Privatizing China: socialism from afar*. Ithaca, N.Y.: Cornell University Press.

L'esprit et le Diable : porosité et discernement dans deux Églises charismatiques chinoises

Résumé

L'autrice explore les rencontres avec l'au-delà et les notions d'esprit dans deux Églises de style charismatique en Chine. Les fidèles de l'Église du Village de Zhao, dans la province rurale du Henan, ont davantage tendance à penser que l'esprit est perméable à la corruption par le Diable. Ceux de l'Église Vivante de Shanghai sont plus influencés par des notions psychologiques délimitées de l'esprit comme entité et, bien qu'ils considèrent aussi qu'il est perméable aux êtres spirituels, c'est son fonctionnement interne qui leur apparaît comme l'obstacle central au discernement, et non l'action extérieure du Diable. Alors que les fidèles de Shanghai mettent en avant une vérification rétroactive graduelle des signes spirituels potentiels, ceux du Henan recherchent un rythme de réponse immédiate. Dans le même temps, les fidèles de Shanghai décrivent moins de rencontres sensorielles et incarnées (voix divine, douleur, guérison) que ceux du Henan. On peut partiellement comprendre de telles différences de théories de l'esprit, de rythmes vertueux et de distribution dans l'appareil cognitif spirituel des chrétiens à travers les modes d'engagement privilégiés par ces Églises, et partiellement aussi par les irrégularités de parcours de l'abolition et de la résurgence du fait religieux en Chine, avec une présence plus forte des genres psychothérapeutiques dans les villes et de la médiumnité dans les zones rurales au cours des dernières décennies. Ces variations de personnalité et de contact avec l'au-delà, allant jusqu'à une très grande porosité, coexistent ainsi au sein d'un environnement athéiste, après l'une des campagnes de sécularisation les plus radicales que l'on ait vu mener par un État moderne.

Journal of the Royal Anthropological Institute (N.S.), 95-113

6

Empowered imagination and mental vulnerability: local theory of mind and spiritual experience in Vanuatu

Rachel E. Smith *University of Cambridge*

'Theory of mind' in developmental psychology focuses on how children develop the ability to infer others' beliefs, desires, and intentions. Anthropologists have taken up the notion of 'theory of mind' to explore the way cultural differences in representations of beliefs, desires, and intentions affect everyday lives. In Oceania, anthropologists have noted that inferences about others' intentions are not accorded a privileged role in social interaction. In Vanuatu, I find, it is often the material, rather than immaterial, aspects of relatedness that are elaborated upon. People think about knowledge, creativity, meaning, and intention not as confined to a bounded mental or inner domain, but as discoverable through the body, and in the world at large. I argue here that this propensity to locate meaning and moral purpose as external to the mind corresponds to a 'porous' view of self and mind, and that this in turn may open people to experience vivid, intense, and often tangible forms of spiritual encounter.

In developmental psychology, 'theory of mind' (psychological ToM) is understood as a basic human capacity underpinning social interaction by enabling people to construe others, to explain and predict their actions in terms of mental states. More recently, anthropologists (Bloch 2013; Keane 2015; Luhrmann *et al.* 2011; Robbins & Rumsey 2008) have taken up what we have come to call 'local theory of mind' in broader ways to explore cross-cultural variations in the ways people think about thinking, and to ask whether these differences in representation appear to be related to people's everyday lives. In Oceania, numerous anthropological accounts point to a tendency for people to deny mental inference and intention a privileged place in social life (Robbins & Rumsey 2008), provoking debate about whether people were speculating any less about others' intentions (Bloch 2013: 120; Keane 2015: 125; Luhrmann *et al.* 2011: 11). Ni-Vanuatu do not confine faculties such as knowledge, creativity, meaning, and intention to a bounded 'mind' or 'self' (as in many secular Western folk models, Luhrmann *et al.* 2011: 6), but find them within and through the body and the world, a world of spirits. I will argue that this propensity is associated with a model of mind that is 'porous', and with vivid, intense, and often tangible spiritual experiences.

    To make this argument, I draw on research conducted as part of the Mind and Spirit project; a Templeton-funded, Stanford-based comparative and interdisciplinary project under the direction of T.M. Luhrmann (PI), drawing on the expertise of anthropologists, psychologists, historians, and philosophers. The project asks whether different understandings of 'mind', broadly construed, might shape or be related to the ways that people attend to and interpret experiences they deem spiritual or supernatural. We took a mixed-method, multi-phase approach, combining participant observation, long-form semi-structured interviews, quantitative surveys among the general population and local undergraduates, and psychological experiments with children and adults. We worked in five different countries: China, Ghana, Thailand, Vanuatu, and the United States, with some work in the Ecuadorian Amazon. In each country, we included a focus on an urban charismatic evangelical church, with additional work in a rural charismatic evangelical church, and in another urban and rural religious setting of local importance.[1]

Vanuatu is a small island nation of around 280,000 people in the Southwest Pacific, characterized by astonishing diversity. There are at least 110 distinct indigenous languages, matched by a wide array of social arrangements, including kinship systems, political structures, and ritual practices. In choosing research sites, I aimed to reflect some of this variety and also choose relatively autonomous settings: that is, those which Ni-Vanuatu had led in recent decades (as opposed to foreign missionaries). For the urban and rural charismatic Christian settings, I approached the 'New Covenant Church' in the capital, Port Vila, and on the island of Tongoa, in central Vanuatu, where the church was founded by an ex-Presbyterian evangelist during a charismatic revival in 1978. This self-described 'indigenous' church has been so shaped by prophetic visions that it is unrecognizable from the Presbyterian church. For the contrasting rural site, I visited the kastom[2] villages of Randoa and Bunlap in South Pentecost (north-central Vanuatu). By '*kastom*' (Bislama[3]: from 'custom') villages, I refer to rural populations that have resisted the establishment of Christian churches, and consciously maintained spiritual beliefs and practices they consider indigenous and associate with an ancestral way of life (Jolly 1994; Lane 1965). The majority have no formal education. That is not to say they represent a 'pre-Christian' society: they articulate their contemporary practices with and against those of Christians, and many rituals have changed, been discontinued, or revived. For the comparative urban population, I was based at the Presbyterian Church of Vanuatu (PCV), the main church in Port Vila. PCV is the largest and oldest denomination in the archipelago, independent since 1948. Owing to space limitations, I will discuss this church only briefly.

So what could constitute a 'local theory of mind', given these diverse settings? I have focused on common tendencies or similarities that appear across different contemporary Vanuatu locations. This is not to suggest that Vanuatu is homogeneous, or that different forms of Christianity, education, and political economic change have not had a profound influence on people's sense of self and morality, or their spiritual beliefs and practices. Rather, I aim to construct a kind of 'frame' or 'deep picture', in Charles Taylor's (2007: 549, 557) terms, within which people develop modes of thought and experiences, comparable to the 'immanent frame' Taylor posits for the modern North Atlantic. Taylor's approach is useful in discussing 'local theory of mind' because he attempts to construct for a particular 'epistemology': 'an underlying picture which is only partly consciously entertained, but which controls the way people think, argue, infer, make sense of things' (2007: 557). For Taylor, a deep picture underlies, or supports, a range of more specific 'pictures', including different predispositions or 'spin' towards 'openness' or 'closure', that structure how people view the world,

Journal of the Royal Anthropological Institute (N.S.), 114-130
© Royal Anthropological Institute 2020

and make sense of themselves and their subjective experiences in different social contexts.

Taylor (2007: 3) sought to explain why it is that in some social milieus, what it means to believe in God (or spiritual entities) corresponds to different understandings of mind and self, and how this affects the 'conditions of experience'. He asked why in the modern North Atlantic 'believing' has become a matter of deliberation, and a more difficult undertaking. Taylor (2007: 363, 553) connects this to specific historical processes of 'disenchantment' in the region over the last five hundred years, including the rise of Reformed Christianity, in which more people began to dismiss ideas about magic and spirits, and the development of 'closed world structures', in which the world was seen as ordered by impersonal, natural laws. In the process, he suggests (2007: 27, 33-6), more people came to see moral order as originating in the self, or mind. Thoughts, feelings, and intentions were imagined as confined to individual human minds, conceived of as bounded inward spaces sharply separated from bodies, other persons, and the 'outer' world. This mind-centric 'buffered self' developed new forms of interiorization: more attention to, and description of, phenomena in mental and emotional terms. The 'immanent frame' does not entail a singular secular sceptical 'West': the rise of charismatic Christianity – with its emphasis on being 'spirit-filled' – can be seen as a modern instance of (re-)enchantment (Meyer 2012: 109; Taylor 2007: 552).

Across my diverse fieldsites, Ni-Vanuatu described their world in ways that resonate with what Taylor (2007: 30-6, 553) calls an 'enchanted' world: one animated by spirits (good and bad) and moral forces, and in which meaning is often independent of the thinking subject, or self. Taylor suggests that the enchanted world creates the conditions for a 'porous' self in which there is no clear boundary between self and other, or mind and world. Meaning and moral purpose can be found not only in human minds, but also in the physical and spiritual world beyond, and this melding of mind and world corresponds to the way the self and mind are imagined as porous to spiritual influence, good and bad.

In evoking 'theory of mind' in the context of spiritual experience, I examine not only the ways people draw inferences about, and share intentionality with, fellow humans, but also the ways they impute 'intention' (encompassing capacities such as thinking, judging, and creativity) beyond the human. In the first half of this essay, I focus on how, across diverse settings in Vanuatu, people tended to describe much mental and emotional phenomena in embodied terms, elaborate on material – rather than immaterial – aspects of social relatedness, and found moral purpose and meaning in the physical world, and the actions of nonhumans. This is congruent with Melanesian philosophies (e.g. Nanau 2017; Sanga 2017) that see the mind as intimately intertwined with body and spirit, social relationships, and place, landscape, and environment.

I then turn to the implications of these insights for the central question of the Mind and Spirit project: how this 'local theory of mind' relates to spiritual experience. I ask why Ni-Vanuatu more often reported spiritual experiences with vivid multisensory and palpable dimensions than in some other settings, especially Shanghai and California (Ng and Brahinsky, this volume). Then I argue that the interpretation of perception as experience of something 'out there' or as inner mental phenomena may involve different modes of informed guesswork or abductive reasoning about subjective experience, which may accord with particular cultural and historical suppositions about the self, others, and the world.

Journal of the Royal Anthropological Institute (N.S.), 114-130
© Royal Anthropological Institute 2020

Embodied and extended minds

In recent decades, phenomenologically inclined philosophers, psychologists, and neuroscientists have argued that mind is fundamentally embodied (Clark 2010) and extended (Clark & Chalmers 1998), that cognition is distributed between people (Hutchins 1995), and that meaning can be seen as embedded in the world (Haugeland 1993). These 'situated' theories of cognition are quite different from Western secular folk models, which often describe the mind as a domain of interiority more sharply separated from the body and the world (Luhrmann *et al.* 2011). 'Situated' theories may offer grounds for anthropologists to re-theorize ethnographic phenomena in the light of scientific insights into human cognition. In any event, these new approaches seem more open than the secular folk theory to accommodate the distinctive ways in which my Ni-Vanuatu interlocutors described knowledge, meaning, and intention as embodied, socially embedded, and extended into the world. I will describe the Ni-Vanuatu approach before speculating about what this might tell us about the cultural dimensions of spiritual experience, and cognition more generally.

Body and spirit

People across Vanuatu often discuss cognition and emotion in bodily terms. In the languages of north-central Vanuatu (where my fieldsites are located) – such as Sa, in South Pentecost – strong cognitive operations, feelings, and desires are often located in the 'insides' (north-central Vanuatu: *lo-*), or internal organs such as the gut (François 2013; Ross, Pawley & Osmond 2016). Worrying ('thinking too much') and unreleased negative emotions, such as anger, were often said to cause sickness. This bodily language for interiority could also imply a degree of unknowability or opacity of others' mental and emotional states, as concealed within. However, rather than encouraging an inward focus in dealing with emotion, people would emphasize the importance of an outward-facing social orientation. Interviewees frequently commented that if anger could not be 'forgotten', it should be resolved in a collective meeting presided over by a chief, and a material exchange would help restore social harmony.

The embodied notion of 'mind' or 'thinking' is dependent on but distinct from the 'soul' or human 'spirit', which can separate from the body. As is common around the world, in the north-central Vanuatu languages the spirit or soul is often referred to by a word that also refers to 'shadow' or 'reflection' (Codrington 1891: 252; Lane 1965 on South Pentecost). This human spirit-double can detach from the body and travel around, not only when one is close to death, but also in altered states of consciousness. These journeys can be a source of knowledge and spiritual revelation. Body and spirit are thus integral to thinking, knowing, and feeling.

Across Melanesia, embodied experience is also a means of sensing the spiritual, or making predictions (Nanau 2017: 183; Sanga 2017: 106). The full range of sensory capacities are understood as instruments of attaining knowledge through revelation: 'seeing', 'hearing', 'smelling', and 'feeling' what might be otherwise hidden (see also Gegeo & Watson-Gegeo 2001: 63). Sensations, including palpitations, sweating, dizziness, or goosebumps, may indicate the presence of a malevolent being, such as a sorcerer or a spirit.

Christians and *kastom* adherents alike discussed deriving knowledge through interpreting signs in the body (compare Ng, this volume, on Henan province): sensations on the left-hand side of the body usually portend a bad omen, whereas sensations on the right indicate good news. Most of my interviewees from the South

Pentecost *kastom* communities claimed they could make more specific inferences through patterned bodily sensations: they would feel twitches or spasms in certain body parts that would foretell a particular social event. The location of these twitches indexed a characteristic of the inferred subject. Telkon,[4] a young man from Randoa, told me that a twitch in his hand foretold an infant's death; the location in the hand signified parents holding a babe-in-arms. Others said certain sensations could reveal that a particular relative would visit, for example. This suggests that people often understand themselves to predict others' actions and social outcomes through embodied experience, rather than purely 'mental' inference.

Substantial connections

What anthropologists call 'opacity of mind' presents an apparent paradox for a study of an Oceanic society. On one hand, anthropologists have noted that the attribution of intentions, desires, and other mental and emotional states to others is avoided, or not a major concern for people across the Pacific. For instance, Fajans (1987) argued that the Baining appeared little concerned with questions of others' intentions and emotions (see also Lillard 1998: 13; Strathern 1988: 117). On the other hand, despite a lack of emphasis on others' mental states, anthropologists of Melanesia have long observed Melanesians to be intensely relational and socially orientated.

'Opacity statements' in which people deny they can know the intentions or interiority of others are widespread in the literature on Oceania. In Papua New Guinea, Robbins (in Robbins & Rumsey 2008) found that Urapmin refrained from speculating about the thoughts and intentions of others. However, there is some debate about whether these injunctions are ideological, or whether they reflect accrued psychological differences (Bloch 2013: 121; Keane 2015). My own experience is that Ni-Vanuatu are well able to infer others' intentions and emotional states: I have always found people highly intuitive and empathic. The 'opacity doctrine' seems less pronounced in Vanuatu than is reported elsewhere in the Pacific: I heard people talk about the plans and intentions of others. However, they may experience, or at least describe, intersubjective inferences in less 'mind-centric' ways than North Americans, for instance.

The apparent contradiction between intense sociability and the apparent reluctance to infer mental states can be better understood if, like Bloch (2013: 14-16), we can choose to see the inference of people's mental states (psychological ToM) as just one of the ways in which people everywhere understand themselves to share intentionality and knowledge, and experience themselves as 'going in and out of each other's bodies' (Bloch 2013). People everywhere are faced with the problem of where the self ends and others begin (Stephen 2009: 98),[5] but in kinship-ordered societies like those of Vanuatu, the emphasis on consubstantiality may give people a 'more specific and elaborate awareness of the lack of boundary between individuals' (Bloch 2013: 16).

Ni-Vanuatu do not necessarily emphasize mental inference when assessing others' intentions and predicting social action. Rather than view mind-to-mind inferences as the basis and precondition for sociability, they see interconnectedness as prior. People tend to address everyone by kin terms, which are typically expressed in the form of inalienable possession in Vanuatu languages, like body parts. They often elaborate on the consubstantial and material aspects of relatedness, rather than mental states, when discussing kinship and social relations (also Lambek & Strathern 1998: 18).[6] This emphasis on flows of substance inspired Strathern (1988) to theorize Melanesian personhood as 'dividual' in that people know themselves as composed of relations, in contrast with the 'individual' as self-proprietor that underlies much Western social theory. While she acknowledged that Melanesians often saw intentions and the 'mind' as hidden, she argued Melanesians 'make visible' their intentions in the context of their social relationships through concrete actions like work, or exchanges, motivated by the regard of others (1988: 164, 272). Material exchange objects circulate as external 'equivalents' to flows of substance (1988: 208).

Such is the porosity between kin that people concern themselves to differentiate and mediate relations with certain kin through material exchanges, as well as modes of avoidance and respect (Wagner 1977). In *kastom* South Pentecost, the debts incurred by the transmission of blood and breast milk from the mother precipitate a cycle of exchanges to the mother's family (see also Jolly 2001). People also make payments called *solsol* temat[7] to their mother's agnates following a death, otherwise the spirits of that *buluim* (kin group) may attack them. Likewise, when a baby is born, payments to the mother's family will prevent harm to him or her. As in many patrilineal communities in northern Vanuatu (Patterson 2001), and elsewhere in Melanesia (Wagner 1967), one's mother's agnates hold a spiritual influence over one's well-being, and people maintain respectful distance through ritual exchanges and avoidance behaviours.

Avoidance does not indicate an absence or weakness of social relatedness. Rather, it expresses and modulates the intensity of bodily connectedness and spiritual influence. Avoidance and mediation may be important factors in why people accentuate shared substance through exchange, while de-emphasizing mental inference.[8] In my rural interviews, I asked people about the possibility and propriety of inferring another's mental state. Whilst I heard very few 'opacity statements' declaring an inability to know another's 'insides' that are prevalent elsewhere in Oceania (Robbins & Rumsey 2008), people were more likely to say that it was improper to make mental inferences about those categories of kin with whom one should observe avoidance and respect. This seems consistent with a view of mind as embodied and interior, in a society in which one avoids touching or even referring to body parts, and there are prohibitions on entering private spaces, of kin with whom one should observe avoidance.

Prohibitions and proscriptions (Bislama: *tabu*) also reveal the intensity of relatedness and consubstantiality by showing how private behaviours are thought to directly affect others' bodily and spiritual states. In South Pentecost, a father avoids certain foods and sexual intercourse to ensure a son's healing after a circumcision ritual (*taltabwean*) (Jolly 2001: 184). And families observe mourning practices, like abstaining from cleaning, to anchor the spirit of a relative in the village for twenty days. *Tabu* like these are essential to regulating proper relations between people, and between people and spirits.

In all the churches in which I interviewed, congregants also expressed a sense of interconnection and mutuality with fellow Christians. Oneness rather than difference was emphasized in the church context: church members speak of themselves as united in one body, and address each other as brothers and sisters. They often prayed for unity of heart and mind, and in New Covenant, there was a strong sense that if some in the group were not submitting fully, the whole church could not progress spiritually. Many Christians described receiving messages and prophecies to share with others. This sense of unity and kinship was often expressed in bodily terms. Some New Covenant members claimed to feel in their body when others fell ill or were in pain. Often, congregants spoke of feeling in their heart the needs or desires of a fellow church member, and felt compelled to meet those desires with gifts. In both *kastom* and Christian contexts, then, people claim capacities to sense others' thoughts, feelings, and desires over distances not so much through 'mind reading' as through outward signs and embodied sensations.

Papua New Guinean theologian Joshua Daimoi suggests that rather than the implicit individualism of the Cartesian assertion, 'I think therefore I am', a Melanesian philosophy would begin with the premise, '"I am" because "they are"' (2001: 11).[9] He argues that the Melanesian universe is socially and spiritually ordered. Across all four sites, my Ni-Vanuatu interlocutors described making moral, social, and spiritual inferences and predictions through attention to bodily states, behaviours of others (including animals and spirit-beings), and events in the physical world. This contrasts with the North Atlantic 'immanent frame' that Taylor (2007: 558) describes, in which knowledge of self is considered prior to that of others, and ideas about the 'transcendent' must be weakly or tentatively positioned at the far end of a long chain of inferences.

Extended mind: intention and meaning in the world

Far from indicating a lack of orientation towards social relatedness, the Melanesian de-emphasis on mental inference appears to be reinforced by a heightened relational and spiritual sensibility. Solomon Island scholar Kabini Sanga describes the 'indigenous Mala'ita philosophical mind' and self that underpins their social world. In a traditional genre, Sanga depicts a world-view that is subjective, contextual, and laden with values and emotions. The physical and the metaphysical are intertwined: 'To ascertain reality you'd ask: What is this thing? Is it social? Is it psychological? Is it spiritual? . . . You understand your world as relational and spiritual' (Sanga 2017: 105).

In Vanuatu, events that would be defined as solely 'natural' or 'physical' in a scientific world-view operate with intent or moral purpose. Ill health or misfortunes may be interpreted as God or ancestral spirits intervening in social affairs. When I interviewed a Presbyterian deacon from Lamen Island, the location of my doctoral fieldwork, I asked her some questions about some of my observations from that time. When a coconut tree fell on an older woman, some people on Lamen suggested ancestral spirits caused it to fall because she was angry at her son's choice of partner. What did the deacon think? She nodded: 'We believe our ancestors are still around, or those that died before us stay to help us. If something happened that tied you with another family, and you had done wrong, you would see – something could happen to you'. She added that a close family member could suffer the consequences instead, adding, 'We on the island would say . . . these signs appear clearly in front of your eyes so you can see – like if something broke or fell down . . . that you should desist. You should not do that'.

Ni-Vanuatu could be described as 'hyperhermeneutic' (Keane 2015: 84-5): they view the world as imbued with intention, symbolic meaning, and ethical import. People identify material 'signs' (*saen* in Bislama) in the surrounding environment. It is common to see animal behaviours as conveying meanings or foretelling socially significant events, such as a pregnancy, a death, or an accident. In interpreting such events, people typically refer to socially agreed interpretations. Some signs were widespread across Vanuatu, others were local. In all my interview locations, people said that a native kingfisher (Bislama: *nasiko*) would foretell important news, typically a death. In South Pentecost *kastom*, sacred snakes (Sa: *taltil loas*) were seen as 'persons' or spirits who could bring messages to their human counterparts. During the time I was lodging with Telkon and his family, such a snake appeared beside the house. Telkon took it as a message that the kitchen – which had been in disrepair since a cyclone – should be mended. While Ni-Vanuatu refer to socially recognized conventions when interpreting 'signs', they

Journal of the Royal Anthropological Institute (N.S.), 114-130
© Royal Anthropological Institute 2020

are not 'symbols' in the sense of arbitrary mental representations, but index spiritual agency, or aspects of a hidden reality (Kripal 2014: 267). Next, I discuss the way Ni-Vanuatu often attribute knowledge, meaning, and inspiration to spiritual inspiration or influence, rather than seeing them as products of a bounded mind, unconnected to the external world.

Empowered imagination and porous minds

So far, I have argued that Ni-Vanuatu inhabit a relational world imbued with spiritual and moral intention. As Taylor (2007: 33) argued, the idea that meaning is immanent in the external world tends to require a conception of self and mind as porous, or permeable to spiritual insight and influence. In this section, I discuss Ni-Vanuatu porosity of mind in terms of an openness to spiritual influence as a source of not only knowledge and creativity, but also vulnerability to sorcery and spiritual attack.

Spiritual revelation and the empowered imagination

In Vanuatu, as elsewhere in Melanesia, spiritual experiences such as dreams and visions may be 'means of exploration, of knowledge and of creation, which give access to a convincing aspect of reality, that is as objective and valid as that provided by other human methods of knowing' (Métais in Clifford 1992: 179). Dreams are frequently a source of knowledge and inspiration, and a means of foretelling the future and averting danger. In the *kastom* villages of South Pentecost, dreams were a potential channel for communication with ancestral spirits, sometimes accompanied by the travel of one's own spirit. Telkon's younger brother, Wari, told me that in a dream his spirit had travelled with an ancestral spirit, which had revealed an *ôt loas* (Sa: restricted/sacred ancestral site [Garde 2015: 141]). The interpretation of dreams as emanating from ancestors can be understood as part of a wider recognition of interconnection and dependence on social others, including spirits (Bloch 2013: 13).

Creative inspiration is often seen as derived not from individual ingenuity, but from spiritual inspiration. Telkon's father, Ruben, was a carver. He told me he received the designs for some carved masks, called *cubuan*, through dreams, which he felt did not come from himself. He later confirmed his sense of spiritual revelation when a European collector showed him photographs of *cubuan* masks in museums resembling the ones he was inspired to carve. Ruben was also a song composer, and rather than seeing his creative process as emanating from within, he said that songs were revealed to him by 'good' spirits (*armat en tô*), often as he was walking along the road, cooking, or performing everyday activities. Ruben explained; 'The spirit comes and gives it to me . . . If it was just in my mind, I couldn't compose it'.

The Christians I interviewed also cultivated openness to spiritual revelation, although more typically from God, Jesus, angels, and the Holy Spirit. The New Covenant congregants in particular described their church as 'born of visions'. Its founder recorded a series of profound visions, through which he was guided in every aspect of the new church, from its structure, to the 'uniforms', the style of music, and leadership styles. He described ten 'raptures' in which his spirit had left his body and travelled, with Jesus or angels revealing aspects of the new church, including the location for the revival. The motto of the church is 'Let the Holy Spirit Guide You', and this emphasis on revelation and guidance through the Holy Spirit was evident at every church gathering. Services were punctuated by people leaping up to the front to share messages and 'inspiration' to their fellow congregants. 'Prophets' would describe dreams and visions. Gifted 'text

Journal of the Royal Anthropological Institute (N.S.), 114-130
© Royal Anthropological Institute 2020

receivers' shared Bible verses. Leaders shared words of 'inspiration': teachings that came to them spontaneously from the Holy Spirit. Others were spiritually guided to lead the congregation in a particular song. Their songs not only sounded heavenly: they were 'received' from the Holy Spirit, or angels, transcribed, and shared by people with this special gift.

Despite the differences in geographical origins, in exposure to education and to religious teachings, there were clear resonances between *kastom* and New Covenant interviewees in terms of epistemological emphasis on spiritual revelation, including in dreams and visions, song receiving, and healing and divination (as I will describe). This openness to spiritual revelation was recognized and appreciated by an early Presbyterian missionary on the southernmost island, Aneityum:

> The Aneityumese recognise the inspiration of the poet; not the inspiration of genius, as accepted by a sceptical or a secular philosophy, but a personal inspiration, a natmas, a personal spirit, distinct from the man's own soul, speaking through the lips of the poet. It is really the Scriptural idea of inspiration. (Inglis 1887: 151).

The distinction the missionary Inglis makes between the biblical interpretation of 'inspiration' as God-given, vis-à-vis the secular sceptic's understanding of inspiration or creativity as self-generated, exemplifies the way the origins of creativity and knowledge may be inferred differently by a porous as compared to a buffered self. This resonance may have become even more pronounced with the expansion of charismatic churches like New Covenant that emphasize gifts of the spirit.

I term the propensity to view some mental or bodily states as spiritually derived sources of revelation, and to interpret physical events as 'signs', the 'empowered imagination'. Rather than a secular post-Cartesian understanding of '(mere) imagination' as a self-generated product of the mind, often connoting fantasy or the 'unreal' (Graeber 2007: 10; Luhrmann *et al.* 2011: 6), the 'empowered imagination' is the capacity to be taken out of oneself, or brought into relationship with other forms of being as a source of knowledge, inspiration, and meaning (Kripal 2014: 245, Taylor 2007: 8). The empowered imagination implies a lack of strong boundaries between mind, or self, and those of (often spiritual) others, and with the wider world. However, the porosity and permeability of self to spiritual influence can also be destructive: Christian and *kastom* interviewees alike described vulnerability to a range of nefarious spirits and sorcery.

Vulnerability

The Ni-Vanuatu emphasis on consubstantiality between people and on the permeability or openness of mind and body to spirit has a dark side: it opens up the person to spiritual attacks, and to sorcery (Biersack 2017). In *kastom* South Pentecost, even 'good spirits' (*armat en tô*), if angered, can pose a danger. Over breakfast, Telkon told me about a disturbing dream he had the previous night. He dreamt an old man had his hands around his baby daughter's neck, and said, 'If you're thinking of leaving, I'm taking her'. The young baby's eyes were rolling back in her head. Telkon replied, 'No, I'm not going!' and the old man said, 'I can see in your body[10] that you will go'. Telkon had been threatening to take the family to Vila because of a local argument, and interpreted the dream as a spirit telling him not to leave. He worried that the dream was a bad omen for his family: even if the dream 'passed over' his daughter, something could happen to one of his brothers' children. So he fetched a leaf to 'block' the dream, and decided to remain in the village.

In addition to 'good spirits', there were more unambiguously malevolent spirit-beings (*armat en sanga*, literally 'bad spirits', and *ôrka*) that inhabited areas beyond village limits. These creatures could transform their face or body into those of relatives to trick people, and could cause madness. Young infants were especially vulnerable. When I accompanied Telkon and his wife the first time he took his baby daughter to see his parents-in-law in another village, the couple picked special leaves to ward off attack from *ôrka* and *armat en sanga*. They rubbed some on their young children's faces and held some like a bouquet in front of the infant.[11]

To counter such threats, people in South Pentecost deploy 'security' and 'protection' for the village by 'blocking' paths to the village, and guarding doors to dwellings. Regarding the aforementioned spirit-snake, *taltil loas*, Telkon said, it 'is a security in the village and it's protecting us in the village. If the people of Randoa all leave, the snakes will cover the tracks entering into the village so others cannot enter with evil spirits and ruin our houses'. Men could also install spirits to guard the *mal* (Bislama: *nakamal*; men's house) through planting special kinds of wood on either side of the door. However, even such 'protection' could occasionally cause harm. Spirits like these can become *tegar*, meaning they can enter human bodies and cause illness and pain. One day, an old man developed a pain down his left side, and Telkon took one of the *mal* spirit-guards to be behind it. The old man had been walking about in the early morning, when spirits are said to roam around. As the man who had placed the guards, Telkon was responsible for removing the *tegar*. He addressed the spirit while brushing down the old man's left arm: 'Come out, you've made him sore. I'll take you back'. Sometimes *tegar* can make one mad, as when someone fails to meet obligations to their mother's agnates, and the spirits are angered. People were also physically and mentally vulnerable to magic and sorcery. One type of magic, called *temat* in Sa language, caused people to lose motivation and drive. Ruben said *temat* could be used to promote peace in a situation in which people would not let go of their anger: 'When I say *temat*, I give *temat*, it's like a peace talk', he said, 'it can make conflicts subside'. However, it could also be used in a malevolent way: making people's 'thoughts go down' to prevent them from working, or cause their business to fail.

Across Vanuatu, commonly recognized types of sorcery exploit people's mental porosity, targeting their inner self, or interiority (Eriksen & Rio 2017: 203). Some, like *temat*, act on people's motivations, preventing them from completing projects, such as house building. *Su* allows the sorcerer to enter a home undetected, often to steal or rape: it prevents the occupants from waking up. Love or attraction magic, *masing* in Bislama, is used in nefarious ways: for example, by an old or unattractive man to snare a young woman. Similarly, *swit maot* (Bislama: 'sweet mouth') can give the holder beguiling powers of persuasion.

Sorcery attacks in Vanuatu, as elsewhere in Melanesia (Biersack 2017; Munn 1992: 224; Stephen 2009), may be understood as a kind of 'anti-kinship': the negative potential of mutuality, interpenetration, and consubstantiality. Unlike in Ghana (Dulin, this volume), people tend not to fear sorcery from immediate family and in-group members. More often, people point to a distrust of 'strangers', often saying sorcery can be worse in town. Nevertheless, accusations tend to extend to people on the limits of kinship, perhaps affines, or those from other clans, villages, or islands, with whom one lives in contiguous space. Those people who are 'outside' but who can observe your movements or extend substances such as food may present the most danger. This vulnerability may be heightened by a sense of a limit on one's ability to know another's true intentions.[12] When discussing sorcery with a young Presbyterian man, he made a statement that points to a sense of 'opacity' of others' intents in this context: 'Our great-great-grandfathers used to say, "You only see the front, you don't know what is behind". He might come and talk to you, be your friend. But then he may turn his back on you and ruin you'.

Hidden intentions may, however, be revealed in other ways, such as the identification of a sorcerer through dreams. If people are unable to ascertain the cause themselves, they may visit specialists known in Bislama as *kleva* (*loas* in South Pentecost). *Kleva* (from 'clever') are like seers or shamans who may make their spirit-double travel in dreams or visions to gain revelation about a problem, such as suspected sorcery or spiritual attack, or the location of lost objects. The *kleva* can often find the offender and 'block' their action through leaf medicines or other techniques. They can act as healers, particularly for spiritual conditions seen as untreatable by Western medicine. Many Christians visit *kleva*, though churches may insist God and the Holy Spirit should be the main source of healing, security, and salvation. Others use prophets and prayer healers much as they might the *kleva*: to cure illness, 'block' sorcery, exorcize spirits and demons, and find lost objects. When my research assistant was trying to locate her lost iPhone, she visited two prayer healers.

New Covenant has a twenty-four-hour healing centre in its Port Vila headquarters, where church members with a gift for healing pray over patients. Talented healers are said to have 'x-ray' vision, seeing what is going on deep within people's bodies (see Eriksen & Rio 2017: 200). One pastor called the centre a 'hospital of the Holy Spirit', though it deals with a wider range of afflictions than public hospitals. The centre's sign promises to free sufferers from several different kinds of 'cursing' inhibiting their 'physical', 'spiritual', and 'material' well-being. When people become New Covenant members, they go through a stage called 'Breaking of Cursing'. They would spit on an orange thorn, which was then burned, symbolizing the end to the curses. Some of these curses affected whole families, even islands, for generations. In Tongoa, a woman called Meriam told me that when she first joined New Covenant, the Founder revealed that her family were cursed because her grandfather had murdered someone. The curse had affected Meriam's father's brothers, who had 'lost their heads a bit'. It had made Meriam short-tempered until she was baptized, when she felt the curse lift. Although ideas of generational curses are biblical, they seemed reinforced by Ni-Vanuatu emphasis on collective responsibility and mutuality with kin and ancestors.

Christianity did not banish local spirits from existence, although it was partially successful in 'diabolizing' them. Christians often refer to even ancestral spirits as 'devils' and would not usually admit propitiating them or using any magical techniques. However, Christianity may have reinforced existing demonologies as it reconfigured them (Meyer 2012: 88, 96; Rio, MacCarthy & Blanes 2017: 4), even expanding the range of spiritual entities and forces that people contend with. In the New Covenant church, negative emotions and motivations were sometimes seen as originating from outside the person – from a 'spirit of envy', for example. Demons, said to possess people and make them act wickedly or insane, were frequently exorcized at the healing centre. Although demon exorcisms are performed in charismatic denominations globally, arguably they resonate with vernacular practices of removing invasive spirits, such as *tegar* in South Pentecost.

Journal of the Royal Anthropological Institute (N.S.), 114-130
© Royal Anthropological Institute 2020

Captivating pictures and perceptive abductions

This brings me to the main question driving the overall Mind and Spirit project: is there a connection between the 'theory of mind' framework I have presented for Vanuatu and spiritual experience? I want to suggest that distinctly Ni-Vanuatu patterns of empowered imagination and mental porosity are connected to a vivid sense of spiritual presence. The initial data from our interviews suggest that many Ni-Vanuatu interviewees frequently experienced events with a more vivid multi-sensory character, such as external visions, smells, and songs. Urban and rural New Covenant members reported experiencing God as a 'tangible presence' more frequently than other Christian groups in the Mind and Spirit project. Remarkably, every ni-Vanuatu interviewee reported experiences of spiritual presences other than God, such as ancestral spirits, ghosts of relatives, wild spirits, and sorcerers, far more frequently than any other research location.

Interviewees in both the *kastom* villages of South Pentecost and New Covenant church spoke of vivid, tangible encounters with spiritual beings in human form. These accounts had many similarities. In the *kastom* village, Ruben's brother described his encounter on the road with an ancestral spirit-being called Melesia (who features in epic stories, e.g. Jolly 2001: 190); he appeared to be of mixed race, tall with long hair, and was dressed in army gear. They shook hands, and Melesia went on his way. At New Covenant, the founder's daughter, Rebecca, told me how she once met Jesus on the road. He was white, with long hair, wearing sandals and carrying agricultural bags. She shook his hand and felt a rush of wind through her, and instant joy. Rebecca also spoke of encounters with angels, and an apparition of a fellow Christian who was praying for her. The latter was so vivid that she phoned that friend to check if she had visited her home in person. Rebecca was also one of several congregants who reported receiving material gifts (typically foodstuffs) from God.

Why do Ni-Vanuatu describe having more vivid spiritual experiences, and particularly in tangible, material forms? Certainly they are open to, and even *expect*, spiritual experience. Spirits are immanent; they interact with people and intervene in social life. Papua New Guinean philosopher Bernard Narokobi suggested that what some might identify as 'religious experience' is identical with a more foundational Melanesian world-view and cosmology as spiritually ordered: 'I believe an experience, or experience in general, is a total encounter of the living person with the universe that is alive and explosive … An experience for a Melanesian, I believe, is the person's encounter with the spirit, the economics, the politics, and life's total whole' (1977: 7-8). This suggests any experience has spiritual potential.

People across Melanesia tend to experience altered states of consciousness and anomalous events, such as dreams and visions, as more external, sensory, and not-self – not produced from within a bounded mind, a capacity I have termed 'empowered imagination'. To reiterate, the 'empowered imagination' is not experienced as *imaginary*, with the post-Cartesian connotation of unreal and self-generated. Quite the opposite. The 'empowered imagination' can include the propensity to interpret events in the material world as 'signs' conveying meanings and moral purpose, or predicting the future. Subjective experiences, including altered states and events like dreams and visions – particularly those with 'self-alien' (Stephen 1989b: 41) qualities or affordances – are often experienced as having an external reality and meaning, independent of the mind. This can entail modes of thought that Stephen terms the 'autonomous imagination' (1989a: 223; 1989b: 55): the capacity to join inner and outer through harnessing stream-of-imagery thought in ways that bypass ordinary consciousness.

Recent developments in cognitive science that suggest that all perception is a creative fusing of inner and outer can help us make sense of such modes of thought. Cognitive neuroscientist Anil Seth (2017) has explained that perception is a process of inference, or 'informed guesswork', in which sensory signals from the surrounding environment are combined in the brain with prior knowledge and expectations about the world in making predictions about the causes of the signals. For Seth, 'We don't just passively perceive the world. We actively generate it. The world we experience comes as much, if not more, from the inside-out as from the outside-in'. Seth suggests that in terms of perception, there is little to distinguish 'reality' from 'hallucination', except that 'reality' can attain some social agreement. Even our experiences of being a self or having a body can be seen as 'controlled hallucinations'.

The 'informed guesswork' that Seth describes is similar to C.S. Peirce's notion of *abduction*, or abductive reasoning: the generation of explanatory hypotheses, or insights, based on suppositions. Peirce (1997 [1903]: 244) argued that all perception is interpretative, and there is little to separate abductive judgements from judgements about perception in general, except that abductive judgements can be disagreed with. Abductive judgements suggest existing suppositions about 'nature' (Bateson 1979: 142) or how the world is, but are also a means by which people introduce new ideas. Gell (1998: 14-15; cf. Graeber 2015; Taylor 2007: 35) argues that inferences of intention or agency in artwork and religious objects can be understood as abductions, or 'inferential schemes', similar to inferences of others' mental states. Perhaps the inference of intention and meaning in experiences like dreams and visions, or in patterns in the environment, could also be seen as akin to those discussed in psychological ToM. Peirce himself suggested that 'hypnotic phenomena' 'involve the fact that we perceive what we are adjusted for interpreting' (1997 [1903]: 244). This points to the possibility that particular cultural or historical pictures of 'how the world is' (those that obtain some social agreement), and of the mind and self, might 'adjust' or 'nudge' us towards particular interpretations or abductive inferences, including whether particular subjective experiences are products of a bounded mind, or are spiritual in origin.

In Vanuatu, the propensity to infer meaning and intention beyond the mind corresponds to an understanding of self as open to spiritual influence. People often infer outward origins for subjective experiences, independent of their mind or self. In Luhrmann's terms (introduction to this volume), there may be a 'cultural invitation' to experience such events as more sensorially, even materially, present when compared with those with a more buffered, psychologized sense of self, as in Shanghai and California (Ng and Brahinsky, this volume).

Conclusion

In this essay, I have constructed an alternative frame to the 'immanent frame' Taylor describes for the secular North Atlantic, in an attempt to capture a 'sensed context' for distinctly Ni-Vanuatu understandings of mind and self, and experiences. Despite the diversity of Ni-Vanuatu communities in which I conducted this research (including wide variation in the degree of exposure to formal education, different forms of Christianity, capitalism, and urban life), across all sites intention and meaning were not confined to the operations of a bounded mind. Rather, people reported interpreting signs in the body, in altered states of consciousness (such as dreams and visions), and through observations of patterns and events in the surrounding world. They invoked physical and metaphysical ideas of consubstantiality and spiritual influence when discussing kinship and social relations, and making inferences about social action. Physical and environmental events were often laden with moral or spiritual purpose and intention.

I have termed the capacity to infer meaning, intention, and moral purpose in altered states of consciousness, in bodily states, and in world events the 'empowered imagination'. The Ni-Vanuatu propensity to locate meaning and moral purpose as external to the mind corresponds to a 'porous' view of self and mind, opening people up to vivid, intense, and often tangible forms of spiritual encounter. However, the porosity of the mind and self to interpersonal and spiritual influence is double-edged: it can also leave one exposed to spiritual attack, possession, or invasion.

Unlike a Cartesian distrust of the senses and privileging of introspective self-awareness, in Vanuatu, mind may be seen as the more partial, unknowable, and unreliable domain of interiority, while sensory, bodily, and spiritual experiences and events can be a preferred means to accessing hidden knowledge and insight. Indeed, Robert Lane (1965: 251) described the people of South Pentecost as 'empiricists'. Tradition and convention guided interpretation, but did not supersede judgements of sensory experience.

A 'picture' can 'hold us captive'. Quoting from Wittgenstein, this is how Taylor (2007: 557) communicates the difficulty of imagining the world in another way, or making sense of others' beliefs and experiences, adding that this can cause particular problems for the 'ethnologist'. Although I was raised in a charismatic church in Scotland that actively cultivated bodily and emotional experiences in lively worship sessions (like those described by Brahinsky for northern California), I also recognize much of my 'background' is captured in Taylor's 'immanent frame'. I was ever doubtful about the existence of God, and the efficacy of prayer. While some congregants seemed more certain than I did, to 'believe' and 'have faith' was still presented much more as a matter of individual deliberation, and persistent effort, than it appeared in Vanuatu. A prayer group I attended at age 12 taught us to dial back the self and focus on hearing from God, hold fleeting and faint images or words that entered our minds, then ask 'Could this be from God?' Vivid encounters with the divine, like those I had read about in Bible stories or historical pilgrimage sites, seemed beyond reach. Ghosts and magic were (most likely) the stuff of 'fairy tales'.

Any 'picture' offers only a partial perspective. The alternative picture I have sketched here is intended not as a representation of an actually-existing singular 'Vanuatu', but as my attempt to grasp the 'sensed context of [spiritual] experience' underlying my interlocutors' accounts. Over the years I have spent in Vanuatu, I have been struck by how people describe vivid encounters with spiritual beings, not just in church but as they go about their everyday activities. Across all my interviews, nobody told me they doubted the existence of spiritual entities, and everyone reported at least one sensory spiritual experience.

Our limitations in grasping others' perspectives pertain not only across cultures, but also between people. Perhaps 'opacity statements' that deny the possibility of knowing the intentions or interiority of others are an acknowledgement of a difficulty we all face. What psychological ToM points to, I suggest, is that we all rely on a lot of 'informed guesswork', or abductive reasoning, to make inferences about and participate in social worlds, share experience, and co-ordinate action with others, even if this process is only partly conscious. While psychologizing secular theories explain this ability in 'mind-centric' ways, others may focus more on embodied, material, and spiritual aspects of shared experience. At the deepest level, we all 'abduct' the ways we perceive the world, and we all take part in constructing the pictures that appear to captivate us.

NOTES

A relational and intersubjective theory of mind points to how knowledge and thinking is never the product or property of one mind, but is always shared. Many thanks to my Ni-Vanuatu interlocutors and research assistants, all the collaborators on the Mind and Spirit project, to Courtney Handman, and to two anonymous reviewers for sharing the knowledge and insights that inspired this essay.

[1] This paragraph is based on a description drafted collectively by the Mind and Spirit team and used to illustrate the joint nature of the research.

[2] *Kastom* (from 'custom') glosses a range of practices and knowledge deemed 'indigenous' or 'customary', as opposed to knowledge, practices, and goods seen as coming from 'outside'. (Underlining here indicates a Bislama term: see the following note.)

[3] Bislama is Vanuatu's lingua franca. Although much of the lexicon is derived from standard English, its grammar differs significantly. Bislama terms are italicized, underlined, and translated in the text.

[4] Personal names of Ni-Vanuatu interlocutors are given as pseudonyms.

[5] Everywhere can be found aspects of individuality and dividuality, which may be emphasized in different contexts (e.g. Lambek & Strathern 1998: 12; Sanga 2017: 106).

[6] This is an idea partially developed in personal conversation with Joel Robbins.

[7] Words in Sa (the language of South Pentecost) are given in italics.

[8] See Robbins (2017: 472) on how the Urapmin, with their strong 'opacity doctrine', are also concerned to differentiate relations through material exchanges.

[9] See Birhane (2017) for a comparable argument from a cognitive science perspective, drawing on African philosophies.

[10] In Bislama, Telkon used the phrase *hat* ('heart'), but for the Sa version, he said *tarben* ('body'). This may imply people in South Pentecost explicitly infer people's mental/emotional states from exterior signs, such as posture, face, countenance, rather than claiming to 'mind-read' directly. Telkon's wife added that you cannot see inside one's body, but you can tell if someone feels bad from their posture, walk, and so on.

[11] Another vulnerability of infants when travelling is soul-loss; the parents had to remember to call their daughter's name each time we moved on from a rest stop, otherwise her soul might remain behind, causing the baby to cry. Telkon's brother, Wari, later told me babies can see spirits more easily, and this also makes them cry.

[12] If anything, emphasizing the ways humans can act to deceive and mislead others indicates an acute awareness of 'theory of mind': that is, that people not only maintain false beliefs, but also cultivate them in others to their own ends (cf. Bloch 2013: 125)

REFERENCES

BATESON, G. 1979. *Mind and nature: a necessary unity*. New York: E.P. Dutton.
BIERSACK, A. 2017. Afterword: From witchcraft to the Pentecostal-witchcraft nexus. In *Pentecostalism and witchcraft: spiritual warfare in Africa and Melanesia* (eds) K. Rio, M. MacCarthy & R. Blanes, 293-305. London: Palgrave Macmillan.
BIRHANE, A. 2017. Descartes was wrong: 'a person is a person through other persons'. *Aeon* (available online: *https://aeon.co/ideas/descartes-was-wrong-a-person-is-a-person-through-other-persons*, accessed 17 January 2020).
BLOCH, M. 2013. *In and out of each other's bodies: theory of mind, evolution, truth, and the nature of the social*. New York: Routledge.
CLARK, A. 2010. *Supersizing the mind: embodiment, action, and cognitive extension*. Oxford: University Press.
——— & D. CHALMERS 1998. The extended mind. *Analysis* **58**, 7-19.
CLIFFORD, J. 1992. *Person and myth: Maurice Leenhardt in the Melanesian world*. Durham, N.C.: Duke University Press.
CODRINGTON, R.H. 1891. *The Melanesians*. Oxford: Clarendon Press.
DAIMOI, J. 2001. Understanding Melanesians. *Melanesian Journal of Theology* **17**: 2, 6-22.
ERIKSEN, A. & K. RIO 2017. Demons, devils, and witches in Pentecostal Port Vila. In *Pentecostalism and witchcraft: spiritual warfare in Africa and Melanesia* (eds) K. Rio, M. MacCarthy & R. Blanes, 189-210. London: Palgrave Macmillan.

FAJANS, J. 1987. The person in social context: the social character of Baining 'psychology'. In *Person, self, and experience: exploring Pacific ethnopsychologies* (eds) G.M. White & J. Kirkpatrick, 367-97. Berkeley: University of California Press.

FRANÇOIS, A. 2013. Shadows of bygone lives: the histories of spiritual words in northern Vanuatu. In *Lexical and structural etymology: beyond word histories* (ed.) R. Mailhammer, 185-244. Berlin: Walter de Gruyter.

GARDE, M. 2015. 'Stories of long ago' and the forces of modernity in South Pentecost. In *Narrative practices and identity constructions in the Pacific Islands* (ed.) F. Gounder, 133-52. Amsterdam: John Benjamins.

GEGEO, D.W. & K. WATSON-GEGEO 2001. 'How we know': Kwara'ae rural villagers doing indigenous epistemology. *The Contemporary Pacific* **13**, 55-88.

GELL, A. 1998. *Art and agency: an anthropological theory.* Oxford: Clarendon Press.

GRAEBER, D. 2007. Revolutions in reverse. Chicago: Anarchist Library (available on-line: *http://library.uniteddiversity.coop/More_Books_and_Reports/The_Anarchist_Library/David_Graeber__Revolution_in_Reverse_a4.pdf,* accessed 17 January 2020).

——— 2015. Foreword. In *The chimera principle: an anthropology of memory and imagination,* C. Severi (trans. J. Lloyd), xi-xxiii. Chicago: Hau Books.

HAUGELAND, J. 1993. Mind embodied and embedded. In *Mind and Cognition: 1993 International Symposium* (eds) Y.-H. Houng & J. Ho, 233-67. Taipei: Academica Sinica.

HUTCHINS, E. 1995. *Cognition in the wild.* Cambridge, Mass.: MIT Press.

INGLIS, J. 1887. *In the New Hebrides: reminiscences of missionary life and work, especially on the island of Aneityum, from 1850 till 1877.* London: T. Nelson & Sons.

JOLLY, M. 1994. *Women of the place: kastom, colonialism and gender in Vanuatu.* Reading: Harwood Academic.

——— 2001. Damming the rivers of milk? Fertility, sexuality, and modernity in Melanesia and Amazonia. In *Gender in Amazonia and Melanesia: an exploration of the comparative method* (eds) T. Gregor & D. Tuzin, 175-206. Berkeley: University of California Press.

KEANE, W. 2015. *Ethical life: its natural and social histories.* Princeton: University Press.

KRIPAL, J.J. 2014. *Comparing religions: coming to terms.* Hoboken, N.J.: Wiley.

LAMBEK, M. & A. STRATHERN 1998. *Bodies and persons: comparative perspectives from Africa and Melanesia.* Cambridge: University Press.

LANE, R.B. 1965. The Melanesians of South Pentecost, New Hebrides. In *Gods, ghosts and men in Melanesia: some religions of Australian New Guinea and the New Hebrides* (eds) P. Lawrence & M.J. Meggitt, 250-79. Melbourne: Oxford University Press.

LILLARD, A.S. 1998. Ethnopsychologies: cultural variations in theory of mind. *Psychological Bulletin* **123**, 3-33.

LUHRMANN, T.M., R. ASTUTI, J. ROBBINS, *et al.* 2011. Towards an anthropological theory of mind. Position papers from the Lemelson Conference [includes introduction, individual essay and edited collection]. *Journal of the Finnish Anthropological Association* **36**: 4, 5-69.

MEYER, B. 2012. Religious and secular, 'spiritual' and 'physical' in Ghana. In *What matters? Ethnographies of value in a not so secular age* (eds) C. Bender & A. Taves, 86-118. New York: Columbia University Press.

MUNN, N.D. 1992. *The fame of Gawa: a symbolic study of value transformation in a Massim (Papua New Guinea) society.* Durham, N.C.: Duke University Press.

NANAU, G. 2017. '*Na Vanuagu*': epistemology and personhood in Tathimboko, Guadalcanal. In *The relational self: decolonising personhood in the Pacific* (eds) U. Vaai & U. Nabobo-Baba, 177-201. Suva: USP Press & PTC.

NAROKOBI, B. 1977. What is religious experience for a Melanesian? In *Christ in Melanesia, Point* **1**, 7-12. Goroka: Melanesian Institute for Pastoral and Socioeconomic Service.

PATTERSON, M. 2001. Breaking the stones: ritual, gender and modernity in North Ambrym, Vanuatu. *Anthropological Forum* **11**, 39-54.

PEIRCE, C.S. 1997 [1903]. *Pragmatism as a principle and method of right thinking.* New York: SUNY Press.

RIO, K., M. MACCARTHY & R. BLANES 2017. Introduction to Pentecostal witchcraft and spiritual politics in Africa and Melanesia. In *Pentecostalism and witchcraft: spiritual warfare in Africa and Melanesia* (eds) K. Rio, M. MacCarthy & R. Blanes, 1-36. London: Palgrave Macmillan.

ROBBINS, J. 2017. Keeping God's distance: sacrifice, possession, and the problem of religious mediation. *American Ethnologist* **44**, 464-75.

——— & A. RUMSEY 2008. Introduction: Cultural and linguistic anthropology and the opacity of other minds. *Anthropological Quarterly* **81**, 407-20.

ROSS, M., A. PAWLEY & M. OSMOND 2016. *The lexicon of Proto-Oceanic: people: body and mind,* vol. **5**. Canberra: Asia-Pacific Linguistics.

SANGA, K. 2017. *Keleirurufia*: lamenting the indigenous Mala'ita philosophical mind. In *The relational self: decolonizing personhood in the Pacific* (eds) U. Vaai & U. Nabobo-Baba, 103-8. Suva: USP Press & PTC.

SETH, A.K. 2017. How does consciousness happen?' TEDBlog, 26 April (available online: *https://blog.ted.com/how-does-consciousness-happen-anil-seth-speaks-at-ted2017/*, accessed 17 January 2020).

STEPHEN, M. 1989*a*. Constructing sacred worlds and autonomous imagining in New Guinea. In *The religious imagination in New Guinea* (eds) M. Stephen & G. Herdt, 211-36. New Brunswick, N.J.: Rutgers University Press.

——— 1989*b*. Self, the sacred other and autonomous imagination. In *The religious imagination in New Guinea* (eds) M. Stephen & G. Herdt, 41-64. New Brunswick, N.J.: Rutgers University Press.

——— 2009. The Mekeo 'man of sorrow': sorcery and the individuation of the self. *American Ethnologist* **23**, 83-101.

STRATHERN, M. 1988. *The gender of the gift: problems with women and problems with society in Melanesia.* Berkeley: University of California Press.

TAYLOR, C. 2007. *A secular age.* Cambridge, Mass.: Belknap Press of Harvard University Press.

WAGNER, R. 1967. *The curse of Souw: principles of Daribi clan definition and alliance in New Guinea.* Chicago: University Press.

——— 1977. Analogic kinship. *American Ethnologist* **4**, 623-42.

Imagination agissante et vulnérabilité mentale : théorie locale de l'esprit et expérience spirituelle au Vanuatu

Résumé

En psychologie du développement, la « théorie de l'esprit » décrit la manière dont les enfants développent la capacité de deviner les croyances, désirs et intentions des autres. Les anthropologues ont repris cette notion pour explorer la manière dont les différences culturelles de représentation des croyances, des désirs et des intentions affectent la vie quotidienne. En Océanie, ils ont remarqué que la déduction des intentions de l'autre ne jouait pas un rôle privilégié dans les interactions sociales. Au Vanuatu, ce sont souvent les aspects matériels des liens, plutôt que les aspects immatériels, qui sont développés. La connaissance, la créativité, la signification et l'intention n'y sont pas confinées à un domaine mental ou intérieur délimité mais peuvent être découvertes à travers le corps et, plus largement, dans le monde. L'autrice avance que cette propension à situer la signification et le but moral à l'extérieur de l'esprit correspond à une vision « poreuse » de soi-même et de l'esprit, ce qui peut ouvrir à des rencontres spirituelles vivaces, intenses et souvent tangibles.

7

What anthropologists can learn from psychologists, and the other way around

KARA WEISMAN & T.M. LUHRMANN *Stanford University*

The Mind and Spirit project uses methods from anthropology and psychology to explore the way understandings of what English-speakers call 'the mind' may shape the kinds of events people experience and deem 'spiritual'. In this piece, we step back to reflect on this interdisciplinary approach. We observe that, in some ways, both fields are in parallel states of critical self-reflection around explanation and comparison: anthropology in the wake of the postmodern and postcolonial critique; and psychology in response to a pair of recent crises about the overreliance on Western samples and the reproducibility of psychological research. We suggest that combining our methods may go some way towards giving each field more confidence in its research. Joint fieldwork with specific point-by-point comparison is not common in either anthropology or psychology. We found it fruitful and commend it to others.

The Mind and Spirit project is a comparative, interdisciplinary project based at Stanford University, funded by the Templeton Foundation, and led by T.M. Luhrmann (PI). The project draws on the expertise of anthropologists, psychologists, historians, and philosophers to explore whether different understandings of 'mind', broadly construed, might shape the ways that people attend to and interpret experiences they deem 'spiritual' or 'supernatural'. We took a mixed-method, multi-phase approach, combining participant observation, long-form semi-structured interviews, quantitative surveys among the general population and local undergraduates, and psychological experiments with children and adults. We worked in five different countries: China, Ghana, Thailand, the United States, and Vanuatu, with some additional work in the Ecuadorian Amazon. In each country, we included a focus on a charismatic evangelical Christian church in an urban centre, with additional work in a rural church, and in another religious setting of local importance (in both urban and rural locations).[1]

The other essays included in this special issue have focused primarily on ethnographic observations from individual fieldsites (Aulino, Brahinsky, Dulin, Dzokoto, Ng, Smith) and on qualitative comparisons that inform our current sense of what we've learned from the project (Luhrmann). We consider this the initial 'anthropological' take on the

Mind and Spirit project. Future essays will, in turn, introduce the more 'psychological' side of the project, reporting the results of (ongoing) quantitative and experimental work that serves to test the hypotheses emerging from our ethnographic observations.

In our day-to-day work on the project, however, there was not such a stark divide between the anthropological and the psychological; both perspectives informed all aspects of our research from the beginning. The influence of psychology can be felt in the ethnographic observations that are the focus of this volume, much as the influence of anthropology will be felt in our experimental reports. In this essay, we – the project's resident psychologist and chief data analyst (Weisman) and the principal investigator and senior anthropologist (Luhrmann) – turn our attention to the way the team borrowed from each of our respective fields over the course of our long collaboration. We think of each field as working with a *mindset*: a mode of asking and answering questions; a way of thinking about how to plan and conduct research, and identify and interpret evidence. Along with a mindset go a set of methods developed to achieve these goals. We've learned a lot from the way that our respective fields think about what counts as evidence, and about how to collect evidence to answer our questions.

This is hardly the first time that anthropologists and psychologists have collaborated (see, e.g. Astuti & Harris 2008; Astuti, Solomon & Carey 2004; Duncan, Huston & Weisner 2008; Minow, Shweder & Markus 2008; Norenzayan *et al.* 2016; among many others); there are even subfields built out of the commitment to joint exploration (psychological anthropology and cultural psychology). There are some psychologists (like Cristine Legare and Suzanne Gaskins, both involved in the Mind and Spirit project) with extensive experience in anthropological methods and some anthropologists (like Rita Astuti and Pascal Boyer) with extensive experience in psychological methods. Yet systematic collaboration on so large a scale as the Mind and Spirit project is still relatively rare. Most anthropologists still work as lone wolf researchers. In our view, more of us should seek out such opportunities – not only because such collaborations are fascinating, but also because psychology and anthropology are unusually complementary. Both fields are acutely aware of how difficult it is to study and theorize about our fellow humans ethically, responsibly, and carefully, but anthropologists and psychologists have historically chosen to address these challenges quite differently. We suggest that incorporating mindsets and methods from each field can speak to the pressing challenges of the other. Because this journal has a largely anthropological readership, we write here with an eye towards anthropological concerns.

Current challenges in anthropology

Anthropology's most intensive period of self-reflection began several decades ago. At the heart of the postmodern and postcolonial critique lay guilt about replicating colonial dynamics in scholarly practice (see the useful history in Schnegg 2014). Michel Foucault began to dominate the discipline. Scholars shied away from subjecting other people – usually, poorer people with less power – to what they began to see as reductive categories that stripped away their subjectivity. They grew uncomfortable with the idea that friends they made in the field were also data (Behar 1996). They wrote critiques about writing and observing as forms of control (Clifford & Marcus 1986), and they experimented with different forms of representation (e.g. Lavie 1990). They shifted their attention – in Joel Robbins's (2013) striking characterization – from the 'savage subject' to the 'suffering subject'. They began to think of anthropology not so much as a field about explaining difference but more as a means to witness the injustices inflicted by some societies on others. George Marcus and Michael Fischer's *Anthropology as cultural critique* became a disciplinary bestseller.

The field has learned a great deal from these critiques. Anthropologists have grown acutely conscious of the power asymmetry between the one who conducts the research and the one about whom the research is conducted. They have sought out ways to collaborate with their research participants, from co-authoring to creating a form of fieldwork now known as 'participatory', in which researchers work as partners with local participants on problems of direct interest to them (Jessee, Collum & Gragg 2015; Ross, Sherman, Snodgrass, Delcore & Sherman 2011). Anthropologists have grown more sophisticated about the politics of representation and more sensitive to the risks of latent racism and sexism. They have grown far more conscious of the researcher's unconscious bias.

And yet these new sensitivities have come at some cost. In particular, anthropologists have become hesitant to explain causally and to compare directly (Borofsky 2019a). They rarely compare groups of people or particular cultural contexts explicitly, because they are so aware of the many ways comparison can go astray: for example, by treating one group (often White Americans or Europeans) as the norm or standard from which the 'other' might vary; or by imposing the categories of one context (often an American or European context) onto the behaviours and experiences of another context. Even in subfields like medical anthropology, where anthropologists sometimes collaborate with medical scientists, direct comparison across groups of people is not the norm.

As a result, these days in the corridors of anthropology departments one can hear rumblings about the field's refusal to ask big, broad questions, like why Europe was so successful in acquiring wealth and power (Diamond 1997), or what social forces equalize income inequality across time and space (Scheidel 2017). In a recent paper, a group of young anthropologists writes, 'Of all the social and historical sciences, anthropology is perhaps that which is most formally aligned with the very idea of the comparative ... Yet in practice, social and cultural anthropology may be one of the least comparative disciplines' (Miller *et al.* 2019: 284). 'Where have all the comparisons gone?' bemoans Robert Borofsky (2019b). Another senior scholar, Marshall Sahlins, goes so far as to suggest that anthropologists have given up the attempt to *explain* the differences they observe:

> The large increase in the number of North American anthropologists since the 1950s has been matched by their interest in increasingly varied and arcane cultural singularities ... the gourmandization of hummus in Israel, the biopolitics of the US war on fat, pyramid schemes in postsocialist Albania, spatiality in Brazilian hip-hop and community radio, the occupy movement in Žižek's hometown, and new uses of the honeybee (2013: xi-xii).

'Where did anthropology go?' asks Maurice Bloch (2005). There are, he writes, no shared questions, and anthropology graduate students have learned that the very effort to generalize is wrong: that is, that they should not offer general explanations of anything. Roy D'Andrade (1995) argued that anthropology had come to this point because the postmodern critique led anthropologists towards moral stances – witnessing, giving testimony to pain. Debate disappeared because everyone agreed in the moral stakes; as D'Andrade would say, everyone thinks that oppression is bad.

Such claims, of course, are not wholly fair. The paper on the Occupy movement in Žižek's home town, which Sahlins presents as evidence of contemporary anthropology's interest in the particular rather than the general, was really trying to compare two

Journal of the Royal Anthropological Institute (N.S.), 131-147
© Royal Anthropological Institute 2020

models of activist democracy in order to consider the way politics might be reimagined. One could make similar points about the other papers he mentions. And yet many anthropologists might agree that the discipline has been cautious about explanation and comparison for decades.

Some trends in contemporary anthropology even explicitly reject explanation as a kind of epistemic violence. The leader of the recent 'ontological turn', Eduardo Viveiros de Castro, argues that the very attempt to explain what people mean in terms that are different from theirs is a kind of ethnocentric imperialism:

> The most Kantian of disciplines, anthropology, is practiced as if its paramount task were to explain how it comes to know (to represent) its object – an object also defined as knowledge (or representation). Is it possible to know it? Is it decent to know it? Do we really know it, or do we see it (and ourselves) through a glass, darkly? There is no way out of this maze of mirrors, mire of guilt. Reification or fetishism is our major care and scare: we began by accusing savages of confusing representations with reality; now we accuse ourselves (or, rather, our colleagues) (2004: 483-4).

The ethnography at issue in this quotation is one in which people make apparently incredible claims: for example, that a child looks at what seems to be her human mother, sees a jaguar's tail between that human's legs, screams, and then sees the jaguar (which no longer looks like her mother) bound away into the forest (Vilaça 2005). Viveiros de Castro seems to insist that the claim (the jaguar shape-shifted into a human) should be taken at face value (jaguars are able to make themselves appear to be human) and the attempt to explain it in any other way is morally wrong.

Patricia Greenfield, a partial insider trained as both anthropologist and psychologist, published an essay in 2000 that described what she saw as anthropology's 'breast-beating and self-flagellation' (2000: 564). Looking at the discipline's reaction first to Clifford Geertz's (1973) interpretivism and then to the postmodern critique that followed, she saw a field struggling with sharp critiques that objectivity is impossible, that cultures aren't unitary wholes and so cannot be studied as such, and that observation is always political. She suggested that psychology may have been less daunted by the postmodern critiques of the period because psychologists specified their methods so explicitly and were so clear that their claims were always inferences from limited evidence – and so the acknowledgement of bias was built into the structure of the research.

We think that Greenfield has a point. On the Mind and Spirit project, we found that when we adopted a more psychological mindset, focusing in on specific findings produced by methods we knew to be limited, it became easier for us to see how much anthropological methods could accomplish despite their limitations – and that this was liberating both for the psychologists and for the anthropologists in the group.

These observations may be timely. In anthropology there are stirrings now towards a new comparativism. There has been great excitement about Philippe Descola's (2013) comparison of the way social worlds imagine the relations of humans to the natural world. Peter van der Veer (2016) published his Lewis Henry Morgan lectures on the value of comparison in anthropology. Matei Candea has produced a text entitled *Comparison in anthropology: the impossible method* which lays out challenges and offers solutions. Candea writes: 'A new wind of epistemological confidence is blowing through the discipline, and comparison is explicitly reclaimed and brandished as the distinctive anthropological method' (2018: 1-2). These efforts are indeed chastened by what Sylvia Yanagisako – in her own essay on the importance of comparison – calls 'the recognition that contemporary local communities, ethnic groups, religions and what we once called "culture areas" are not autonomous, self-regulating, self-reproducing or self-developing systems' (2007: 1). This new comparativism avoids claims about the way one geographical area or type of person differs from another in general, but instead focuses on claims about the way specific phenomena – the imagined relationship between human and nonhuman animals, panic disorder, psychosis – differ in different communities, and why. This may enable us to move beyond the limitations of the cautious consensus of recent years without repeating the mistakes of the past.

Here we explain what we found useful from each other's fields, and how our process became (to borrow Lévi-Strauss's pleasing phrase) good to think with.

The psychologist's focus on specific findings

Psychologists conduct experiments. They make a single intervention – they pass out a survey, they tell people a story, they ask them to select one out of four pens – and from the participant's response, they draw a conclusion. Compared to anthropologists, they work with a very small amount of evidence. This has led the field to pay close attention to the specifics of what a researcher did and what happened, and to hone in with great scepticism on the relationships between the limited data and the inferences drawn by the researcher. This is the psychological mindset we found useful in our work on the Mind and Spirit project.

For example, professional talks in psychology departments often focus on just a few experiments. This gives the audience a very clear topic: what did the speaker find out, and are their conclusions reasonable? Perhaps there is a talk in which a speaker presents the results of an experiment suggesting that reading fiction (Phenomenon A) causes greater donations to charity (Phenomenon B) by virtue of putting readers in a more empathetic frame of mind (Mechanism C). An audience of psychologists would likely respond to that talk with attempts to counter the speaker's argument by explicitly proposing 'alternative explanations' for the observations presented. For instance: 'What if it only looks like A causes B because of some additional variable D that you didn't manipulate or measure?'; 'You claim your experiment manipulated Phenomenon A, but you also manipulated Phenomenon E, which could affect B for a totally different reason that's unrelated to A'; 'You claim to be measuring Mechanism C, but I don't think that you did'. The specificity cuts the claim down to size. The question becomes: from these specific observations, what kind of inference makes sense? What is the boldest claim we can make with the data, given how small a slice of the world it really is? In some ideal form (though perhaps not in practice), a psychological experiment produces one clear, single finding – and the job of the scholar is to figure out what it means.

With this comes an expectation that the logic of a psychological explanation and the nature of psychological evidence should be exquisitely clear. Rita Astuti (pers. comm., January 2016) remembers her own surprise when she began reading psychological studies about the young child's developing understanding of biological inheritance. There was an initial paper that presented a claim and the evidence to support it; and then another that questioned the interpretation of the evidence and presented a new experimental design, producing new evidence that supported a slightly revised claim; and then yet another paper. Astuti remembers that she laid them out one after another in her living room, and that she felt she had never seen anything so structured and cumulative in the recent anthropological scholarship she had read in graduate school. Her own work has since become a paradigmatic example of clarity for anthropologists.

Journal of the Royal Anthropological Institute (N.S.), 131-147
© Royal Anthropological Institute 2020

Anthropologists, of course, are sceptical and concerned with detail, but the ethnographic method produces so many observations (thousands of pages of notes, hundreds of published pages) that it can be hard to know what to scrutinize or even what method was followed. Once there are many ethnographers working in many sites, one can struggle to locate an intellectual footing.

It is hard enough to make sense of a single rich, nuanced fieldsite. To compare across sites without specific points to compare is very difficult. In the back of our minds as we planned our work on the Mind and Spirit project was the glorious failure of *The people of Rimrock* (Vogt & Albert 1966), one of an earlier generation's ambitious comparisons. The project set out to compare 'values' in five local communities around (as it happened) the Vogt family ranch in New Mexico. The book was ethnographically rich. But the research never defined 'value' – it allowed each researcher to define the term as he or she felt best – and it never defined a clear question about what social features might give rise to different values. As a result, the conclusions of the project – the work of many anthropologists over many years – were disappointingly vague. 'Each piece is a gem', the *American Anthropologist* reviewer said with frustration, 'yet the resulting mosaic lacks overall cohesion' (Graves 1967: 751).

In the Mind and Spirit project, the act of focusing in on specific findings produced by methods we knew to be limited helped us to move on from ongoing debates about whether comparison was possible. For instance, as the fieldworkers were in the process of making ethnographic observations and conducting semi-structured interviews, the group began to get the impression that participants in Ghana might have had particularly vivid experiences of God's voice. But the experiences and conversations different fieldworkers were having in their different fieldsites were so rich and nuanced, so attuned to that particular place, that it was difficult to make a direct comparison; indeed, the whole goal of site-by-site comparison seemed dubious. When we added to this mix a specific quantitative finding – that participants in Ghana tended to say 'yes' to more questions about God's voice than participants in other sites – we found ourselves getting down to work. We had focused discussions about how to understand this *particular* observation, taking into account both concerns about the methodology and the possibility of real differences. This focus gave rise to some very structured discussions about different representations of thoughts and their power, which in turn led to a discussion about the ontological anxiety among the US charismatics, and how it stood out against a different way of handling secular scepticism in China, and against the behaviour of the Thai participants who often commented 'it depends' when Felicity Aulino tried to pin them down on what they thought was real.

In the beginning, before the team did fieldwork, we had heated arguments about whether it was possible to compare the way people thought about minds. What, after all, was a 'mind'? But in order to conduct site-by-site comparisons in the style of psychologists, we had to commit to shared questions in the interviews. When results came back, and the fieldworkers reconvened, we had to ask ourselves whether our findings were informative, or just artefacts of the way we asked those questions. These discussions yielded specific critiques and concrete ways to address them, feeding into a virtuous cycle of gathering observations, critiquing methods, forming interpretations, and testing those interpretations. The struggle about whether we could compare became a puzzle about what we had seen.

We have sought to think like sceptical psychologists – descending on a finding like wolves on a carcass (to use a metaphor offered by another team member, Michael

Lifshitz) – in thinking about the central claim we have presented in this volume: that people who conceptualize the mind as more 'porous' tend to have more frequent and more vivid spiritual experiences than people who conceptualize the mind as more 'bounded'. The fact that work in a wide range of fieldsites supports this general interpretation – and the fact that such a diverse group of researchers has come to any consensus about this issue at all – gives us more confidence in the claim.

Still, we continue to challenge ourselves to imagine how our data could be interpreted differently. To give an example: what if it only looks like porosity is related to spiritual experience because social worlds that imagine minds as porous are also social worlds in which people interrupt their sleep more often? Research finds that interrupted sleep leads to more frequent and vivid spiritual experiences; on the boundary between sleep and waking, many people report voices and visions and other remarkable events (Ohayon, Priest, Caulet & Guilleminaut 1996). So we included a sleep questionnaire in our survey packets, and we plan to do more work to disentangle the relationship.

To think of oneself as having *findings to explain* is quite different from setting out to draft the perfect ethnography. Luhrmann remembers her own graduate training, and the burden of the idea that she had to write everything down and put it into one book that would explain everything about those people. It was obviously an impossible task. A finding is a specific observation, made in specific circumstances, which may – or may not – be important, offer insight, be useful. You cannot hold the illusion that you are writing the final word on the subject. Instead, presenting specific findings invites a broader discussion about what sense to make of them. When you have findings, you open a conversation.

Methodological tools for promoting specificity and scepticism
Because experiments are so prima facie limited (a small pool of subjects, a single measurement), psychologists are often acutely aware that their methods (and all methods) are limited. They have developed some principles that can help anthropologists who choose to use psychological methods to use them in a way that increases their confidence in what they find.

Gathering converging evidence. The use of more than one method to answer a question can be a powerful approach because the more kinds of evidence that support the claim, the more confident the researcher can be in this claim. Psychologists call this 'converging evidence': observations collected by different methods that converge on a particular interpretation, each method providing a check on the validity of the others. In the Mind and Spirit project, we interviewed people in depth about their spiritual experience, in part to determine how frequently people in certain settings experienced particular events. The fact that pen-and-paper surveys with large samples of different participants came up with similar rates helps us to feel more confident in the findings from interviews. When results from these different approaches converge, our observations become more believable, both to ourselves and to our audiences in both fields. All methods have flaws. We have found it less anxiety-arousing and more satisfying to have data from multiple methods, each with its own limitations, rather than a single method that would have had to be – but never could have been – perfect (and equally perfect in all fieldsites).

To be clear, anthropologists have used mixed methods throughout the history of the field. Margaret Mead, for example, used a remarkable array: linguistic probes, drawings, experiments with new technologies like photography and film, and so forth. Still, today mixed methods are relatively rare (Hay 2015). A few decades ago, even methods classes were rare in anthropology doctoral programmes. The fieldworker was imagined as a kind of sponge: one became intimately involved in the field and returned to squeeze it all out onto the page. In advocating for gathering converging evidence, then, we are harkening back to this more expansive vision of how anthropologists can learn in the field.

Standard protocols: doing things the same way every time. In a psychological experiment, the gold standard is to write a protocol detailing the experiment from start to finish, such that any researcher faced with any participant would conduct the experiment exactly the same way. This often includes 'scripts' to be memorized by every experimenter involved in the study, which cover how to greet participants, how to describe the purpose of the experiment, how to explain what is expected during the task, and how to answer any questions they might raise. The protocol might specify aspects of the physical set-up of the interaction, such as places where the experiment may or may not be conducted, whether lights should be on or off and doors open or closed, how the experimenter should be positioned relative to the participant, how many inches should separate the participant's face from a computer screen, the precise location and timing of presenting any 'stimuli' to the participant, and so forth.

The goal of such a protocol is to anticipate common 'low-level' alternative explanations for some set of observations and rule these alternatives out in advance. A standard protocol addresses the following realities of human observation and interaction: (1) individual researchers differ (e.g. Researcher A is generally friendlier; Researcher B tends to explain things more clearly); (2) individual participants differ (e.g. Participant A is taller; Participant B is left-handed; Participant C tends to speed through written instructions when bored); and (3) the physical and social context can have large impacts on behaviour (e.g. dark rooms make people sleepy; people pay attention to things that are placed directly in front of them; loud and unpredictable noises are distracting; being treated kindly makes people more co-operative). By specifying in advance an ideal version of how an experiment should unfold, experimenters hope to minimize the chances that these factors will skew the results of the study or obscure interesting findings.

We sought to use standard protocols in many aspects of the Mind and Spirit project. Before fieldworkers left for the field, we discussed in detail how to choose comparable congregations for the charismatic Christian samples. We drew up guidelines to ensure that fieldworkers in different sites would speak to a similar range of interlocutors in each setting within their primary fieldsites (e.g. setting goals for a mix of ages and genders). We spent months developing, refining, translating, and back-translating an extensive protocol for structured interviews, the goal being for each fieldworker to ask each of their interlocutors the same set of questions in the same order, using a similar set of strategies across individuals and across fieldsites to probe interlocutors' understandings of 'the mind' and their spiritual experiences. To the extent that we followed these guidelines and protocols, they are now helping us rule out a variety of alternative explanations for our observations in each fieldsite, as well as the similarities and differences across fieldsites: for example, that differences across sites are reducible to differences in the 'charismatic-ness' of different Christian samples, the age or gender of interlocutors in different sites, variations in the wording of our questions across sites, and so on.

In practice, to do things in the same way in different places sometimes requires the researcher to adapt methods to fit a particular sample – in other words, to institute superficial differences in order to preserve deeper similarities. If, in California, you ask people about a story in which there is a man you call 'John', in Shanghai you should call the man something like 'Xiaofeng'. A vignette that features a child playing with a pretend 'choo choo' won't work in a place without trains. And things can get more complex: how can you ask Buddhists the same questions about religion that you pose to Christians? The introduction recounts some part of our own wrestling with these matters. Our solution has been to use some methods that are strictly standardized and others that are more open-ended. In both cases, we sit with the results and try to work through why they came out as they did.

Fixed orders, counterbalancing, and randomization. Another useful strategy we borrowed from psychology is to structure (some of) our interactions with participants in ways that minimize the risk that the results arise from bias in the method itself. Consider a situation in which a researcher wants to know if people in a particular setting tend to prefer A or B (e.g. do people at this church prefer to pray alone or with others?). A common concern among psychologists about such questions, in which a researcher asks a participant to select one of two options, is that the order of presentation of these options matters. If a researcher presents the question verbally – 'Do you prefer to pray alone or with others?' – interlocutors might be drawn to the second option because of the relative stress put on the first vs second options (try comparing this question to 'Do you prefer to pray with others or alone?'). Likewise, if a researcher presents the question visually – e.g. showing a picture of praying alone on the left, and a picture of praying with others on the right – interlocutors might tend to point to the picture on the side of their dominant hand (which for most will be the picture on their right). And if a researcher asks this question directly after a series of questions about the importance of community, interlocutors might be more inclined to say they prefer praying with others than they would if the question about prayer had come first.

One response to this concern is to accept that the way a question is posed will introduce bias and to ensure that bias is held constant across all participants by asking the question the same way every time. This is often a wise strategy when response options are naturally ordered (e.g. 'yesterday, today, or tomorrow' makes more sense than 'today, tomorrow, or yesterday'), or when a series of questions flows best in a certain order. In the structured interviews, the standard protocols described in the previous section included a single fixed order in which to ask questions, because the group determined that this would make these detailed, wide-ranging conversations easier to compare than if different interlocutors were asked about their experiences in different orders. The order of the questions surely influenced interlocutors' responses. By fixing this order, however, we can be assured that this bias was comparably present in every interview, such that when the interviewer first asked about hearing God's voice (for example), it was in the context of a similar conversation for all interlocutors in all sites.

In other situations, researchers might actively try to mitigate such response biases in advance. In the previous example of asking about prayer preferences, psychologists might 'counterbalance' the order of the response options ('alone' vs 'with others') by deciding to alternate between orders such that every second participant hears the question in the reverse order, or they might 'randomize' the order by flipping a coin to determine which to use for each participant. In the Mind and Spirit project, we randomized the sequence of questions in many of our pen-and-paper surveys; we counterbalanced the order of surveys, experiments, and other tasks in our extended interactions with a single participant; and we alternated genders of characters in the vignettes that participants were asked to reason about or explain (to give just a few examples). These kinds of strategies ensure that roughly equal numbers of participants heard, saw, or otherwise experienced our 'studies' in each of the various ways they could unfold – helping us to feel that anything that we observe in the aggregate may be true above and beyond what happened in a particular interaction.

Stepping back, we found that using these tools associated with the psychological mindset helped us to structure our conversations and feel more confident about our observations.

A parallel set of challenges in psychology

As it happens, these days psychology has its own fraught relationships with comparison and explanation.

Let us turn first to the challenge of comparison. The field of psychology has been built almost exclusively on studies with participants who are Western, educated, industrialized, rich, and democratic ('WEIRD'; Henrich, Heine & Norenzayan 2010; see also Nielsen, Haun, Kärtner & Legare 2017). This has remained true despite incisive critiques stretching back to the 1970s (e.g. Cole & Scribner 1974; Fiske, Kitayama, Markus & Nisbett 1998; Rogoff 2003; Shweder 1995).

It is not surprising that psychologists gravitate towards what the field calls 'convenience samples' (college undergraduates and the adults and children who live near American and European universities, many of them White and middle class). They are indeed physically convenient: close to hand and relatively easy to recruit. They are also convenient in a deeper sense: the researcher and participant speak the same language, and can read each other's gestures and facial expressions; researchers have strong intuitions about what experimental probes will 'work' for these participants, and are sensitive to what questions might seem too strange, academic, or personal. In a word, psychologists, like most other people, are fluent in their own cultures, and utilize this fluency in their research with participants within those cultures.

Make no mistake: cultural fluency has undoubtedly improved the quality of psychological research. Without it, researchers can easily ask participants to complete tasks that to them seem incomprehensible or perverse, such as filling out pen-and-paper surveys when they have never done so, or reasoning about fictional characters in hypothetical scenarios when this kind of speculation is alien, or even discouraged, in their normal social lives (see Cohen 2007; Greenfield 1997a; Heine, Lehman, Peng & Greenholtz 2002). Lacking fluency, researchers can easily misunderstand individual participants' responses to these tasks, or misinterpret general tendencies in their sample of interest – often erring in the direction of interpreting variation from the standard established in prior work as a 'deficit' (see, e.g., Foley 1997).

But psychologists are increasingly concerned about the fact that the majority of researchers and participants in the field are fluent in a single dominant culture: what might be called Euro-American middle-class culture. For most of the history of experimental psychology, it was assumed – and hardly ever even stated – that people in this context are reasonable representatives of 'human nature' more broadly; that the fundamentals of cognition, development, social relationships, and affective experience are universal and can be studied without being situated in a particular social-cultural context; and that whatever varies across cultural contexts is patina, and not an appropriate subject of psychological inquiry. In recent years, more and more psychologists have publicly disputed these assumptions, and have turned to cross-cultural comparison to shed new light on continuity and variability in the human experience. However, such work has been (often justifiably) criticized for being less than rigorous (e.g. because an experimental method ends up seeming more fluent in one cultural context than another) or difficult to interpret (e.g. because researchers lack the cultural expertise to understand the similarities and differences in the responses of different groups of participants).

The second challenge, often referred to by psychologists as 'the reproducibility crisis', has been spurred by the troubling revelation that many of the findings published in top psychology journals have been found not to replicate. That is, researchers who attempt to repeat some previously published study often fail to obtain the published result (according to some estimates, up to half of the time; Open Science Collaboration 2015). The goal of modern psychological science is to push the field's collective understanding closer to something like truth by conducting scientific studies that establish some result and lay the foundation for further studies, in an incremental progression towards an accurate model of the world. The possibility that so many psychological results might not be replicable calls into question how much progress the field has actually made towards this goal.

There have been many suggestions for how to respond to the reproducibility crisis, including identifying and explicitly incentivizing best practices in designing and conducting studies (e.g. through new submission formats and special 'badges' appended to journal articles); making data openly available for external reanalysis and reuse; and adopting better statistical practices (e.g. Frank & Saxe 2012; John, Loewenstein & Prelec 2012; Brandt et al. 2014; Cumming 2014; Munafò et al. 2017; O. Klein et al. 2018; Simmons, Nelson & Simonsohn 2011; Simonsohn 2015; Wagenmakers et al. 2018). Nonetheless, the field still struggles to reconcile the goal of using empirical data to support logical, scientific explanations of human behaviour with the realization that this is a much more difficult and error-prone process than many experimental psychologists once believed.

This is where a close alliance with anthropology may prove helpful.

An anthropological mindset and tools for promoting cultural fluency

Anthropologists spend a long time – months, years – in one or more cultural settings outside their academic institution during their fieldwork. They develop considerable cultural fluency in that other site, and a rich sense of that different social world rooted in such extensive experience that it is unlikely to rest on fluke observations that are wildly unrepresentative or untrue. Just as we believe that anthropologists would benefit from the psychological mindset described above, we also believe that psychologists would benefit from this anthropological mindset focused on understanding meaning through immersion in other social worlds.

Conducting multi-site research as a built-in check on repeatability. In the simplest sense, doing elsewhere the research that one usually does at home can teach one about the limitations of that research. Anyone who has attempted to conduct cross-cultural or otherwise comparative research can attest to how much effort it takes to make sure

Journal of the Royal Anthropological Institute (N.S.), 131-147
© Royal Anthropological Institute 2020

that research is conducted the same way in each site. Preparing to conduct the studies included in the Mind and Spirit project forced us to make any physical materials easy to re-create; to standardize our interview protocols and experimental procedures; and to be explicit about techniques that might typically be passed on by word of mouth (e.g. strategies for recruiting and 'warming up' participants). This provided a built-in check, early on, on which aspects of any given study were easy for a new team to implement from scratch and which might need to be specified in greater detail. Several prominent research groups in psychology have capitalized on this general insight, advocating for studies to be conducted in multiple labs in parallel to assess replicability, estimate effect size, and gauge generalizability (Frank *et al.* 2017; R.A. Klein *et al.* 2014). Conducting a study in multiple fieldsites is much like conducting multiple internal replications of that study, thereby improving its repeatability – the probability that another researcher could conduct the same study at a future date (regardless of its outcome). Doing so in sites outside of the United States and Europe would help to solve the field's overreliance on 'WEIRD' samples.

This, of course, raises the issue of 'cultural fluency', described earlier as one of the problems currently facing psychology; but as we have argued throughout this piece, cultural fluency outside of the United States and Europe is a particular specialty of anthropologists, who are uniquely suited to comparing across cultures carefully, conscientiously, and with meticulous attention to noticing and describing cultural variability with nuance. We recommend that when psychologists work abroad, they work with anthropologists, who can provide the cultural fluency that the project needs.

Including qualitative methods to maximize validity. We believe that psychologists would benefit from incorporating more rigorous qualitative techniques into their research, following in the footsteps of their forebears (e.g. William James and Jean Piaget) and drawing on qualitative research to identify important areas of research, form hypotheses, design 'ecologically valid' studies (i.e. studies that resemble familiar situations from participants' everyday life), and guide the interpretations of results. The advantage of a highly structured method (e.g. a formal survey) is that the intervention is identical everywhere – at least in principle. Its disadvantage, of course, is that, in practice, the intervention may be interpreted quite differently in different contexts. We chose to combine highly structured methods with qualitative methods that more accurately assessed local meaning. (For discussions about the risks of structured methods without qualitative methods, particularly in international settings, see Gaskins *et al.* 2017; Greenfield 1997*b*; Hay 2015; Kline, Shamsudheen & Broesch 2018; Tiokhin, Hackman, Munira, Jesmin & Hruschka 2019).

Psychologists already collect and interpret qualitative data in private (see Gelman 2018 for recent remarks to this effect from a prominent statistician and critic of psychological research); as they push towards openness and honesty in their methods, data, and analyses, they should also include more of the qualitative observations that help them to formulate their studies and interpret their findings. Psychologists might even incorporate more of the modern qualitative methods developed by anthropologists and others to improve how they go about deciding what to study, how to study it, and what to make of the results. In these ways, including qualitative methods in the modern psychology toolkit could help psychologists move towards theories and conclusions that meet increasingly high standards of replicability and rigour.

Working as a team

In November 2018 – a few months after the Mind and Spirit team members had moved on to their next projects and positions – we reconvened for a two-day retreat to reconnect, update each other on ongoing research and writing, and so forth. One afternoon we spent an hour or so mulling over the questions 'What can psychology learn from anthropology?' and 'What can anthropology learn from psychology?' Many of those lessons appear in this essay.

Our discussion also sparked a shared realization that much of what we as a team have taken away from the Mind and Spirit project is neither 'from anthropology' nor 'from psychology', but from the alchemy of combining the two fields. There were many times in this conversation when someone pointed to a habit we had adopted in our weekly conversations, a technique we had used in designing our structured interviews, or a way of describing quantitative results as an example of the influence of one field or the other, just to be rejected by representatives from that field ('That's not psychology – I thought it was anthropology!'; 'I thought *you* were the one who suggested that!').

Of course, there are aspects of this project that we recognize as 'pure' anthropology (e.g. each fieldworker's ethnographic observations of his or her primary fieldsite) or 'pure' psychology (e.g. the administration of pen-and-paper surveys to undergraduates in all sites). As we have argued in this piece and as many others have argued before us, we see value in this use of multiple methods. We would add that an approach that emphasizes *converging* methods hinges on maintaining a certain amount of distance between methods, relying on a division of labour between researchers with different areas of expertise and theoretical bents. The primary thesis of the current essay is that anthropologists and psychologists, in particular, have complementary skillsets that, when used together, can improve our research.

Yet not all of our work on this project has been 'multidisciplinary' in this sense. Some of our primary methods have turned out to be hybrids of anthropological and psychological techniques. For example, the long-form interviews about 'thinking about thinking' and 'spiritual experience' that informed all of the pieces in this special issue were more structured and standardized than most anthropological methods, and more open-ended and less standardized than most psychological methods; they were designed to yield a mix of qualitative and quantitative data. Many of the conversations we have amongst ourselves are conversations that would not occur in any of our home departments. The Mind and Spirit project has yielded methodological and theoretical insights that we anticipate carrying with us well into the future, both in our ongoing collaborations with each other and in our independent projects.

Many of these insights emerged from working as a team. When we state this bluntly, it seems obvious (even saccharine). It is hard, however, to convey how differently the intellectual work proceeds when the work is not done at a single person's desk but instead in an ongoing group debate. We invested a good deal of time in interaction. For months at Stanford we met in twice-weekly meetings in person and over frequent 'salon'-style dinners at Luhrmann's home. When fieldworkers were scattered around the world, we held a weekly video-chat (with some of the team waking up at dawn and others struggling to stay awake past midnight). We hosted workshops with leaders in the fields of anthropology, psychology, religious studies, and philosophy, and went on a week-long retreat together to the Esalen Institute (where we met up with another team with similar interests, led by Jeffrey Kripal). These experiences cemented our professional relationships into deep intellectual collaborations and meaningful personal connections.

This was not the same as a lab meeting or a writing group, where individuals bring their own projects to a larger group to get 'external feedback'. Rather, we made research plans together; tried to explain to each other what we thought we were seeing even as we were still squinting to see it; sorted through our 'data' together; and pondered at length (and not without heated debate) how best to make sense of the meaning of our 'findings'.

Such an extended, intensive collaboration is a transformative process, rendered particularly powerful when it includes members of other disciplines. This is because when people in other fields encounter each other's work, they ask questions so basic that the researcher might not usually consider them: *Does the study measure what it is intended to? Is that question reasonable? How do you know what you have seen?* Of course, such questions can come from within one's own field as well. But it can be even more startling and productive to interact with someone from a discipline that thinks differently about evidence – in which what even counts as evidence is different – and to justify one's questions and research to them.

In our view, this is one of the primary benefits of collaborative, comparative work: each fieldworker's interpretations of observations from his or her primary fieldsite offer a check on the observations and interpretations arising from the other fieldsites, and each researcher's attempts to study a phenomenon using the mindset and methods from his or her primary discipline offer a counterpoint to the studies emerging from the other disciplines. Reports from each fieldsite and data from each method generate alternative explanations for other sites and methods, leading everyone to re-evaluate their assumptions and try out new interpretations of their own observations. This comparative process enables us to refine our descriptions of the nuances of particular places and people, while at the same time identifying points of commonality across cultural contexts and scholarly perspectives – both of which inform our emerging general theory.

Orienting ourselves towards generality and truth

We would like to close by briefly considering the following question: what are we after with our observations, interviews, surveys, and experiments?

For the two authors of this essay, the answer is that we aim to draw conclusions that are both *true* and *general*: 'true' in the sense of describing with some degree of accuracy a real phenomenon in the world; and 'general' in the sense of applying not just to one person, or one small group of people, but to humans. At the same time, we consider these goals to be impossible to achieve – not just difficult, but impossible; and not just impossible for a single project, but impossible for an entire research career, even an entire discipline. After all, human observation is limited, while human experience is infinite. 'True' is a complicated word. The observations we have made in the Mind and Spirit project are descriptions of specific individuals, in specific places and times, observed by a group of researchers using a particular set of mindsets and methods. We think that our observations are accurate – within limits. There are surely aspects of our participants' experiences that we have interpreted incorrectly, or failed to see altogether. Such is the nature of human exchange.

In this sense, our claims about theory of mind and spiritual experience are, in some deep way, untrue. Nonetheless, we intend these claims to be *oriented towards* generality and truth – to point in the direction of underexplored aspects of the reality of human experience. For the two of us, at least, this work has affirmed our commitment to tilting at the windmills of comparison and explanation, in hopes that others will take note, inform us of our errors, and push us to do better.

NOTES

Special thanks to Suzanne Gaskins, Cristine Legare, Michael Lifshitz, Hazel Markus, Nicole Ross-Zehnder, Thomas Weisner, Ciara Wirth, and the rest of the Mind and Spirit team, including the authors of the pieces in this special issue and the research co-ordinators, research assistants, data collectors, translators, and participants in each fieldsite and at our home base at Stanford University. Thanks to Sophie Bridgers, and also to Nick Long and several anonymous reviewers, for comments on earlier versions of this essay. In addition to the John Templeton Foundation, Weisman's participation in this project was supported by the National Science Foundation Graduate Research Fellowship Program under Grant DGE-114747 and by a William R. and Sara Hart Kimball Stanford Graduate Fellowship. This essay reflects joint first authorship.

[1] This paragraph is based on a description drafted collectively by the Mind and Spirit team and used to illustrate the joint nature of the research.

REFERENCES

ASTUTI, R. & P. HARRIS 2008. Understanding mortality and the life of the ancestors in rural Madagascar. *Cognitive Science* **32**, 1-29.
———, G.E.A. SOLOMON & S. CAREY 2004. Constraints on conceptual development: a case study of the acquisition of folkbiological and folksociological knowledge in Madagascar. *Monographs of the Society for Research in Child Development* **69**: 3, 1-135, vii-viii; discussion 136-61.
BEHAR, R. 1996. *The vulnerable observer: anthropology that breaks your heart.* Boston: Beacon.
BLOCH, M. 2005. Essays on cultural transmission *(LSE Monographs on Social Anthropology).* London: Berg.
BOROFSKY, R. 2019a. *An anthropology of anthropology: is it time to shift paradigms?* Kailuha, Hawaii: Center for a Public Anthropology.
——— 2019b. Where have all the comparisons gone? Member Voices, *Fieldsights*, 10 September (available online: *https://culanth.org/fieldsights/series/comparison*, accessed 20 January 2020).
BRANDT, M.J., H. IJZERMAN, A. DIJKSTERHUIS, *et al.* 2014. The replication recipe: what makes for a convincing replication? *Journal of Experimental Social Psychology* **50**, 217-24.
CANDEA, M. 2018. *Comparison in anthropology: the impossible method.* Cambridge: University Press.
CLIFFORD, J. & G.E. MARCUS (eds) 1986. *Writing culture: the poetics and politics of ethnography.* Berkeley: University of California Press.
COHEN, D. 2007. Methods in cultural psychology. In *Handbook of cultural psychology* (eds) S. Kitayama & D. Cohen, 196-236. New York: Guilford.
COLE, M. & S. SCRIBNER 1974. *Culture and thought: a psychological introduction.* Oxford: Wiley.
CUMMING, G. 2014. The new statistics: why and how. *Psychological Science* **25**, 7-29.
D'ANDRADE, R. 1995. *The development of cognitive anthropology.* Cambridge: University Press.
DESCOLA, P. 2013. *Beyond nature and culture* (trans. J. Lloyd). Chicago: University Press.
DIAMOND, J. 1997. *Guns, germs and steel: a short history of everybody for the last 13,000 years.* New York: Norton.
DUNCAN, G., A. HUSTON & T. WEISNER 2008. *Higher ground: new hope for the working poor and their children.* New York: Russell Sage.
FISKE, A.P., S. KITAYAMA, H.R. MARKUS & R.E. NISBETT 1998. The cultural matrix of social psychology. In *Handbook of social psychology* (eds) D.T. Gilbert, S.T. Fiske & G. Lindzey, 915-81 (Fourth edition). New York: McGraw-Hill.
FOLEY, D. 1997. Deficit thinking models based on culture: the anthropological protest. In *The evolution of deficit thinking: educational thought and practice* (ed.) R. Valencia, 113-31. Washington, D.C.: Falmer Press.
FRANK, M.C. & R. SAXE 2012. Teaching replication. *Perspectives on Psychological Science* **7**, 600-4.
———, E. BERGELSON, C. BERGMANN, *et al.* 2017. A collaborative approach to infant research: promoting reproducibility, best practices, and theory-building. *Infancy* **22**, 1-26.
GASKINS, S., M. BEEGHLY, K.A. BARD, A. GERNHARDT, C.H. LIU, D.M. TETI, R.A. THOMPSON, T.S. WEISNER & R.D. YOVSI 2017. Meaning and methods in the study and assessment of attachment. In *The cultural nature of attachment: contextualizing relationships and development* (eds) H. Keller & K.A. Bard, 195-230. Cambridge, Mass.: MIT Press.
GEERTZ, C. 1973. *The interpretation of cultures.* New York: Basic Books.

Gelman, A. 2018. What is the role of qualitative methods in addressing issues of replicability, reproducibility, and rigor? Blog post (available online: *http://Andrewgelman.Com/2018/06/19/Role-Qualitative-Methods-Addressing-Issues-Replicability-Reproducibility-Rigor/*, accessed 20 January 2020).

Graves, T. 1967. *People of Rimrock*, review. *American Anthropologist* **69**, 751-2.

Greenfield, P. 1997a. Culture as process: empirical methods for cultural psychology. In *Handbook of cross-cultural psychology* (eds) J.W. Berry, Y.H. Poortinga & J. Pandey, 301-46 (Second edition). Boston: Allyn & Bacon.

——— 1997b. You can't take it with you. *American Psychologist* **52**, 1115-24.

——— 2000. What psychology can do for anthropology, or why anthropology took postmodernism on the chin. *American Anthropologist* **102**, 564-76.

Hay, M.C. (ed.) 2015. *Methods that matter: integrating mixed methods for more effective social science research.* Chicago: University Press.

Heine, S.J., D.R. Lehman, K. Peng & J. Greenholtz 2002. What's wrong with cross-cultural comparisons of subjective Likert scales? The reference group effect. *Journal of Personality and Social Psychology* **82**, 903-18.

Henrich, J., S.J. Heine & A. Norenzayan 2010. The weirdest people in the world? *Behavioral and Brain Sciences* **33**, 61-83; discussion 83-135.

Jessee, N., K.K. Collum & R.D.S. Gragg 2015. Community-based participatory research: challenging 'lone ethnographer' anthropology in the community and the classroom. *Practicing Anthropology* **37**: 4, 9-13.

John, L.K., G. Loewenstein & D. Prelec 2012. Measuring the prevalence of questionable research practices with incentives for truth telling. *Psychological Science* **23**, 524-32.

Klein, O., T.E. Hardwicke, F. Aust, *et al.* 2018. A practical guide for transparency in psychological science. *Collabra: Psychology* (available online: *https://www.collabra.org/articles/10.1525/collabra.158/*, accessed 20 January 2020).

Klein, R.A., K.A. Ratliff, M. Vianello, *et al.* 2014. Investigating variation in replicability: a 'many labs' replication project. *Social Psychology* **45**, 142-52.

Kline, M.A., R. Shamsudheen & T. Broesch 2018. Variation is the universal: making cultural evolution work in developmental psychology. *Philosophical Transactions of the Royal Society B*, **373**: **1743** (available online: *https://royalsocietypublishing.org/doi/full/10.1098/rstb.2017.0059*, accessed 20 January 2020).

Lavie, S. 1990. *The poetics of military occupation: Mzeina allegories of Bedouin identity under Israeli and Egyptian rule.* Berkeley: University of California Press.

Marcus, G.E. & M.J. Fischer 1986. *Anthropology as cultural critique.* Chicago: University Press.

Miller, D., E. Costa, L. Haapio-Kirk, *et al.* 2019. Contemporary comparative anthropology – the why we post project. *Ethnos* **84**, 283-300.

Minow, H., R. Shweder & H. Markus (eds) 2008. *Just schools: pursuing equality in societies of difference.* New York: Russell Sage.

Munafò, M.R., B.A. Nosek, D.V.M. Bishop, *et al.* 2017. A manifesto for reproducible science. *Nature Human Behaviour* **1**, 1-9.

Nielsen, M., D. Haun, J. Kärtner & C.H. Legare 2017. The persistent sampling bias in developmental psychology: a call to action. *Journal of Experimental Child Psychology* **162**, 31-8.

Norenzayan, A., A.F. Shariff, W.M. Gervais, A. Willard, R. McNamara, E. Slingerland & J. Henrich 2016. Parochial prosocial religions: historical and contemporary evidence for a cultural evolutionary process. *Behavioral and Brain Sciences* **39**, 43-65.

Ohayon, M., R.G. Priest, M. Caulet & C. Guilleminaut 1996. Hypnagogic and hypnapompic hallucinations: pathological phenomena? *British Journal of Psychiatry* **169**, 459-67.

Open Science Collaboration 2015. Estimating the reproducibility of psychological science. *Science* **349**: 6251.

Robbins, J. 2013. Beyond the suffering subject: toward an anthropology of the good. *Journal of the Royal Anthropological Association* (N.S.), **19**, 447-62.

Rogoff, B. 2003. *The cultural nature of human development.* Oxford: University Press.

Ross, A., K.P. Sherman, J. Snodgrass, H.D. Delcore & R. Sherman 2011. *Indigenous people and collaborative stewardship of nature.* Walnut Creek, Calif.: Left Coast Press.

Sahlins, M. 2013. Foreword. In *Beyond nature and cultue*, P. Descola (trans. J. Lloyd), xi-xiv. Chicago: University Press.

Scheidel, W. 2017. *The great leveler: violence and the history of inequality from the Stone Age to the twenty-first century.* Princeton: University Press.

Schnegg, M. 2014. Anthropology and comparison: methodological challenges and tentative solutions. *Zeitschrift für Ethnologie* **139**, 55-72.

Journal of the Royal Anthropological Institute (N.S.), 131-147
© Royal Anthropological Institute 2020

SHWEDER, R. 1995. Cultural psychology – what is it? *The culture and psychology reader* (eds) N.R. Golberger & J.B. Veroff, 41-86. New York: University Press.

SIMMONS, J.P., L.D. NELSON & U. SIMONSOHN 2011. False-positive psychology: undisclosed flexibility in data collection and analysis allows presenting anything as significant. *Psychological Science* **22**, 1359-66.

SIMONSOHN, U. 2015. Small telescopes: detectability and the evaluation of replication results. *Psychological Science* **26**, 559-69.

TIOKHIN, L., J. HACKMAN, S. MUNIRA, K. JESMIN & D. HRUSCHKA 2019. Generalizability is not enough: insights from a cross-cultural study of social discounting. *Royal Society Open Science* **6**: 2 (available online: *https://royalsocietypublishing.org/doi/10.1098/rsos.181386*, accessed 20 January 2020).

VAN DER VEER, P. 2016. *The value of comparison*. Chapel Hill, N.C.: Duke University Press.

VILAÇA, A. 2005. Chronically unstable bodies: reflections on Amazonian corporalities. *Journal of the Royal Anthropological Institute* (N.S.) **2**, 445-64.

VIVEIROS DE CASTRO, E. 2004. Exchanging perspectives: the transformation of objects into subjects in American ontologies. *Common Knowledge* **10**, 463-84.

VOGT, E.Z. & E.A. ALBERT (eds) 1966. *The people of Rimrock*. Cambridge, Mass.: Harvard University Press.

WAGENMAKERS, E.J., M. MARSMAN, T. JAMIL, *et al.* 2018. Bayesian inference for psychology. Part I: Theoretical advantages and practical ramifications. *Psychonomic Bulletin and Review* **25**, 35-57.

YANAGISAKO, S. 2007. Comparative ambivalence. Unpublished typescript.

Ce que les anthropologues peuvent apprendre des psychologues, et réciproquement

Résumé

Le projet « Esprit et Esprit(s) » utilise les méthodes de l'anthropologie et de la psychologie pour explorer la manière dont les acceptions du mot anglais *mind* (esprit) peuvent modeler les types d'événements que l'on peut vivre et qualifier de « spirituels ». Le présent article prend du recul pour réfléchir sur cette rencontre entre les disciplines qui se trouvent toutes deux confrontées à des réflexions critiques sur leurs approches explicatives et comparatives : l'anthropologie dans le sillage de la critique postmoderne et postcoloniale, et la psychologie, suite à des remises en cause récentes de la surreprésentation d'échantillons occidentaux et de la reproductibilité des recherches. Les autrices suggèrent que la combinaison des méthodes pourrait aider à conforter chaque discipline dans la validité de ses recherches. Le travail de terrain conjoint, procédant par des comparaisons spécifiques point par point, n'est habituel ni en anthropologie ni en psychologie. Cette démarche s'est toutefois avérée fructueuse et recommandable.

Thinking about thinking: the mind's porosity and the presence of the gods

T.M. Luhrmann *Stanford University*

The Mind and Spirit project found that the way a social world invites its members to experience thought appears to have consequences. When the boundary between inner awareness and outer world is culturally represented as porous, so that thoughts can be construed to move in and out of the mind as if they had agency and power, people are more likely to describe their experience of invisible others as if those others could be experienced with the senses. They are more likely to say that a god or spirit spoke in a way they could hear with their ears, or that they sensed a presence in the room.

What is thought? Not: what is cognition, what is the neuroscience of consciousness, from which perspective not only trees but also lizards, amoebas, and even rocks can be said to think, but what is thought as a human experience? The answer must include that thought involves a relationship between a felt sense of an inner reality and of an outer one. Consciousness is awareness. Awareness involves one who is aware and something of which one is aware. Thoughts are acts of awareness, although some thoughts may lurk *sub voce* in our consciousness.

The way the thinker understands such awareness has consequences. In our work, we saw that when the boundary between mind and world is represented as porous, so that thoughts can move in and out of the mind as if thought had agency, people are more likely to describe their experience of the invisible as if it were more sensory, more palpable, more there in the world. It is as if thought itself had more heft, so that it could act in the world and be perceived (for invisible others are often known through thoughts and impressions) as more substantial. Cultural differences in the perceiver's understanding of perception appear to shape the nature of sensory experience. These observations arise out of the fieldwork, the interviews, and (although we do not discuss them here) the more structured empirical research. In this concluding discussion, I want to step back to set these observations in a theoretical context and to move towards a social explanation.

Here is William James on what he calls the five characteristics of thought:

1. Every thought tends to be part of personal consciousness.
2. Within each personal consciousness thought is always changing.

Journal of the Royal Anthropological Institute (N.S.), 148-162
© Royal Anthropological Institute 2020

3. Within each personal consciousness thought is sensibly continuous.

4. It always appears to deal with objects independent of itself.

5. It is interested in some parts of these objects to the exclusion of others, and welcomes or rejects – *chooses* from them, in a word – all the while. (1950 [1890]: 225, emphasis in original)

James points out along the way that phrases like 'personal consciousness' are words whose meaning we know until we try to define them – and then they become the most difficult problems in philosophy. Still, it is clear that there is something very basic in the phenomenological difference between the awareness of the thought and the object of the thought, even when thought takes itself as an object. We often characterize that difference as inner and outer, an interior domain of subjective experience and the external world. 'The universal conscious fact is not "feelings and thoughts exist", but "I think" and "I feel"' (James 1950 [1890]: 226).

If the blunt sense of an inner and an outer is human, the way in which inner and outer are imagined is social and particular. Consider two dimensions along which that relationship could be imagined: vulnerability and potency. 'Vulnerability' here is the sense that some thoughts come in to the mind from outside. These thoughts are not generated by the thinker or communicated to the thinker in ordinary ways. When people in a local social world speak of divine inspiration, divination, telepathy, clairvoyance, the ability of one twin to know when the other twin is hurt: in that social world, people accept that for some people, under some circumstances, knowledge enters awareness from the outside in unusual ways. Typically, they assume that there are often constraints about which people are thought to have these capacities, and which thoughts are viable candidates to be understood as thoughts which come from the outside. Not just anyone has those gifts, and nor do they apply to all thoughts. We know of no social world in which people hold that no thoughts are self-generated, or that all thoughts come always from gods or demons.

There are often similar constraints around 'potency', the idea that wishing can have a direct effect on the world. The healer, the shaman, the man of God, the sorcerer, the witch: at the heart of their abilities is often the power of an inner intention to have direct causal impact on an outer world. Again, this potent power is usually limited: it requires special people, special words, special gestures, special tools, special training. At the same time, in many social worlds there also lurks the idea that anyone – if they are angry enough or envious enough – may find that their anger or envy seeps out to poison others even if the angry/envious person never utters a word, and the idea that all minds, if not protected, will be vulnerable.

Our team used the word 'porosity' to describe cultural invitations to imagine minds as vulnerable and thoughts as potent: the sense that the boundary between mind and world is permeable, usually in specific ways. They are invitations around what I have called the conflicting intuitions about our thoughts and feelings: the intuition that our inner experience is entirely our own versus the intuition that some thoughts and feelings come to us directly from the outside; the intuition that thoughts and feelings do not affect the world directly versus the intuition that they do. Most of the time people feel that their thoughts are their own, and that their thoughts cannot leak into the world like a toxic force. But the opposite concepts are not phenomenologically alien. Most of us – perhaps all of us – have had at least a passing sense, at some point in our lives, that we have had a thought we did not generate, or imagined that a wish had an impact on the world. In some social worlds, these intuitions are developed into culturally supported ideas about witches, diviners, prophets, and so forth.

Journal of the Royal Anthropological Institute (N.S.), 148-162
© Royal Anthropological Institute 2020

The term 'porosity' comes from Charles Taylor's characterization of non-secular, non-modern selves: 'A crucial condition [for the modern self] was a new sense of the self and its place in the universe: not open and porous, vulnerable to a world of spirits and powers, but what I want to call "buffered"' (2007: 27). By 'buffered' self, Taylor means a bounded self: a person with a mind imagined not only as an inner, mental space directly separate from an outer world – as if there was a wall between them – but also as the source of fundamental meaning. As he put it, for the modern self: 'My ultimate purposes are those which arise within me, the crucial meaning of things are those defined in my responses to them' (2007: 38). Here is another characterization:

> The rise of the buffered identity has been accompanied by an interiorization: that is, not only the Inner/Outer distinction, that between Mind and World as separate loci, which is central to the buffer itself; [but also] the growth of a rich vocabulary of interiority, an inner realm of thought and feeling to be explored (2007: 539).

For Taylor, the 'porous' self is what the 'buffered' self is not. The porous self has a less developed sense of interiority, of the importance of inner experience for identity, of a boundary between the inside and the outside world.

The essays in this special issue demonstrate that there are many different kinds of porosity. The team writes as if, on the one hand, porosity is on a continuum. There are more and less porous minds, more and less permeable mind-world boundaries. And yet in different settings the fieldworkers also found themselves writing of different ways in which porosity is understood. The porosity imagined in a Thai world is contingent on prior behaviour in a manner quite different from the fear of vulnerability we see in Vanuatu. We found that there are both general characteristics of thoughts that are understood to cross the mind-world boundary, and characteristics that are specific to a local social world. In general, thoughts that are judged more spontaneous are more likely to be attributed to an external source than thoughts associated with effort and deliberation. In a Christian world in which people expect that God will speak back to them, thoughts that pop into the mind suddenly are more likely to be judged as words from God. (I saw this as well in my earlier work with evangelical Christians; Luhrmann 2012). We believe that we see that anger and envy are more likely to be judged as more potent than other thoughts, at least in most places, and perhaps that thoughts spoken aloud (but not heard by others) may be more potent than thoughts spoken in the mind. Yet there are also many understandings about the nature of these potent, permeating thoughts that are specific to local social worlds.

For example, in Vanuatu, Rachel Smith found that people were invited by their local social worlds to experience certain kinds of thoughts as spiritual revelations about the state of the world, a capacity she calls 'empowered imagination'. That ambiguous boundary between inner thought and outer world also made them susceptible to more nefarious influences. Her participants often denied that ordinary people could use their thoughts to affect the world directly, but they deeply feared the sorcery of others. (They also often denied the existence of witchcraft or sorcery in their own village, but said that it existed in others.) They feared that they themselves were vulnerable to others who might instil thoughts and emotions in them that were not their own – that they could be made to fall in love, or lose their will. The mind itself could be seen as weak, and for Christians, this required surveillance against manipulation. More than other groups, urban Ni-Vanuatu Christians treated fantasy in children and adults as a kind of lie when asked about a child's imaginary friend or an adult who took a bite out of a cookie on Christmas Eve to show their child that Santa had visited the house. 'I will not encourage them to live with lies and pretence', one participant remarked. Asked whether adults should think about things that were impossible, many said that this would be neither right nor important, as if to imagine was a waste of time. 'Because what you see happening now is important, but what you have not seen – don't think too much about it', responded another.

In Ghana, participants seemed intensely worried about the supernaturally potent thoughts of others. Unlike the social world in Vanuatu, these dangerous others – witches – were often close kin, so that danger lurked within intimacy. More so than in Vanuatu, as Vivian Dzokoto shows, the person is imagined as having made a definitive moral choice, so that the mind is either 'bad' or 'good'. She and John Dulin both observe that the difference between inner mental experience and outer material world seemed less salient to their participants. Dulin calls this a 'bundling' of mind and world. His participants often vacillated between describing experience as internally or externally located. Here is an example from an interview done by his Ghanaian research assistant (in Fante):

Participant:	You hear it with your ears.
Interviewer:	In your ears?
Participant:	Yes.
Interviewer:	Okay. So you definitely hear it with your ears.
Participant:	Yes.
Interviewer:	So it's the voice in your head or not.
Participant:	The voice is definitely in my head.

The interviewer then went on to explain how some people hear the voice up close, and some hear from afar, and some people say they hear the voice in their mind. Then the conversation continued:

Participant:	Well, I hear it in my mind.
Interviewer:	You hear it in your mind.
Participant:	Yes.
Interviewer:	Did you hear it with your ears?
Participant:	You hear it with your mind and so you use your mind to ...
Interviewer:	So do you hear it with your ears or not your ears?
Participant:	You hear it with your ears.
Interviewer:	Do you turn your head to see who is speaking?
Participant:	Yes, you can definitely turn to see.

This is someone for whom the mind/world boundary is simply not that meaningful, as it was, for example, among our American participants.

People in the United States spoke and behaved quite differently. There, our Christian participants imagined a bounded mind which cut them off from God. They needed God to 'break through' and show them that he was real. They were deeply worried that perhaps no God was present. (Josh Brahinksy calls this 'ontological anxiety'.) When they answered questions about whether someone's angry feelings could affect someone else's body directly, these Christians first said, almost unthinkingly, that this was impossible. Then, Brahinksy found, after a while it was as if they remembered that they were evangelical Christians and so ought to believe in demons and cursing and the like. In some interviews it seemed hard for them to reason about a mind porous to spirits. That is, they believe that their mind should be vulnerable to demons but continued to describe their mind as if it were not – the kind of reversion from theological correctness to everyday understanding that Barrett and Keil (1996) documented in everyday reasoning about God. They had relatively few sensory experiences of God. When these American participants answered questions about whether children and adults should imagine things that were not real or even possible, it was quite clear that they had no worries that what one imagined could somehow slip out of the mind like a potent force, except in the most indirect way, by inspiring the dreamer to act. Here is one participant:

> I think it is important [to imagine impossible things] because at some point, things stop being impossible. I know I'm focusing more on things on earth than in the greater scheme of things, but if you told someone in the 1800s that we would have boxes with colors that talk to them, they'd look at you as if you were a madman. To think of the impossible is important because that's how it eventually or potentially becomes possible.

These American Christians routinely said that it was a good idea for a father to take a bite out of a cookie his daughter left for Santa:

> Because I think it's fun to dream, just like kids dream. My son's lost a tooth, right? The tooth fairy still exists, we give him a dollar under the pillow. It's exciting, it's fun. And I think adults are the same way.

Another said: 'Because it is fun, because it gives the feeling of magic, that you just don't get too often as an adult'. These are not people who worry that what someone else imagines might be dangerous in and of itself, the way people sometimes did elsewhere.

In China, Emily Ng shows that both porous and more buffered (bounded) orientations can exist among people within the same country. She sees the presence of an imagined psychological mind in urban Shanghai, and observes that it was imported from the West in the nineteenth century and has grown more popular in recent years with the rise of urban psychotherapy. She also saw that in the rural area in which she worked, her participants understood mind differently. Her urban Christian participants experienced themselves as hampered by the mind. The mind lay between them and God. They reported relatively little in the way of sensory experiences of God. Ng's rural Christian participants did not share this hesitation – and their spiritual experiences of God were markedly more sensory. In rural China, God's voice has an immediacy that demands action; in urban Shanghai, humans are often thought to be mistaken in their judgement of God's voice, and the pastor urges caution before they act.

Our Thai participants seemed to imagine what English-speakers call mind quite differently. Felicity Aulino presents the ways mental events are understood to be intimately connected to events in the world, even while her participants idealize a state in which inner awareness is not ruffled, disoriented, or subject to another mind's invasion. Aspiring middle- and upper-class Christians did not aspire to be slain in the spirit or overwhelmed by emotion the way American charismatic evangelical Christians often do. Their goal was to be calm. Aulino described them as holding a 'kaleidoscopic' model of mind. She thought that her participants imagined the domain of mental events as created through multiple interactions which are both morally charged and also shaped by their situational context. She calls this 'constitutive' porosity. Her participants described less external experience of invisible others – and possibly, a less bundled experience of thought and world – than those in Ghana and Vanuatu.

Porosity, then, is both general and particular. We saw that our participants in Ghana and Vanuatu were more likely to commit to the idea that someone's angry thoughts can affect another person's body directly. They developed these ideas in different ways.

Nevertheless, our work found that people who were more likely to assent to porosity – to talk about minds as vulnerable and thoughts as potent – were also more likely to say that they had experienced the presence of invisible gods and spirits in a more sensory way. How might the representation of thought shape the way thought-like events are experienced, thus shaping something as basic as the way people perceive what they take to be real? This raises the question of mechanism and takes us to kindling.

Spiritual kindling

We have been working with the hypothesis that the way people pay attention to thought-like events changes those events; that different cultural models (the local theory of mind) invite people to pay attention to mind and body in different ways, and that these different cultural models are associated with different mental events. A sceptic might say: are you not simply suggesting that the shape of spiritual experience changes in different social settings? And of course we are. But we are also suggesting more: that local culture, as well as individual practice and individual differences, changes the *nature* of experience. It is a complex process because spiritual experiences are varied and because different people have different proclivities and vulnerabilities. Still, we suggest that as people pay attention differently, certain patterns of experience become more habituated and more fluent for members of that social group. I have called this process 'spiritual kindling' (Luhrmann 2020). (In the current work, we see '*cultural* kindling' [cf. Cassaniti & Luhrmann 2014] as the more general process through which cultural models shape subjective experience, and *spiritual* kindling as an account of the cultural shaping of spiritual events.)

The term 'kindling' was first used explicitly to describe epileptic seizure, but psychiatric scientists argue that it captures a pattern observed by the great psychiatrist Emil Kraepelin, who observed that to the extent that actually demoralizing events – a job loss, a break-up, a bad relationship – play a role in a first episode of depression, they play a less important role in later ones (Kendler, Thornton & Gardner 2000). The body's response to the first blow predisposes its response to the second, as if it leaves kindling behind to build another blaze. Over time, the response is habituated. A smaller spark sets the fire burning. Kindling is an act of learning which changes the way the body responds. The premise behind the Mind and Spirit project is that cultural invitations may kindle spiritual experiences.

Why might the mental event identified as God's voice feel more auditory, have more of a hearing quality, in some social worlds than in others? Psychological work on 'reality monitoring' tells us that hearing an audible voice in the absence of a material and sensory cause depends to some extent on judgement – and that judgement changes the event. Suppose some words enter awareness – perhaps, 'slow down'. The research suggests that this is when the subject asks, in a micro-moment of attention, did I generate these words or did they come from somewhere else? Did the words 'slow down' spring from my mind, or were they spoken in the world? This work suggests that what we pay attention to affects our judgement. The more someone recalls a quality of gruffness in the words, the more they are likely to judge – in that micro-moment – that the words were not their own internally generated thought, but an external spoken voice. Those micro-moment judgements – in the mind or in the world, of the self or of another – alter the way the words are remembered and thus how they are experienced phenomenologically: as an auditory voice or as an inner thought (Bentall 2003; Johnson & Raye 1981; see Bilu 2013 for an anthropological example).

Journal of the Royal Anthropological Institute (N.S.), 148-162
© Royal Anthropological Institute 2020

Note that there are two kinds of judgements here: who generated the mental event (me versus not-me) and where it originated (inside versus outside). Mostly, humans experience thoughts as self-generated and located inside, and things other people say to them as non-self-generated and located in the world. In fact, one could say that those differences are what define thought in contrast to the words of other people. Yet people do have experiences that violate these expectations, and it is in the domain of these violations that one finds both faith and madness. An outside, not-me voice spoke to Moses. The outside, not-me voices of madness are often people who talk, whisper, shout around you, but whom you cannot see.

There are also 'not-me inside' thoughts – events experienced as not one's own but originating inside the mind. The symptoms of psychosis include 'thought insertion'; people with psychosis talk of 'inside voices'. Many Christians also say that God speaks 'inside the mind' although they are not mad. When Martin Luther King Jr sat at his kitchen table in the winter of 1956, terrified by the fear of what might happen to him and his family during the Montgomery bus boycott, he heard in his mind the voice of Jesus promising, 'I will be with you'. He went forward. Those with psychosis also report 'me outside' thoughts: their thoughts are broadcast out loud and outside. 'Me outside' experiences are perhaps less common outside of madness, although one could argue that the shamanic experience of the mind leaving the body has some similarities. I do not at all want to suggest here that faith experience is psychotic; the relationship between faith and madness is complex (for a richer discussion, see Luhrmann 2017). The point is that unusual thought-like events occur in both faith and madness. They do so across the globe.

The Mind and Spirit project observes that the boundary between mind and world – the distinction between 'inside' and 'outside – can be understood differently in different social worlds, and we suspect that these differences in cultural representation alter the way ambiguous, unusual thought-like events are interpreted and experienced.

There are two points to make. First, humans have ambiguous, unusual thought-like events which seem to exist in an uncertain domain between mind and world (between me-and-internally-generated, like a thought, and not-me-and-externally-generated, like a god's audible voice). This is an observation about the phenomenological experience of humans in general. For example, many of the American Christians I worked with would describe moments in which they felt they heard God, and say that they felt that God's voice was not in their mind – but also not in the world (Luhrmann 2012). They spoke, in other words, as if they had phenomenological experiences of powerful moments of communication that felt to them to exist in a 'borderland' between what was inside and what was outside. Here are two examples of this uncertainty:

Interviewer: When you heard that, would you describe that as hearing it through your ears? Or was it inside your head?

Participant 1:   That's a good question. It's hard ... it may have been through the ears. You know. It's hard to recall ... It was almost like you're talking. You know, 'cause I had a conversation with it.

. . .

Interviewer: Would you say that that's something that you hear in your mind or do you actually hear it through your ears?

Participant 2:   I think I hear it in my mind. It's hard to differentiate between, because the thing is that I know that I hear it, but it is how I would associate it to actually hearing it in

> comparison to it being in my mind, is that typically I would have directionality. When I physically hear it, I would have directionality. [And he didn't have that sense.]

The speakers are uncertain about whether the phenomenological event came from inside or outside the mind in other social worlds.

In my own work with charismatic evangelical Christians in Accra, Ghana and Chennai, India (Luhrmann 2017) – the pilot work for this larger project – I also saw that people experienced the borderland between mind and world in talking about gods and spirits. Here are some examples:

> *Chennai subject*: It was semi-audible for me. It was more inside, again, but it was – I even looked behind and I knew – I cannot see, I cannot see, and [yet] I know. [Here it is worth noting that people typically do not turn their head unless they feel a sensory quality – what an earlier participant called 'directionality'.]
>
> *Accra participant*: It comes audibly in my mind, and I just hear, 'Who are you serving?' [It is] sort of in between. I haven't heard audibly but in my mind and in between your spirit talks to you. Then you know that at this point it's not your flesh dictating things to you but it's your spirit that is talking to you.

There is likely something very basic, very human about the experience of (some) phenomenological events that are neither 'inside' nor 'outside' the mind.

At the same time (and this is the second point), there is also something deeply cultural about the way that the inbetween is understood. This is an observation about cultural ideas which shape this common human experience of the borderland of the mind. My American Christian participants very clearly held in their mind a cultural model of a sharp distinction between mind and world. They readily understood questions about inside the mind versus outside the mind, and they volunteered comments that suggested that the idea of a boundary was highly salient. This is what Josh Brahinksy also found with his American participants who talked about 'the wall' and the need for God to 'break through'.

My participants in Accra and Chennai did not share this cultural model of a sharp boundary between mind and world. Those in Chennai seemed to use what Jean Briggs (1998) called a 'covert category' to describe the borderland itself – by which I mean that they kept referring to something like a borderland as 'spirit sense', even though not all of them used the category nor referred to it quite in that way. The clearest example came through a quotation I used in the introduction, from Pastor J.:

> *Tanya*: Did you hear [the voice of God] with your ears? Or – ?
>
> *Pastor J.*: Yes. Yes. With my ears.
>
> *Tanya*: Oh. Audibly.
>
> *Pastor J.*: Audibly, I heard [God speak]. I heard this question: 'Do you want to be in a job, working for a company? Or do you want to be my servant feeding my sheep? Or do you want to be a pastor working with the church?'
>
> *Tanya*: That's amazing. So did you like turn your head to look to see who was speaking? Or did you know it was God?
>
> *Pastor J.*: No. No. No. What I mean by audible is not a sound that is coming from outside. I could clearly *know in my spirit sense* this question coming through my mind – that I'm hearing a clear stated question that's coming to my mind.

Other Chennai participants also talked about sensing things 'in my spirit sense' or about an experience 'wide awake inside of me strong'. They had more articulated language than the Americans to refer to that borderland domain between mind and world.

Journal of the Royal Anthropological Institute (N.S.), 148-162
© Royal Anthropological Institute 2020

In Accra, it seemed that my participants just were not interested in the mind/world distinction and almost defaulted to a sense that when God spoke they ought to be hearing him with their ears. This is the quotation in which this sensibility is most clear:

Interviewer: Have you ever heard God speak in a way that you can hear with your ears?

Participant: Yes. Many times it's his word confirmed to me. Hear somebody say the word in my ears.

Interviewer: Okay. So they weren't actually speaking, but you heard it with your ears? And is it like a sentence?

Participant: Sometimes a whole verse of scripture. And the very last one that I heard was, 'Casting thy imaginations on every thought that rises up against the word of God'.

Interviewer: How commonly does it feel like that's almost auditory? Or actually auditory? So you hear it with your ears?

Participant: As soon as I'm conscious of it – [her hands sweep out from her head and down, away from her body]

Interviewer: It stops?

Participant: As soon as I'm conscious. When I'm conscious that I am hearing God speak, I hear it.

Interviewer: Oh [reinterpreting the gesture] then it pops out and becomes more auditory?

Participant: Yes.

Many participants in Accra spoke as if there was a kind of continuum between mind and world, and as if one's sense of how audible the words were had more to do with who was generating them (you or God) than with how they sounded. At the same time, they resisted the idea that God spoke audibly whenever they experienced his voice. Many spoke of hearing God speak in their minds. Those who did hear God speak audibly did not do so frequently. Like the Americans, they could remember only a handful of experiences. But in Accra people reported an auditory quality to God's voice more often than did those in Chennai, and those in Chennai did so more often than those in the United States – and from the follow-up questions, it seems that there were phenomenological differences here.

In short, from my own work in the United States, in Chennai, and in Accra, I would say that the experience of God is kindled differently in these different places. In the United States, God's voice was predominantly kindled as an internal experience; hearing God speak out loud was often tagged as 'crazy', even though God did sometimes speak audibly and people were moved by that experience. In Chennai, the kindling of God's voice included the borderland, and in Accra, the kindling of God's voice seemed readily to include a felt auditory quality. In each setting, God was still understood to speak more often in the mind than in the world, but people's phenomenological expectations of God's voice were more constrained to the interior in the United States than in either Chennai or Accra – and that seemed to alter their actual experience.

The work of the Mind and Spirit project suggests that moments of human phenomenological ambiguity and cultural invitations around the mind-world boundary interact to change the felt sensory quality of the event. What we see in this phase of the Mind and Spirit research is that the greater the cultural emphasis on porosity, the more people seem to experience that inbetween – where much of the experience deemed supernatural has its expression – in sensorially vivid ways. In social worlds where ideas about witchcraft or sorcery are common, people are more likely to say that they have heard gods and spirits with their ears, seen a vision, or experienced invisible beings as if they were present to them. Again, this is not – or not just – the effect of how religious participants are, as all our participants are deeply religious. Nor are the differences simply the effect of different ways of naming, different discourses or interpretations, as we probed carefully about the phenomenological features of the events. We suggest that the ways people understand the relationship of their inner awareness and what they identify as the external world may lead to significantly different phenomenological events.

Why does this matter? In many ways, the anthropological arguments about ontology (the what-is-real question) have been about the politics of interpretation. The scholarship associated with the ontological turn has largely focused on rebuking those who treat the strange beliefs of other societies as obviously false. Eduardo Viveiros de Castro made the case forcefully: 'Anthropologists must allow that "visions" are not beliefs, nor consensual views, but worlds seen objectively, not worldviews, but worlds of vision' (2016: 133). To be sure, the initial debate over the ontological turn focused on whether the natural world was really fundamentally different in Amazonia and Europe. James Laidlaw (2012) put it this way in a review of Morton Pedersen's *Not quite shamans*: 'The implication is that the very stuff of reality ... is different in these two realms'. Yet it seemed clear to most readers that none of the anthropological contributors to the ontological turn really did believe that women could become jaguars in Amazonia, but not in Europe. In a new summary of their position, Martin Holbraad and Morten Pedersen were markedly more restrained. 'This is the crucial concern of the ontological turn: It is about creating the conditions under which one can "see" things in one's ethnographic material that one would otherwise not be able to see' (2017: 4). The focus, in short, has been on the way anthropologists see.

The profound question raised by the ontological turn remains: whether cultural interpretations change the nature of reality for individuals in more than superficial ways. That has been where the Mind and Spirit project has lived, in the curiosity about whether cultural differences in the perceiver's understanding of perception can shape the nature of sensory evidence itself. This is a question that – for all the anthropological insistence that different people see the world differently – we still need to demonstrate in precise detail and is of intense interest not only to anthropologists, but also to psychologists, philosophers, and others. We need not only to consider that the representations of the mind/world with which Western anthropologists frame their questions are themselves products of a particular social world, but also to explore – with specific detail – how those different representations change the intimate phenomenology of human perception.

This is the thrust behind Philippe Descola's grand comparative study, *Beyond nature and culture*. His central discussion of the mechanisms of the process occurs in chapter 4. There he seeks to show that the culturally different representations of human and nature shape basic mental schemas through which humans apprehend the world. This was of course a Lévi-Straussian claim, but Lévi-Strauss did little (beyond the brilliant discussion in the seventh chapter of *The elementary structures of kinship*, 1969 [1949]) to give it specificity. Descola asks:

> But what is the form of this structural subconscious? Is it present in each mind in the form of cognitive imperatives that remain tacit despite being culturally determined, or is it distributed among the properties of the institutions that reveal it to the observer? How is it internalized by each individual and by what means does it act in such a way that it may determine recurrent behavior patterns that can be translated into vernacular models? (2013: 96).

Descola answers, in effect, that we know that there are cognitive schemas common to all humans, and that there are also psychic, sensorimotor, and emotional dispositions that are internalized through experience in a specific social and environmental setting

(2013: 103). Some of these more culturally specific schemas are consciously available to those in the group, but some are not. 'Many cultural models are not transmitted as bodies of precepts but are internalized little by little, without any particular teaching, although this does not prevent them from being objectified quite schematically when circumstances demand it' (2013: 103). They become 'the tacit frameworks and procedures of objectivization by means of which actors in the system themselves organize their relations to the world and to Others' (2013: 110). The rest of his book is an ethnographic argument that there are deep differences in representation that follow the logic he lays out.

The Mind and Spirit project takes the next step by providing evidence that different ways of representing human-world relationships shape something so basic as sensory evidence, perhaps the most basic human ability and the basic means through which humans judge what it is to be real. The more porous the representation of the boundary between mind and world, the more sensory the experience of invisible others.

Now let me raise a hard question: why is porosity more common in some worlds than in others?

The social setting of porosity

Moments when the mind seems vulnerable and thoughts seem potent are, I have suggested, common in human experience. Most humans have times when anger comes out of the blue or explodes within us like a force, even when we are alone in the room. Most humans have had instances when we behaved as if wishing intensely could change the world, even when we didn't 'really' believe that it would. What social conditions provide the incentives to nurture these human events into shared cultural models and common social practices? Our team suspects that this answer is complicated, and that different conditions encourage different kinds of porosity. Nevertheless, it is true that anthropologists and historians have studied witchcraft deeply for many years, and that witchcraft is a prime example of porosity. Turning to some of the ideas/hypotheses advanced by anthropologists and historians of witchcraft could thus shed useful light on the some of the ways in which social settings may encourage certain cultural elaborations of porosity.

Anthropological work on witchcraft in traditional societies, usually carried out in Africa, found two features commonly associated with rich ideas about witchcraft: small agricultural communities and unstable political succession (Douglas 1970). These days anthropologists tend to be sceptical that witchcraft accusations were a 'social strain gauge' (Marwick 1970) that emerged out of conflict and became the means to express that conflict in relatively safe ways. It is still empirically true that culturally elaborated ideas about witchcraft are found more often in agricultural communities, in which people could not move apart from each other, than in hunter-gathering or pastoralist communities, in which people in conflict can simply part ways. It was the historian John Demos who most vividly described the charged intimacy within small agricultural communities in his portrait of a New England town, isolated in a small and dangerous wilderness.

> The brickmaker who rebuilds your chimney is also the constable who brings you a summons to court, an occupant of the next bench in the meetinghouse, the owner of a share adjacent to one of yours in the 'upland' meadow, a rival for water-rights to the stream that flows behind that meadow, a fellow member of the local 'train band' (i.e. militia), an occasional companion at the local 'ordinary' [pub or tavern], a creditor (for services performed for you the previous summer but not as yet paid for),

a potential customer for wool from the sheep you have begun to raise, the father of a child who is currently a bond-servant in your house, a colleague on a town commitment to repair and improve the public roadways ... And so on. Do the two of you enjoy your shared experiences? Not necessarily. Do you know each other well? Most certainly (Demos 1982: 312).

The scholarship suggests that ideas about supernaturally dangerous others seem more salient in a world in which people fear, but which they cannot leave. Mary Douglas put the consensus thus: '[Witchcraft] accusations clustered in areas of ambiguous social relations' (1970: xvii) – in social domains of hard-to-resolve conflict. Likewise, one might expect that in social worlds in which there is less precarity (less danger, less premature death, more political stability) there might be less invitation to develop ideas and practices around the supernatural malice of other people.

Of course, this is complicated. The remarkable flare-up of accusations in the fifteenth and sixteenth centuries in Europe (and a bit later in the American colonies) that came to be known as the 'witchcraze' made it clear that while witchcraft accusations emerged around hard-to-resolve conflict, often in agricultural villages, the idea of the witch became salient for different reasons in different settings. On mainland Europe, the flames were fanned by religious tensions, and in England, by guilt about the treatment of the poor (Thomas 1971). In both cases, witchcraft first had to become legally prosecutable, rather than being understood as a foolish superstition (as it had been seen by elites before the Inquisition). In late seventeenth-century Salem, perhaps the best-studied example, scholars identified these elements in the mix: tension between Salem Village and Salem Town (Boyer & Nissenbaum 1974); women displaced and dispossessed by the French Indian wars (Karlsen 1998); a hallucinogenic mould that grew on the rye after a wet summer (Caporael 1976); and more. Out of this work emerged the idea that witchcraft accusations flourished in times of social unrest (Cohn 1975) – a claim Mary Douglas trenchantly described as 'superbly untestable' (1970: xx). At the same time, the historical story made it clear that the idea of the supernatural power of malevolent thought was always available, but that it became more believable at certain times – and that when the idea became believable, it could be like a match to tinder.

Are there other general principles about the conditions in which ideas about witchcraft flourish? Peter Geschiere (1997; 2013) suggests that witchcraft ideas are fostered in settings with a paucity of social trust. One of the many puzzles about witchcraft accusations in general is that they have exploded in urban sub-Saharan Africa (Comaroff & Comaroff 1999; Niehaus 2001). Geschiere points out that one of the peculiarities of witchcraft ideas in Africa (as compared to the Navajo, or in Europe, or, for that matter, sorcery in Oceania, where one's blood relatives are thought less likely to use sorcery against one) is that the witch is imagined as an intimate – a member of the family, not a neighbour, or in a distant town. (Levine [1973] argues that this coupling of witchcraft with intimacy arose out of the joint polygamous households once common in much of sub-Saharan Africa.) As a result, Geschiere argues, the way witchcraft is imagined in sub-Saharan Africa speaks to something fundamental in human experience. We all get deeply upset at intimates. Another reason why witchcraft ideas thrive in urban sub-Saharan Africa may be that Pentecostalism dramatically reinforces ideas about demons in movies, radio, and church services that are like theatrical productions (Meyer 2015; Rio, MacCarthy & Blanes 2017). Still, the obvious difficulty of social life in these cities suggests that there may be something to the idea that conditions of social mistrust breed environments in which ideas of malevolence can grow.

Journal of the Royal Anthropological Institute (N.S.), 148-162
© Royal Anthropological Institute 2020

These observations also point to a powerful inhibitor of witchcraft ideas: secularism – and possibly the pluralism and industrialization that often accompany it. It is likely harder to believe in the porosity of malevolent others in a secular world because such a world inhibits all kinds of ideas about actions that it deems supernatural. To be clear, porosity is not the same as religiosity. One can be deeply religious without holding a porous model of mind. One can even be Pentecostal without holding a porous model of mind. It is true that porosity undergirds many common ideas associated with religion (divination, prophecy, cursing, witchcraft, etc.), but that is not to say that porosity is the same as being religious. Still, those who are not religious at all are likely less inclined to believe in the supernatural potency of a witch's angry thoughts, and less likely to imagine themselves as vulnerable to a curse. One can be superstitious but not religious, but the less religious one is, the less rich one's supernatural commitments are likely to be.

There is much more work to do. There are likely a range of arguments for why an interest in prophecy, divination, oracles, sorcery, mesmerism, and all other forms of potency and vulnerability, positive or negative, might rise and fall. There are a myriad of ways that dominant power structures within societies could have an interest in, or give rise to, ideas about the porosity or bufferedness of the mind. While spiritual or mental experience is certainly not *reducible* to such interests, an attention to power relations might be helpful for understanding why certain experiences are or are not kindled.

Conclusion

We – the Mind and Spirit team – see the anthropology of mind as laying out a fundamental question: how do different social worlds shape the intimately felt experience of awareness? How is the quality of our present consciousness shaped by the way we have come to imagine thoughts, feelings, mind? We see an anthropology of mind as the attempt to capture differences in subjectivity which have emerged through historical change, social contact, and religious engagement. These differences are not timeless but rather always in historical flux. An anthropology of mind allows us to pay close attention both to local understandings of subjective experience and to ways that encounters with others seem to alter them. In riposte to the challenge laid out to us in the introduction, we see these differences as more than superficial. But to demonstrate these differences is hard.

This is why the anthropologists among us found it helpful to work with psychologists (Kara Weisman and Vivian Dzokoto, of course, but also Suzanne Gaskins, Alison Gopnik, Paul Harris, Cristine Legare, and Hazel Markus, among others) in consultation with a philosopher, Neil van Leeuwen, and historian, Ann Taves. (Joanna Cook, Julia Cassaniti, Joel Robbins, and Thomas Weisner were among our anthropological advisers.) The question of how cultural models and social practices change human experience is central to anthropology. You could even say that this is the central question of the field. But it is challenging to argue that social and cultural differences go so far as to alter something as basic to human life as sensory awareness, because the claim can so easily be dismissed: as a local theory of vision, rather than as a shift in sensory experience. The more we can bring to bear evidence organized by an empirical logic that other fields find persuasive, the more effective our anthropological arguments will be. We still believe that the method of anthropology – its ground-up, experience-near observation – is uniquely suited to studying the human condition.

This work is a call to arms for comparison. It is also a call for a method of comparative phenomenology. Anthropology offers the most fine-grained practice of observation and listening in the world. We sit and watch and listen, at length. Comparative phenomenology is the practice of describing with the pragmatic phenomenological precision William James modelled for us: careful, precise, specific. Like no other discipline, we can describe and compare the texture of human experience and learn from it the ways in which culture gets under the skin. This is the invitation our method extends to us, and to the scholarly world.

REFERENCES

BARRETT, J. & F. KEIL 1996. Conceptualizing a nonnatural entity: anthropomorphism in God concepts. *Cognitive Psychology* **31**, 219-47.

BENTALL, R. 2003. *Madness explained: psychosis and human nature.* London: Penguin.

BILU, Y. 2013. 'We want to see our king': apparitions in messianic Chabad. *Ethos* **41**, 82-95.

BOYER, P. & S. NISSENBAUM 1974. *Salem possessed: the social origins of witchcraft.* Cambridge, Mass.: Harvard University Press.

BRIGGS, J. 1998. *Inuit morality play: the emotional education of a three year old.* New Haven: Yale University Press.

CAPORAEL, L. 1976. Ergotism: the Satan loosed in Salem? *Science* **192**, 21-6.

CASSANITI, J. & T.M. LUHRMANN 2014. The cultural kindling of spiritual experiences. *Current Anthropology* **55**: S10, S333-43.

COHN, N. 1975. *Europe's inner demons: an enquiry inspired by the great witch-hunt.* New York: New American Library.

COMAROFF, J. & J. COMAROFF 1999. Occult economies and the violence of abstraction. *American Ethnologist* **26**, 279-303.

DEMOS, J. 1982. *Entertaining Satan: witchcraft and the culture of early New England.* Oxford: University Press.

DESCOLA, P. 2013. *Beyond nature and culture* (trans. J. Lloyd). Chicago: University Press.

DOUGLAS, M. (ed.) 1970. *Witchcraft: confessions and accusations.* London: Routledge.

GESCHIERE, P. 1997. *The modernity of witchcraft: politics and the occult in postcolonial Africa* (trans. P. Geschiere & J. Roitman). Charlottesville: University of Virginia Press.

——— 2013. *Witchcraft, intimacy, and trust: Africa in comparison.* Chicago: University Press.

HOLBRAAD, M. & M.A. PEDERSEN 2017. *The ontological turn.* Cambridge: University Press.

JAMES, W. 1950[1890]. *The principles of psychology.* New York: Dover.

JOHNSON, M. & C. RAYE 1981. Reality monitoring. *Psychological Review* **88**, 67-85.

KARLSEN, C. 1998. *Witchcraft: confessions and accusations.* London: Routledge.

KENDLER, K., L. THORNTON & C.O. GARDNER 2000. Stressful life events and previous episodes in the etiology of major depression in women: an evaluation of the 'kindling' hypothesis. *American Journal of Psychiatry* **157**, 1243–51.

LAIDLAW, J. 2012. Ontologically challenged: a review of M.A. Pedersen, *Not quite shamans. Anthropology of This Century* **4** (available online: http://aotcpress.com/articles/ontologically-challenged/, accessed 21 January 2020).

LEVINE, R. 1973. Patterns of personality in Africa. *Ethos* **1**, 123-52.

LÉVI-STRAUSS, C. 1969 [1949]. *The elementary structures of kinship* (trans. J.H. Bell, J.R. von Sturmer & R. Needham). Boston: Beacon.

LUHRMANN, T.M. 2012. *When God talks back: understanding the American evangelical relationship with God.* New York: Knopf.

——— 2017. Diversity within the psychotic continuum. *Schizophrenia Bulletin* **43**, 27-31 (available online: *https://academic.oup.com/schizophreniabulletin/article/43/1/27/2548951*, accessed 21 January 2020).

——— 2020. *How God becomes real: kindling the presence of invisible others.* Princeton: University Press.

MARWICK, M. (ed.) 1970. *Witchcraft and sorcery: selected readings.* London: Penguin.

MEYER, B. 2015. *Sensational movies: video, vision, and Christianity in Ghana.* Berkeley: University of California Press.

NIEHAUS, I. 2001. *Witchcraft, power, and politics: exploring the occult in the South African Lowveld.* London: Pluto.

RIO, K., M. MACCARTHY & R. BLANES (eds) 2017. *Pentecostalism and witchcraft: spiritual warfare in Africa and Melanesia*. New York: Palgrave Macmillan.

TAYLOR, C. 2007. *A secular age*. Cambridge, Mass.: Belknap Press of Harvard University Press.

THOMAS, K. 1971. *Religion and the decline of magic: studies in popular beliefs in sixteenth- and seventeenth-century England*. London: Penguin.

VIVEIROS DE CASTRO, E. 2016. *The relative native: essays on indigenous conceptual worlds*. Chicago: HAU.

Penser la pensée : porosité de l'esprit et présence des dieux

Résumé

Le projet « Esprit et Esprit(s) » a permis d'observer que la manière dont un monde social invite ses membres à appréhender la pensée semble avoir des conséquences. Quand la frontière entre conscience intérieure et monde extérieur est représentée, culturellement, comme quelque chose de poreux, où l'on peut imaginer que les pensées entrent et sortent de l'esprit comme si elles étaient dotées d'agencéité et de pouvoir, les sujets sont davantage enclins à décrire leur perception d'autres invisibles comme si ces autres pouvaient être perçus par les sens. Ils disent plus souvent qu'ils ont entendu « de leurs oreilles » un dieu ou un esprit parler ou qu'ils ont senti une présence dans une pièce.

Index